PLURALISM IN A DEMOCRATIC SOCIETY: LEGAL, ETHICAL, AND HUMAN RIGHTS PERSPECTIVES

YUKIO SAKURAI

COMMON GROUND

First published in 2026
as part of the Aging & Society Book Imprint

Common Ground Research Networks
University of Illinois Research Park
2001 South First Dr, Suite 201 L
Champaign, IL 61820 USA

Library of Congress Cataloging-in-Publication Data Forthcoming

ISBN:978-1-969318-31-3 (HBK)
ISBN: 978-1-969318-32-0 (PBK)
ISBN: 978-1-969318-33-7 (PDF)
DOI: https://doi.org/10.18848/AGSCBI/B9

Cover Design: Phillip Kalantis-Cope

ACKNOWLEDGMENTS

This book is the culmination of seven years of research, reflection, and dialogue on global governance across multiple disciplines and contexts. Growing up in postwar Japan, while witnessing economic transformations, social inequalities, and recurring disasters, and later spending a decade abroad, provided both perspective and comparative insight. These experiences enabled me to situate Japan's challenges within a broader international framework of democratic resilience and pluralist governance.

I am deeply indebted to the many colleagues, international researchers, and interlocutors whose probing questions, constructive critiques, and thoughtful insights have continually refined my analysis and inspired a multidimensional perspective. I would like to express my sincere gratitude to Dr. Masahiro Kohara, Emeritus Professor at the University of Tokyo, for his invaluable comments and profound insights, as well as for our enduring friendship over the past forty-five years.

I wish to express my deepest thanks to my family, whose patience, encouragement, and steadfast support supported me through the inevitable challenges of sustained scholarly work. Without them, this book would not have been possible. Any shortcomings, inconsistencies, or oversights remain entirely my own.

Yukio Sakurai

DESCRIPTION

This book examines how democracy is sustained and challenged in the twenty-first century, drawing on comparative analyses of Japan and Turkey. It contends that contemporary democracy is most vulnerable not to abrupt collapse but to gradual erosion, wherein pluralism and accountability weaken even as formal institutions remain intact.

Significance of Study

The study makes three primary contributions. First, it demonstrates that the vitality of democracy depends on more than constitutions and elections; it requires open information, accountable governance, and inclusive social structures. Second, it reconceptualizes sovereignty as relational, shaped not only by national autonomy but also by global interdependence and ethical obligations. Third, it underscores that the protection of human rights cannot rely solely on legal frameworks but must be grounded in institutions and civic practices that sustain pluralism. Collectively, these insights position pluralism as both the foundation and the measure of democratic resilience.

Limitations of the Study

Several limitations warrant acknowledgment. The analysis prioritizes conceptual and qualitative depth over quantitative evidence. Its focus on Japan and Turkey, while yielding rich insights, restricts comparative breadth by excluding other global regions. Moreover, certain influential global dynamics—such as digital transformation, human rights challenges, and socio-economic inequality—are addressed only selectively and not systematically. Consequently, the findings capture a snapshot of democracy's evolving trajectory rather than its full complexity.

Future Tasks

The study identifies several avenues for further research. Scholars should explore how digital technologies and artificial intelligence reshape the public sphere and influence democratic processes. Theories of sovereignty should more fully incorporate dimensions of interdependence and vulnerability. Comparative research should expand geographically to encompass a broader range of democratic experiences. In practice, policymakers and citizens must enhance civic education, support independent media, and embed pluralism into everyday governance.

Concluding Reflections

This book concludes with a dual perspective of caution and hope. The caution lies in the fact that democracy can erode quietly, imperceptibly hollowing out its own foundations. The hope resides in the potential for resilience, fostered through transparency, robust institutions, accountability, and active civic engagement. Above all, pluralism must be enacted as a lived practice rather than merely affirmed as a principle. Through such a commitment, democracy can endure and adapt amid the uncertainties of the contemporary world.

CONTENTS

Contents

Contents

LIST OF PUBLICATION

Chapter 1:
Sakurai, Yukio. 2025. "The Triangle of Concealment and Conformity: Information Control, Media Dependency, and Democratic Resilience in Japan's Recent Crises."

Chapter 2:
Sakurai, Yukio. 2026. "Autocracy 2.0 and the Informational Turn in Democratic Backsliding: A Comparative Analysis of Japan and Turkey."

Chapter 3:
Sakurai, Yukio. 2022. "Shinzo Abe's Politics in Japan: Characteristics and Implications." *Political Reflection Magazine* 8, no. 4: 27–32. CESRAN. https://politicalreflectionmagazine.com/vol-8-no-4/.

Chapter 4:
Sakurai, Yukio. 2018. "Turkey's Possible Future Directions After the 2017 Referendum: Autocracy or Democracy?" *The International Journal of Interdisciplinary Civic and Political Studies* 13, no. 1: 33–45. CGRN. https://doi.org/10.18848/2327-0071/CGP/v13i01/33-45.

Chapter 5:
Sakurai, Yukio. 2025. "The Evolution of Japan's Limited Sovereignty: From the Era of Unequal Treaties to the Japan-U.S. Alliance." *The Rest: Journal of Politics and Development* 15, no. 2: 163–81. CESRAN. http://hdl.handle.net/10131/0002001987.

Chapter 6:
Sakurai, Yukio. 2025. "The Impact of Third Parties on Japanese Politics and Sovereignty: Limited Sovereignty Theory and Political Party Mediation."

Chapter 7:

Sakurai, Yukio. 2025. "The Challenges of Local Politics in Japan: Focusing on Self-Government, Political Succession and Ethics." *The International Journal of Interdisciplinary Civic and Political Studies* 20, no. 1: 91–108. CGRN. https://doi.org/10.18848/2327-0071/CGP/v20i01/91-108.

Chapter 8:

Sakurai, Yukio. 2026. "Japan's Immigration Governance: Legal Reform, Social Integration, and Democratic Accountability." *Yokohama Journal of Social Sciences* 30,no. 3: 43-164. *https://doi.org/10.18880/0002002454.*

Chapter 9:

Sakurai, Yukio. 2025. "The Silent Influence: How Sub-Societal Structures Shape Sexual Violence in Japan." *The International Journal of Interdisciplinary Civic and Political Studies* 20, no. 2: 115–33. CGRN. https://doi.org/10.18848/2327-0071/CGP/v20i02/115-133.

Chapter 10:

Sakurai, Yukio. 2021. "Possible Challenges to the Welfare State in a Post-COVID-19 Society: An Illustration from a Citizen's Perspective." *The International Journal of Interdisciplinary Civic and Political Studies* 16, no. 2: 21–35. CGRN. https://doi.org/10.18848/2327-0071/CGP/v16i02/21-35.

Chapter 11:

Sakurai, Yukio. 2019. "Turkish Politics and Human Rights Law: Focusing on Transformation." *The International Journal of Interdisciplinary Global Studies* 14, no. 2: 1–25. CGRN. https://doi.org/10.18848/2324-755X/CGP/v14i02/1-25.

Five articles were previously published by Common Ground Research Networks (CGRN) in the United States, two by CESRAN in the United Kingdom, one by the Association of Yokohama International Social Science Studies (AYISSS) in Japan, and the remaining three have been newly prepared for inclusion in this volume. The author has received permission from the publishers to reproduce the previously published articles in this volume.

TABLE AND FIGURE

ACRONYMS

ABCD encirclement	America, Britain, China, and Dutch encirclement (a term referring to the pre–World War II economic blockade against Japan)
AI	Artificial Intelligence
AKP	Justice and Development Party (Adalet ve Kalkınma Partisi, Turkey)
BBC	British Broadcasting Corporation
CHP	Republican People's Party (Cumhuriyet Halk Partisi, Turkey)
COVID-19	Coronavirus Disease 2019
EU	European Union
FETO	Fethullahist Terrorist Organization (designation by Turkish government)
GDP	Gross Domestic Product
GHQ	General Headquarters (Allied Occupation Headquarters in Japan after WWII)
ICRRA	Immigration Control and Refugee Recognition Act (Japan)
IMF	International Monetary Fund
ISA	Internal Security Agency (Japan)
LDP	Liberal Democratic Party (Japan)
LGBT	Lesbian, Gay, Bisexual, and Transgender
MHLW	Ministry of Health, Labour, and Welfare (Japan)
MHP	Nationalist Movement Party (Milliyetçi Hareket Partisi, Turkey)
MOFA	Ministry of Foreign Affairs (Japan)
NATO	North Atlantic Treaty Organization
NGO	Non-Governmental Organization
NHK	Japan Broadcasting Corporation (Nippon Hōsō Kyōkai)

OECD	Organization for Economic Co-operation and Development
OSCE	Organization for Security and Co-operation in Europe
OTIT	Organization for Technical Intern Training (Japan)
PKK	Kurdistan Workers' Party (Partiya Karkerên Kurdistanê)
PRC	People's Republic of China
QUAD	Quadrilateral Security Dialogue (Australia, India, Japan, and the United States)
SCAP	Supreme Commander for the Allied Powers
SOFA	Status of Forces Agreement
TEPCO	Tokyo Electric Power Company
TTTP	Technical Intern Training Program (Japan)
UBI	Universal Basic Income
UK	United Kingdom
UN	United Nations
UNHRC	United Nations Human Rights Council
UPR	Universal Periodic Review
U.S.	United States
USFJ	United States Forces Japan

INTRODUCTION

Pluralism in a Democratic Society: Legal, Ethical, and Human Rights Perspectives examines a central dilemma of the twenty-first century: whether democratic systems can preserve their resilience and legitimacy amid intensifying volatility and contestation. Contemporary democracies face growing pressures arising from armed conflicts, economic stagnation, social fragmentation, and the widening gap between rapid technological change and comparatively static political institutions. At the same time, regimes that retain the formal structures of democracy while hollowing out its substantive core are gaining prominence, prompting fundamental questions about the nature, meaning, and practice of democracy itself.

In response to these challenges, this volume adopts a comparative framework, focusing on Japan and Turkey as case studies that exemplify broader global patterns of democratic stress, adaptation, and transformation. The analysis is organized around three overarching questions: whether democracy can maintain vitality under conditions of unpredictability; how national independence can be reconciled with citizen welfare within an increasingly interdependent international environment; and how fundamental human rights can be effectively safeguarded amid evolving political, social, and technological conditions.

Rather than treating these questions in isolation, the chapters draw upon insights from law, political science, sociology, and ethics to articulate a holistic account of democratic sustainability. Taken together, they demonstrate that the endurance of democracy depends not only on constitutional design and institutional capacity but also on cultural practices, ethical commitments, and the ability of societies to respond constructively to global interdependence and internal pluralism.

Part I. Democracy, Information, and Resilience

This section investigates the conditions under which democracies maintain resilience in moments of crisis and examines how institutions adapt under informational and political pressure.

Chapter 1 introduces the Triangle of Concealment and Conformity, a conceptual model that explains how government information control, media dependency, and expert conformity intersected to shape Japan's responses to the Fukushima nuclear accident, the COVID-19 pandemic, and the Russo-Ukrainian war. Across these cases, state actors, media institutions, and professional communities coproduced narratives that prioritized stability, authority, and risk avoidance over transparency. Such strategies may preserve public order in the short term, yet they ultimately weaken public welfare, democratic trust, and institutional resilience. The chapter argues for institutionalized transparency, strengthened media independence, diversification of expert knowledge, and enhanced citizen information literacy.

Chapter 2 extends this analysis through a comparative examination of Japan and Turkey, demonstrating that democratic erosion often proceeds not through overt coercion but through adaptive institutional change. In Japan, bureaucratic governance, executive expansion, and juridified policymaking incrementally narrow pluralism. In Turkey, charismatic-populist leadership and rapid centralization have produced more visible and abrupt institutional transformation. Both cases reveal how information management—now increasingly mediated by digital infrastructures and algorithmic systems—enables elite insulation and restricts civic agency. The chapter highlights informational governance as an emerging global challenge that transcends regime type.

Chapter 3 examines the political legacy of Shinzo Abe. Abe consolidated executive authority, reframed Japan's security doctrine, and reshaped public expectations regarding leadership. Yet his leadership also provoked concerns regarding constitutionalism, accountability, and institutional balance. His sudden death exposed the vulnerabilities inherent in personalized leadership systems, suggesting that democratic resilience depends not only on institutional design but also on political culture, norms of accountability, and mechanisms of leadership succession.

Chapter 4 analyzes Turkey's trajectory following the 2017 referendum that ushered in a presidential system. The chapter identifies two competing paths: the consolidation of competitive authoritarianism or a gradual shift toward dialogical democracy catalyzed by international engagement. External mechanisms—such as EU accession processes and UN oversight—together with domestic political contestation will shape Turkey's institutional direction. The analysis underscores that democratic outcomes are contingent, shaped by the interaction of internal dynamics and external pressures.

In sum, Part I demonstrates that the vitality of democracy cannot be reduced to electoral procedures or constitutional form. It depends equally on the circulation of credible information, leadership accountability, and the openness of public discourse. Democratic backsliding frequently occurs through legal, administrative, and informational mechanisms that preserve institutional façades while hollowing out pluralism and contestation.

Part II. National Independence, Sovereignty, and Citizen Well-Being

This section explores the evolving relationship between sovereignty, national independence, and citizen welfare within a globalized and interdependent international order.

Chapter 5 situates Japan's sovereignty within a long historical arc—from nineteenth-century treaty inequality to the postwar US–Japan alliance. Across these periods, sovereignty has been constrained through both external imposition and internal accommodation. Contemporary alliance politics show sovereignty not as fixed authority but as a relational and negotiated practice shaped by geopolitical structures. Persistent tensions between strategic dependence and democratic legitimacy highlight the need to reassess sovereignty in terms of citizen welfare and constitutional accountability.

Chapter 6 applies Krasner's limited sovereignty framework to Japan–China relations, analyzing cooperative, infiltrative, and normative constraints on Japanese policymaking. Through Komeito's mediating role, transnational networks, and extensive economic linkages, the chapter shows how institutionalized influence produces diplomatic restraint and policy convergence. By demonstrating how "productive power" shapes preferences and norms, it reveals how democratic sovereignty may erode subtly through coordination and normalization, underscoring the need for transparency and strengthened civic oversight.

Chapter 7 turns to Japan's local politics. With more than 34,000 local politicians, Japan possesses an extensive system of self-government, yet one increasingly challenged by hereditary succession, demographic decline, and ethical lapses. Democratic renewal thus requires revitalizing local governance through political openness, ethical standards, and participatory opportunities for new entrants. Demographic pressures—including aging and depopulation—threaten administrative capacity, highlighting the necessity of grassroots democratic revitalization.

Chapter 8 examines Japan's immigration policy. By framing migration as "policy on foreign nationals," the state avoids acknowledging immigration as a structural reality, thereby obscuring social implications and reinforcing executive control. Governance in this domain lacks legal clarity, public deliberation, and robust rights protections. The chapter argues for foundational immigration legislation, inclusive integration measures, and strengthened oversight mechanisms, situating immigration policy within broader debates on labor, dignity, and democratic pluralism.

Together, the chapters in Part II show that sovereignty, independence, and citizen well-being must be continually recalibrated. Sovereignty is meaningful only when it secures dignity, welfare, and participatory inclusion. In the twenty-first century, sovereignty must be understood as relational, conditional, and oriented toward pluralistic democratic governance.

Part III. Human Rights, Ethics, and Social Structures

This section analyzes how human rights can be effectively protected within societies marked by inequality, entrenched institutional norms, and intensifying global crises.

Chapter 9 examines sexual violence in Japan through the lens of sub-societal structures. Insular groups—ranging from sports associations and workplaces to cultural industries—reinforce norms that sustain impunity and silence victims. Despite recent legal reforms, cultural and structural barriers impede accountability. The chapter calls for stronger whistleblower protections, external auditing mechanisms, and independent human rights institutions to dismantle these persistent silences.

Chapter 10 evaluates the welfare state in the post–COVID-19 context. The pandemic exposed institutional vulnerabilities and highlighted citizens' deep reliance on social protection systems. Recognizing individuals as embedded in networks of interdependence, the chapter argues that welfare policies must promote both social ethics and active citizenship. Sustaining welfare provision requires not only administrative capacity but also international cooperation and civic responsibility.

Chapter 11 concludes with an analysis of Turkey's human rights trajectory. Despite adopting extensive legal frameworks, the Turkish state continues to restrict media freedom, suppress opposition, and weaken institutional autonomy. These dynamics show that legal codification alone is insufficient to guarantee rights realization. Without cultural transformation, political commitment, and enforceable accountability, rights remain largely symbolic. The chapter emphasizes pluralism as a foundational principle for substantive human rights protection.

In sum, Part III demonstrates that human rights cannot be secured through legal entitlements alone. They require supportive social structures, cultural practices grounded in equality, and ethical commitments recognizing human vulnerability and interdependence. Rights become meaningful only where pluralism enables diverse voices to be protected, recognized, and incorporated into public life.

Intellectual Significance of the Volume

This volume offers an intellectual contribution by integrating three thematic categories—democracy and resilience, sovereignty and citizen well-being, and human rights and social structures—into a broader conceptual framework centered on pluralism. These categories are not discrete; rather, they are deeply interwoven, illuminating both the fragility and the adaptability of democratic systems. Together, they demonstrate that democracy is sustained not by formal institutions alone but through the dynamic interplay of information flows, sovereign authority, welfare responsibilities, and rights protections situated within diverse and evolving social structures.

Democracy, Information Control, and Rights

The first theme foregrounds the ways in which information management, institutional functioning, and accountability mechanisms shape democratic vitality. These dynamics intersect directly with questions of sovereignty and human rights. Japan's crisis governance demonstrates how secrecy, media dependency, and technocratic decision-making can erode public accountability, thereby weakening democratic oversight of sovereign power. Turkey's model of informational autocracy similarly constrains civil and political rights, illustrating that the health of democracy must be assessed not solely by electoral processes or formal institutional arrangements but also by the normative conditions under which sovereignty is exercised and rights are protected. This theme thus highlights the centrality of transparency, communicative openness, and institutional integrity to democratic resilience.

Sovereignty, Welfare, and the Ethics of Interdependence

The second theme underscores that sovereignty is neither absolute nor static; it is relational and contingent, shaped by external constraints, strategic alliances, and internal responsibilities. Japan's reliance on the United States for security illustrates how geopolitical interdependence influences domestic accountability and policymaking autonomy. Likewise, immigration policy and post-COVID welfare reforms reveal that economic sovereignty must be reconciled with global interdependence through cooperation, fiscal solidarity, and civic responsibility. In this light, sovereignty emerges as an ongoing ethical negotiation—balancing self-determination with interdependence, national priorities with transnational obligations—in ways that directly affect citizen well-being and social cohesion.

Human Rights, Social Structures, and the Informational Turn

The third theme emphasizes that the realization of human rights cannot be separated from the democratic and sovereign contexts within which they are embedded. Rights require supportive social environments and pluralistic institutional structures. Japan's sub-societal concealment of sexual violence and Turkey's legislative adoption of rights frameworks without meaningful implementation highlight the persistent gap between formal recognition and lived experience. The informational turn—marked by new modes of communication, surveillance, and political mobilization—further complicates this relationship. Pluralism becomes essential: rights flourish only when diverse voices can be expressed, institutions remain open and responsive, and accountability mechanisms operate effectively.

Pluralism as a Legal, Ethical, and Human Rights Imperative

The intersection of these themes reveals the volume's central concern: the vitality of pluralism in democratic society. Pluralism is not merely the coexistence of differing viewpoints but a foundational principle that sustains institutional legitimacy, underpins ethical governance, and enables the meaningful realization of rights. From legal, ethical, and human rights perspectives, pluralism performs both diagnostic and normative functions: it exposes the subtle erosion of democratic norms and offers a framework for reconciling sovereign authority with citizen welfare, while ensuring that rights are protected in practice rather than merely in form. In this sense, pluralism stands as a critical resource for democratic renewal in an era of uncertainty.

To Readers

This book offers both a warning and an invitation. It warns that democracy is endangered less by sudden collapse than by the quiet, incremental hollowing out of its substantive foundations beneath intact institutional façades. Yet it also affirms that resilience is attainable. Transparency, independent oversight bodies, ethical accountability, and engaged citizenship constitute practical tools for revitalizing democratic life. The central message is that pluralism must be lived rather than simply declared—embedded in law, enacted in ethical practice, and realized through the effective protection of rights. Readers are invited to recognize the subtle forms of democratic erosion that accompany contemporary political life and to cultivate the conditions that allow plural voices to thrive. Preserving democracy in uncertain times requires treating pluralism not only as a normative ideal but as an active practice to be defended, renewed, and shared.

PART I

Democracy, Information, and Resilience

CHAPTER 1

The Triangle of Concealment and Conformity: Information Control, Media Dependency, and Democratic Resilience in Japan's Recent Crises

Abstract

This chapter examines three contemporary crises in Japan: the Fukushima Daiichi Nuclear Accident (2011), the COVID-19 pandemic (2020–), and the Russo-Ukrainian War (2022–). Across these cases, a common structural pattern emerged, conceptualized here as the *Triangle of Concealment and Conformity*, in which government information control, media dependency, and expert conformity interact to shape public discourse. Drawing on political science, media studies, and social psychology, the study analyzes how this triangle operates, revealing that information control, although often justified as promoting short-term stability, undermines public welfare and erodes democratic foundations. This dynamic is interpreted through the lens of *Autocracy 2.0*, which describes governance that preserves the appearance of liberal democracy while subtly managing the public sphere. The chapter concludes that effective crisis management requires transparency, pluralism, and institutional safeguards. It proposes four policy measures to strengthen democratic resilience: legal mandates for immediate data disclosure, enhanced media independence, guaranteed plurality within expert communities, and strengthened citizen information literacy.

Keywords: Triangle of Concealment and Conformity, Information Control, Media Dependency, Autocracy 2.0, Crisis Management

1 Introduction

Crises place extraordinary pressure on democratic governance, compelling states to reconcile the normative imperative of transparency with the perceived necessity of information control. In democratic theory, timely and accurate disclosure is central to maintaining legitimacy and enabling citizens to make informed judgments. Yet governments frequently justify restrictions on information in the name of preventing panic or safeguarding national security.

The tension deepens when mass media and expert communities—actors normatively expected to serve as independent checks on state power—align with official narratives. Such alignment narrows the public sphere, constrains pluralistic deliberation, and erodes reciprocal trust between the state and its citizens (Guriev and Treisman 2019). Trust is foundational to democratic stability, as it presupposes that citizens can rely on authorities to act transparently and honestly (Levitsky and Way 2010). Recurrent suppression of critical information, however, raises fundamental questions about the resilience of democratic institutions and the reliability of governmental claims during crises.

This dilemma has been particularly visible in Japan's recent experience of three crises. During the 2011 Fukushima Daiichi Nuclear Power Plant Accident, delayed disclosure of radioactive dispersion data hindered timely evacuation decisions, illustrating the life-threatening consequences of concealment (Tokyo Electric Power Company [TEPCO] and Government Investigation Committee 2012). In the COVID-19 pandemic from 2020 onward, divergent scientific perspectives were systematically suppressed under the rubric of "misinformation," limiting the public's capacity to evaluate policy and risks autonomously (Yamaguchi 2021). Since the onset of the Russo-Ukrainian War in 2022, domestic political and media discourse has converged around a pro-Ukraine orientation, while alternative diplomatic perspectives have been stigmatized as "pro-Russian," restricting debate over foreign policy options and economic consequences (Sahashi 2022).

Taken together, these cases reveal a recurring structural pattern: centralized government control of information, media dependency, and expert conformity. This configuration, conceptualized here as the "Triangle of Concealment and Conformity," exposes a paradox of crisis governance: while coordination and effective communication are indispensable, the very mechanisms designed to preserve stability can undermine trust, suppress pluralism, and weaken citizens' capacity for informed judgment. The triangle thus constitutes both a functional tool of crisis management and a source of structural fragility in democratic systems.

The analysis highlights two broader contributions. First, it demonstrates that seemingly disparate crises in Japan can be understood within a unified explanatory framework, contributing to debates on informational autocracy, crisis governance, and the subtle vulnerabilities of democratic systems (Levitsky and Way 2010; Guriev and Treisman 2019). Second, it underscores the democratic costs of information control, particularly the erosion of trust and the constriction of the public sphere, while pointing toward the necessity of policies that foster transparency, pluralism, and citizen agency in future crises.

2 Methodology

This study employs a comparative qualitative methodology to analyze the structural dynamics of information control in Japan across three recent crises: the Fukushima Daiichi Nuclear Power Plant Accident, the COVID-19 pandemic, and the Russo-Ukrainian War. The research design is informed by prior studies on Japan and Turkey, particularly investigations into Autocracy 2.0 (Yang 2024), competitive authoritarianism (Levitsky and Way 2010), informational autocracy (Guriev and Treisman 2019), and technocratic governance. These frameworks provide insight into the subtle mechanisms through which democratic institutions can be preserved in form while power becomes increasingly centralized, and public discourse is constrained. The study situates Japan's experience within broader debates on informational autocracy, democratic backsliding, and the transformation of the public sphere under stress.

The empirical analysis draws on a combination of primary and secondary sources to examine interactions among government, media, and expert communities during crises. Primary sources include official documents and reports, such as the Fukushima Nuclear Power Plant Accident Investigation Report (TEPCO and Government Investigation Committee 2012), ministry statements, and public briefings by the Expert Meeting on COVID-19, providing authoritative accounts of policy decisions and information management. Secondary sources comprise mainstream media coverage and scholarly literature on political communication, Autocracy

2.0, competitive authoritarianism, and press dependence, enabling assessment of reporting patterns, narrative framing, and expert conformity.

Analytical procedures integrated qualitative content analysis with structured case comparison, coding for timing and accuracy of disclosure, alignment with official narratives, and social or normative pressures on experts. A comparative matrix systematically examined similarities and differences across crises, including the nature of each crisis, forms of information control, media behavior, and effects on public welfare, with triangulation across sources enhancing the reliability and validity of the findings.

3 Theoretical Framework

3.1 Political Science Perspective: National Security and the State of Exception

Crisis governance often involves governmental attempts to monopolize information to preserve authority and legitimize extraordinary measures in response to unpredictable shocks, a dynamic reminiscent of Schmitt's ([1922] 2005) concept of the state of exception, in which normal legal frameworks are suspended to protect the political order. While such practices are framed as necessary to prevent public panic or safeguard stability, they simultaneously erode the transparency that underpins democratic legitimacy. In Japan, policymaking frequently operates through a council-based system, in which experts appointed by ministries study agenda items and issue reports following deliberations across multiple meetings.

This governance style fosters close, symbiotic relationships between ministries and experts. Ministries gain insight into expert perspectives, while experts receive research funding, public visibility, and potential future positions within governmental institutions. Consequently, ministries cultivate a trusted circle of experts whose recommendations reliably align with policy objectives. These opinions are presented under the names of individual experts and their institutions, lending an appearance of independent legitimacy; in practice, however, they often reflect a co-produced outcome between experts and the ministry. In this sense, experts function as public representatives of pre-determined policy agendas, providing an authoritative façade that legitimizes ministerial decisions while constraining genuine deliberation.

3.2 Media Studies Perspective: Informational Autocrats

Normatively, the media is expected to function as the "fourth estate," safeguarding democracy by holding power to account. Yet in practice, structural dependencies often undermine this role, particularly in contexts where governments exercise subtle but pervasive forms of information control. Guriev and Treisman's theory of informational autocracy highlights how regimes preserve legitimacy not through overt repression but by shaping the informational environment, ensuring that citizens are exposed primarily to favorable narratives (Guriev and Treisman 2019).

In Japan, the press-club system exemplifies this arrangement: accredited journalists gain privileged access to ministries and industrial associations, but such access is conditioned on adherence to established norms that discourage adversarial reporting. During crises, this reliance is amplified, as media outlets frequently replicate government messaging rather than scrutinizing it, effectively functioning as extensions of official communication.

The organizational structure of Japan's major media corporations further reinforces this dynamic. Media conglomerates operate across newspapers, television, and radio, often diversifying into cultural and sporting events, while television broadcasting, in particular, is subject to government authorization under the Broadcasting Act of 1950 and dependent on exclusive frequency allocations. This framework subjects the media to ongoing oversight by political authorities, constraining its autonomy and limiting its ability to act as an independent democratic check.

Moreover, media consumption patterns exacerbate the problem: older generations remain reliant on newspapers and television, whereas younger citizens primarily consume information via digital platforms. Political actors exploit this divide, especially during elections, by leveraging traditional media to secure support from older voters. In this symbiotic relationship, ruling party politicians and government agencies benefit from the compliance of established media outlets, while media organizations maintain privileged access and regulatory stability. Even NHK (*Nippon Hoso Kyokai*, a national broadcasting corporation), although formally mandated as an independent public broadcaster, is subject to government influence through the appointment of its leadership by the prime minister and the National Diet, creating a de facto relationship of control.

3.3 Social Psychology Perspective: Collectivism and Conformity Pressures

Crisis conditions generate powerful social pressures to conform, rooted in cultural and institutional norms of collectivism. In such contexts, maintaining group harmony often takes precedence over individual expression, and dissenting views may be stigmatized as "unscientific" or "alarmist." Within expert communities, these dynamics foster self-censorship, as scholars and practitioners anticipate social sanction or reputational loss for challenging dominant positions. Conformity pressures extend into civil society, where mechanisms such as campaigns against "misinformation" and informal surveillance practices—including the so-called "self-restraint police"—reinforce prevailing narratives and marginalize alternative perspectives (*Mainichi* 2020).

Digital platforms further intensify conformity pressures. Although individuals theoretically enjoy the freedom to upload videos and comments, crisis situations often lead to heightened content regulation. Posts deemed contrary to government policy or dominant discourse may be deleted, frozen, or subjected to opaque moderation standards imposed by platform providers. Such practices produce a chilling effect on citizens' willingness to voice dissent, particularly on sensitive issues such as nuclear power, vaccination policy, or the war in Ukraine. In turn, this environment reinforces a culture of self-censorship, as individuals internalize conformity norms and withhold perspectives that might disrupt collective consensus.

3.4 Integrated Perspective: The Triangle of Concealment and Conformity

These perspectives addressed in the previous section reveal a recurrent structural configuration in crisis governance. Governmental concealment for administrative expediency, media dependence on official sources, and conformity pressures rooted in collectivist norms and amplified by digital platforms interact to form what may be called the Triangle of Concealment and Conformity. This triangle operates less through overt coercion than through mutually reinforcing dynamics that curtail pluralism while maintaining the appearance of democratic process.

At its core, the triangle highlights a paradox of democratic vulnerability: institutions premised on trust between government and citizens are weakened when the very guardians of information act in ways that undermine that trust. Short-term expediency and the preservation of institutional legitimacy are privileged over the long-term welfare of the population. By disregarding ethical responsibility and failing to embrace a sense of noblesse oblige, elites within government, media, and expert communities erode the civic foundations that sustain democracy.

The triangle also reflects the logic of informational autocracy, or "Autocracy 2.0" (Guriev and Treisman 2019; Yang 2024), where legitimacy is preserved less by overt repression than by subtle manipulation of information and discourse. Within this structure, concealment is legitimized through expert endorsement, conformity is normalized through media reproduction, and dissent is marginalized by social sanction and platform regulation. The outcome is a governance regime that retains formal democratic institutions yet functions in practice to limit deliberation and accountability.

The integrated perspective thus emphasizes that the challenge lies not only in institutional design but also in ethical commitment. Without firm adherence to principles of truth, transparency, and responsibility, even established democracies are vulnerable to patterns of information control that hollow out their normative core. The Triangle of Concealment and Conformity may offer a conceptual lens for understanding these dynamics not only in Japan but also in comparative perspective across other democracies experiencing similar tendencies.

4 Case Studies

This section examines three crises in Japan to empirically investigate the operation of the Triangle of Concealment and Conformity. Each case highlights interactions among government, media, and expert communities, while illustrating structural patterns that recur across distinct policy domains. The analysis identifies both immediate crisis management practices and the underlying mechanisms that shape public discourse and citizen trust (Table 1).

Table 1: Comparison of Three Crisis Cases

Item	Fukushima Nuclear Accident	COVID-19 Pandemic	Russo-Ukrainian War
Nature of Crisis	Physical disaster/ technological risk	Infectious disease/public health crisis	International politics/security issue
Pretext for Information Control	Panic prevention/ credibility maintenance	Misinformation prevention/ infection containment	International cooperation/ diplomatic unity
Role of Media	Relayed official safety assurances	Repeated expert committee statements/ excluded dissent	Aligned with Western narratives/ marginalized critique
Discursive Tendency of Experts/ Academics	Safety emphasis/ dissent exclusion	Emphasis on consensus/ dismissal of cautionary views	Sole emphasis on support/ delegitimization of peace advocacy
Form of Information Control	Nondisclosure and delay	Centralized expertise/social surveillance	Self-censorship through normative conformity
Impact on the Public	Delayed evacuation, radiation exposure	Restrictions, economic stagnation, mutual surveillance	Economic burdens, lack of foreign policy debate

Source: Author

4.1 The Fukushima Daiichi Nuclear Power Plant Accident (2011)

On March 11, 2011, a massive earthquake and tsunami precipitated a catastrophic nuclear accident at the Fukushima Daiichi Power Plant. Internally, TEPCO and government agencies quickly recognized the potential for core meltdown and large-scale radioactive contamination (Funabashi and Kitazawa 2012; Kushida 2012). Yet critical information, including projections from the System for Prediction of Environmental Emergency Dose Information (SPEEDI), was withheld from the public. This nondisclosure, officially justified as a measure to prevent panic, obstructed timely evacuation decisions and significantly increased radiation exposure risks (Onishi and Fackler 2011).

A striking feature of the crisis was the divergence between domestic and international media coverage. Japanese outlets largely emphasized government reassurances, while foreign media reported more openly on reactor explosions and raised early suspicions of nuclear fuel meltdown. These discrepancies were widely interpreted as evidence of government influence over domestic reporting, which constrained the range of information available to the Japanese public (Hasegawa 2012).

The mass media, embedded in the press-club system, replicated official statements while facing structural disincentives for adversarial reporting. Press coverage emphasized assurances of safety, and critical inquiries were largely confined to a small minority of outlets. This dynamic reflects the logic of informational autocracy (Guriev and Treisman 2019), in which governments sustain legitimacy not by silencing media entirely but by ensuring that dominant narratives align with official accounts.

Expert communities were subject to parallel conformity pressures. Independent researchers and foreign experts who raised concerns about radiation exposure were frequently stigmatized as alarmist or unscientific (Hasegawa 2012), marginalizing dissenting perspectives. The convergence of government nondisclosure, media replication, and expert conformity exemplifies the operation of the Triangle of Concealment and Conformity, producing informational gaps and delaying protective action for the public.

4.2 The COVID-19 Pandemic (2020–)

The COVID-19 pandemic constituted a crisis marked by uncertainty and rapidly evolving scientific knowledge. The Japanese government established the Expert Meeting on Novel Coronavirus Disease as the primary locus of scientific authority (Shimizu and Negita 2020). Information issued by this body was presented as definitive, while alternative perspectives were frequently dismissed as misinformation. Policy measures—such as voluntary self-restraint orders and vaccination campaigns—were communicated primarily through media channels aligned with official narratives, reinforcing centralized control over public understanding.

Media behavior further amplified this centralization of information. National television and newspapers repeatedly broadcast Expert Meeting recommendations, typically emphasizing compliance and caution. Critical reporting or coverage of dissenting scientific findings remained limited, reflecting both structural dependency on government-sanctioned sources and financial vulnerabilities associated with advertising-based revenue models. Parallel restrictions were visible on digital platforms: for instance, YouTube removed or banned videos that cast doubt on vaccination, framing these measures as part of its anti-misinformation campaign (*Asahi Shimbun* 2021). Whether such actions were the result of independent platform moderation or undertaken in response to explicit or implicit government pressure remains unclear.

Citizens themselves internalized these narratives and, in some cases, engaged in social policing behaviors. The phenomenon of the so-called self-restraint police exemplifies how conformity pressures extended beyond formal institutions into civil society (*Mainichi* 2020; Yoshioka and Maeda 2020). Individuals monitored and sanctioned noncompliant behavior, creating a feedback loop in which the population itself reinforced the Triangle of Concealment and Conformity. This dynamic demonstrates how both ethical norms and social expectations interact with structural information control, producing a hybrid regime of governance rooted in both state-led communication and bottom-up enforcement of conformity.

4.3 The Russo-Ukrainian War (2022–)

The Russo-Ukrainian War presents a contrasting case in which the triangle operates primarily through normative and discursive pressures rather than technical or health measures. Following the outbreak of the conflict, the Japanese government and major media outlets swiftly aligned with Western diplomatic narratives, offering unequivocal support for Ukraine while marginalizing alternative perspectives such as neutral diplomacy or conflict-resolution approaches (Hosaka 2023). NHK's quantitative analysis of evening news coverage confirms this narrowing of discourse, showing a marked emphasis on battlefield developments in Ukraine and Russia, while peace-seeking narratives receded over time (Uesugi 2023).

A striking feature in the Japanese context was the heightened visibility of certain academics—particularly professors of international politics and researchers from national universities and public institutions. These scholars and researchers frequently appeared in mainstream media to advocate unwavering support for Ukraine and to endorse Prime Minister Kishida's alignment with US President Joe Biden. While resonant with official policy, such interventions drew criticism for compromising academic neutrality and professional ethics, transforming scholarly commentary into political advocacy.

Media dynamics reinforced this discursive convergence. Journalists often echoed these academic positions without sustained scrutiny, thereby amplifying dominant narratives. Experts who voiced caution or suggested diplomatic alternatives faced reputational risks and were effectively silenced. Even in the absence of formal censorship, social and professional pressures fostered widespread self-censorship. As a result, citizens were deprived of nuanced information about sanctions, energy prices, and diplomatic options, limiting their capacity for independent judgment.

These developments raise fundamental questions about the orientation of Japanese foreign policy, specifically, whether decisions—such as large-scale financial commitments to Ukraine—are pursued primarily in the national interest or whether they reflect the personal political agendas of the prime minister and the minister of foreign affairs. Such concerns underscore the risks posed when conformity pressures and elite alignment narrow public discourse, thereby weakening democratic accountability in matters of war and diplomacy.

4.4 Comparative Analysis Across Cases

Despite the differing nature of the Fukushima nuclear accident, the COVID-19 pandemic, and the Russo-Ukrainian War, consistent structural patterns emerge across these crises. In each case, government authorities exercised significant discretion over the timing, content, and framing of information disclosure, often privileging political stability, the containment of unrest, and institutional credibility over comprehensive guidance to the public. Domestic media, structurally dependent on official sources, reproduced government-sanctioned narratives and narrowed the range of permissible debate, while foreign outlets more openly reported alternative perspectives, exposing discrepancies in coverage. Expert communities were likewise shaped by professional hierarchies and social expectations that favored consensus and alignment with prevailing government positions (Shibuya et al., 2022). Together, these dynamics restricted the circulation of diverse perspectives, weakened citizens' capacity for autonomous judgment, and steadily eroded public trust in institutions.

The comparative perspective underscores that the triangle operates through varying combinations of formal and informal mechanisms. In the Fukushima and COVID-19 cases, technical regulations, bureaucratic routines, and institutional controls were the primary instruments limiting media scrutiny and expert independence. Restrictions on expression within digital platforms during the pandemic—such as the removal of YouTube videos questioning vaccine safety—further narrowed discursive space, although the extent of governmental influence over such measures remains uncertain.

By contrast, in the Russo-Ukrainian War, overt censorship was largely absent. Instead, normative pressures, reputational sanctions, and the visible advocacy of academics endorsing government's foreign policy became decisive in constraining public discourse (Shibuya et al. 2022). Despite contextual variation, the triangle consistently elevated short-term expediency and the appearance of stability above longer-term democratic commitments to transparency, accountability, and service to the public.

This recurring pattern carries significant normative implications. It demonstrates how democratic systems, even while maintaining procedural continuity, can drift into practices that hollow out substantive legitimacy. When information disclosure is shaped by expediency, when media actors reproduce rather than interrogate official claims, and when experts reinforce orthodoxy instead of subjecting it to scrutiny, the core democratic values of openness, pluralism, and accountability are compromised (Shibuya et al. 2022). Such dynamics not only diminish public trust in government, media, and expert authority but also normalize governance patterns in which ethical responsibilities to citizens are subordinated to the imperatives of control and stability.

From this perspective, the triangle explains more than episodic failures of crisis governance; it reveals a broader democratic paradox. Formal institutions continue to operate and claim legitimacy, yet their practices simultaneously undermine the very conditions—trust, deliberation, and moral responsibility—that sustain democratic life. Recognizing this paradox is crucial, for it frames the central challenge of crisis governance: how to safeguard stability without sacrificing transparency, how to manage uncertainty without silencing pluralism, and how to preserve authority without eroding the ethical duty owed to citizens. These questions establish the normative foundation for the subsequent discussion of the democratic, ethical, and structural vulnerabilities illuminated by the Triangle of Concealment and Conformity (Shibuya et al. 2022).

5 Comprehensive Analysis

The empirical evidence from the Fukushima nuclear accident, the COVID-19 pandemic, and the Russo-Ukrainian War underscores the recurrent operation of what may be termed the "Triangle of Concealment and Conformity." This triangle captures the mutually reinforcing interactions among government, media, and expert communities that structure the production and circulation of information during crises. The pattern is structural rather than incidental: even while formal institutions preserve procedural legitimacy, they repeatedly prioritize expediency over transparency, accountability, and ethical responsibility. In effect, surface stability is sustained at the hidden cost of eroding democratic and normative foundations. This chapter systematically reviews these recurring dynamics thematically across the three cases.

5.1 Government Information Control and the State of Exception

From the standpoint of political philosophy, government information control can be understood through Carl Schmitt's concept of the state of exception, in which ordinary rules are suspended and discretionary authority is asserted in the name of safeguarding order (Schmitt [1922] 2005). The ethical concern is profound.

By withholding or delaying disclosures—such as radioactive dispersion data after Fukushima or infection statistics during COVID-19—authorities implicitly treat public welfare as secondary to administrative convenience. This reflects a failure of noblesse oblige, the moral duty of rulers to prioritize the public good over institutional self-preservation. A structural response would be statutory guarantees of immediate disclosure of life-critical information, thereby constraining discretionary concealment and affirming the public's right to know.

5.2 Media Dependency and the Ethics of Reporting

The media, ideally functioning as a democratic watchdog, is drawn into the triangle through structural dependencies. In Japan, the press-club system and reliance on advertising revenue from government-linked or corporate actors discourage adversarial reporting and incentivize reproduction of official narratives. During crises such as Fukushima and COVID-19, these dependencies became especially pronounced, as reporting prioritized stability and compliance over scrutiny and critique.

The ethical stakes are clear. By privileging reassurance and institutional stability, the media compromises its duty to ensure pluralism, accuracy, and timeliness. Meaningful reform requires strengthening media independence by reducing structural and financial ties to official sources, enabling journalism to reclaim its role as a critical forum for democratic deliberation.

5.3 Expert Communities and Conformity Pressures

Experts, too, face conformity pressures rooted in collectivist norms, professional hierarchies, and reputational risks. Fear of marginalization or public criticism often silences dissenting voices. These pressures result not in open acknowledgment of uncertainty but in the narrowing of discourse, as seen in both scientific risk communication after Fukushima and polarized public health messaging during COVID-19 (Section 4.2).

From an ethical standpoint, experts bear the responsibility to communicate knowledge transparently, acknowledge uncertainty, and articulate minority perspectives when relevant. Institutional safeguards—such as formal dissent-protection mechanisms and structured inclusion of alternative viewpoints—could counteract conformity pressures and enhance the quality of policy deliberation.

5.4 Ethical Fragility and Democratic Resilience

Taken together, the triangle produces outcomes that are consistent but troubling: apparent stability is maintained at the cost of transparency, pluralism, and citizens' capacity for autonomous judgment (Levitsky and Ziblatt 2018). Citizens are not only deprived of information but are also socialized into reinforcing conformity through compliance, reputational policing, and internalization of official narratives.

This reveals an ethical fragility in democratic systems. Government officials, journalists, and experts often pursue short-term incentives of administrative efficiency, career advancement, or social legitimacy while neglecting their longer-term obligations to citizens. Hannah Arendt's notion of "thoughtlessness" aptly captures this dynamic: the uncritical adherence to routines and norms that enables institutionally predictable but ethically unexamined behavior (1963). For genuine democratic resilience, institutional design must be complemented by normative commitments to transparency, accountability, and pluralism.

5.5 Public Trust and Civic Capacity

The consequences of the triangle extend beyond individual crises to the long-term erosion of public trust. Repeated experiences of delayed disclosure, selective reporting, and expert conformity weaken confidence in government, media, and expertise. Once eroded, trust is exceedingly difficult to restore. A crucial counterweight lies in civic capacity. Citizens equipped with information literacy, critical reasoning skills, and participatory opportunities are better positioned to evaluate competing claims, resist conformity, and deliberate constructively. Civic education and participatory initiatives should therefore be recognized as central—not peripheral—to democratic resilience.

5.6 Integrated Recommendations

The preceding analysis points toward four interrelated recommendations:

1. Legal frameworks for transparency—Mandating timely disclosure of crisis-critical data to reduce scope for concealment and affirm the public's right to know.
2. Media independence reforms—Addressing structural and financial dependencies so journalism can act as an autonomous watchdog.
3. Plurality within expert communities—Establishing safeguards that protect dissent and encourage open acknowledgment of uncertainty.
4. Civic information literacy—Expanding education and participatory initiatives that equip citizens to evaluate information critically.

Together, these measures recognize that stability maintained through concealment and conformity is fragile and normatively compromised. Durable democratic resilience requires transparency, pluralism, and ethical responsibility across government, media, and expertise.

6 Conclusion

This study has examined the recurrent operation of the Triangle of Concealment and Conformity across three distinct crises in Japan: the Fukushima Daiichi Nuclear Accident, the COVID-19 pandemic, and the Russo-Ukrainian War. The analysis demonstrates that the interplay of government information control, media dependency, and expert conformity produces the short-term appearance of stability while simultaneously undermining public welfare, pluralistic discourse, and citizen trust. This pattern is structural rather than incidental, reflecting enduring vulnerabilities within democratic governance.

The cases further illustrate that crises function not only as political challenges but also as ethical tests. Government actors often prioritize expedient decision-making and administrative convenience over their moral obligations to the public. Media organizations, constrained by structural and financial dependencies, frequently reproduce official narratives, while expert communities confront social and professional pressures to conform. Collectively, these dynamics limit the conditions for autonomous judgment, critical debate, and sustained confidence in institutions.

At a deeper level, ethical neglect and conformity pressures generate fragility in democratic systems. Stability achieved through concealment is inherently precarious, masking vulnerabilities, while eroding the normative foundations of trust, transparency, and legitimacy.

Resilience in crisis governance requires more than procedural legitimacy; it demands the integration of institutional design with ethical responsibility. Legal frameworks that guarantee timely disclosure, reforms to strengthen media independence, protections for pluralism within expert communities, and the cultivation of civic information literacy together constitute a pathway toward more durable democratic resilience. Societies that confront crises with transparency, pluralism, and ethical commitment can transform moments of vulnerability into opportunities to reinforce democratic trust and legitimacy, rather than allowing expedient concealment to undermine them.

Bibliography

Arendt, Hannah. 1963. *Eichmann in Jerusalem: A Report on the Banality of Evil.* Viking Press.

Asahi Shimbun. 2021. "Fighting Wave of Misinfo, YouTube Bans False Vaccine Claims." September 30. https://www.asahi.com/ajw/articles/14450970.

Funabashi, Yoichi, and Kay Kitazawa. 2012. "Fukushima in Review: A Complex Disaster, a Disastrous Response." *Bulletin of the Atomic Scientists* 68 (2): 9–21. https://doi.org/10.1177/0096340212440359.

Guriev, Sergei, and Daniel Treisman. 2019. "Informational Autocrats." *Journal of Economic Perspectives* 33 (4): 100–27. https://doi.org/10.1257/jep.33.4.100.

Hasegawa, Koichi. 2012. "Facing Nuclear Risks: Lessons from the Fukushima Nuclear Disaster." *International Journal of Japanese Sociology* 21 (1): 84–91. https://doi.org/10.1111/j.1475-6781.2012.01164.x.

Hosaka, Sanshiro. 2023. "Ukraine's Agency in Japanese Discourse: Everything OK with Government and People, While Academia in Trouble." *Journal of Regional Security* 18 (1): 47–58. https://doi.org/10.5937/jrs 18-41778.

Kushida, Kenji E. 2012. "Japan's Fukushima Nuclear Disaster: Narrative, Analysis, Recommendations." Shorenstein APARC Working Paper, December 15. https://ssrn.com/abstract=2118876.

Levitsky, Steven, and Lucan A. Way. 2010. *Competitive Authoritarianism: Hybrid Regimes After the Cold War.* Cambridge University Press.

Levitsky, Steven, and Daniel Ziblatt. 2018. *How Democracies Die.* Crown.

Mainichi. 2020. " 'Self-Restraint Police' in Japan Harassing Business Operating amid Virus Outbreak." May 22. https://mainichi.jp/english/articles/20200522/p2a/00m/0na/023000c.

Onishi, Norimitsu, and Martin Fackler. 2011. "Japan Held Nuclear Data, Leaving Evacuees in Peril." *New York Times*, August 8. https://www.nytimes.com/2011/08/09/world/asia/09japan.html.

Sahashi, Ryo. 2022. *Crisis and International Politics: What the War in Ukraine Asks of Us* [in Japanese]. Iwanami Shoten.

Schmitt, Carl. (1922) 2005. *Political Theology: Four Chapters on the Concept of Sovereignty.* Translated by George Schwab. University of Chicago Press.

Shibuya, Yuka, Chun-Ming Lai, Andrea Hamm, Soichiro Takagi, and Yoshihide Sekimoto. 2022. "Do Open Data Impact Citizens' Behavior? Assessing Face Mask Panic Buying Behaviors during the COVID-19 Pandemic." *Scientific Reports* 12: 17607. https://doi.org/10.1038/s41598 -022-22471-y.

Shimizu, Kazuki, and Masashi Negita. 2020. "Lessons Learned from Japan's Response to the First Wave of COVID-19: A Content Analysis." *Healthcare* 8 (4): 426. https://doi.org/10.3390/healthcare8040426.

TEPCO (Tokyo Electric Power Company) and Government Investigation Committee. 2012. *Fukushima Nuclear Accident Investigation Report* [in Japanese]. TEPCO (Tokyo Electric Power Company) and Government Investigation Committee.

Treisman, Daniel, and Sergei Guriev. 2022. *Spin Dictators: The Changing Face of Tyranny in the 21st Century*. Princeton University Press.

Uesugi, Shinichi. 2023. "Reflecting on the First Year of Russian Military Aggression." NHK Broadcasting Culture Research Institute, August 1. https://www.nhk.or.jp/bunken/english/research/domestic/20230801_6. html.

Yamaguchi, Jun. 2021. *The COVID Crisis and Democracy: The Dilemma of Governance and Freedom* [in Japanese]. Iwanami Shoten.

Yang, David Y. 2024. "China: Autocracy 2.0." NBER Working Paper No. 32993. National Bureau of Economic Research. https://doi. org/10.3386/w32993.

Yoshioka, Takashi, and Yohei Maeda. 2020. "COVID-19 Stigma Induced by Local Government and Media Reporting in Japan: It's Time to Reconsider Risk Communication Lessons from the Fukushima Daiichi Nuclear Disaster." *Journal of Epidemiology* 30 (8): 372–73. https://doi. org/10.2188/jea.JE20200247.

CHAPTER 2

Autocracy 2.0 and the Informational Turn in Democratic Backsliding: A Comparative Analysis of Japan and Turkey

Abstract:

The study examines the phenomenon of democratic erosion within the context of a democratic system, characterized by the presence of democratic elections and institutions. Utilizing theoretical frameworks of Autocracy 2.0 and Informational Autocracy, which emphasizes technocratic governance, information control, and populist legitimacy, the study analyzes how executive authority consolidates within democratic regimes without overt coercion. A comparison of Japan under Shinzo Abe and Turkey under Recep Tayyip Erdoğan reveals two patterns of democratic backsliding: bureaucratically systemized governance in Japan and strong populist leadership in Turkey. The study concludes that contemporary democratic erosion often occurs through the strategic adaptation of existing institutions, as observed in these two distinct patterns. This adaptation is characterized by expanded executive discretion, weakened legislative oversight, and constrained judicial intervention while maintaining the formal appearance of democracy. Additionally, the study finds that control over information flows, increasingly mediated by digital and artificial intelligence (AI) technologies, enables elite dominance and the erosion of democratic agency in Autocracy 2.0. This erosion can only be countered by active civic participation, independent media, and inclusive public discourse. In order to enhance its explanatory power, it is recommended that future research should expand the Autocracy 2.0 framework through cross-regional comparisons and citizen-level perspectives.

Keywords: Autocracy 2.0, Informational Autocracy, Democratic Backsliding, Information Control, Technocratic Governance

1 Introduction

In recent decades, the traditional conception of autocracy as the binary opposite of democracy, marked by the absence of elections, suppression of dissent, and reliance on violence, has undergone substantial refinement (Besley and Kudamatsu 2007). Instead of viewing political regimes through a rigid dichotomy, scholars now emphasize the diversity and adaptability of authoritarian rule (Kelemen 2020). Contemporary research highlights how many regimes combine democratic institutions with authoritarian practices, challenging simplistic categorizations and emphasizing the need for a more nuanced understanding of autocratic governance (Guriev 2024).

In this chapter, democracy is defined in accordance with the classical doctrine articulated by Joseph A. Schumpeter: "the institutional arrangement for making political decisions that realizes the common good by allowing the people to decide on issues through the election of individuals who will assemble in order to carry out the people's will" ([1942] 2006, 250). According to this definition, political systems that deviate from this framework may not qualify as truly democratic. In the twenty-first century, liberal democracies are less challenged by external threats, such as military coups or revolutionary uprisings, and more by developments within their own institutional frameworks. As democratic norms erode, a discernible trend toward new forms of authoritarianism has emerged (Guriev 2024).

According to the 2025 V-Dem Institute Annual Report documents, the global landscape consists of ninety-one autocracies (fifty-six electoral and thirty-five closed) and eighty-eight democracies (twenty-nine liberal and fifty-nine electoral) (V-Dem 2025). Contemporary regimes increasingly rely on aspirational rhetoric, strategic control of information, and technological sophistication rather than overt coercion. Among the emerging models, David Y. Yang's (2024) concept of Autocracy 2.0 has gained analytical prominence. This analytical model depicts an adaptive political form of authoritarianism in which conventional instruments of political pressure are replaced by incentives, bureaucratic administration, and digital governance. Autocracy 2.0 contrasts markedly with earlier variants, referred to as Autocracy 1.0, which relied on coercion, functioned in low-information contexts, and lacked credible institutional commitments.

The concept of Autocracy 2.0, while often linked to authoritarian regimes such as China, has been observed to manifest fundamental mechanisms that are gaining prominence in democratic states experiencing political polarization, economic stagnation, and declining institutional credibility. Japan provides an example of this trend. Recent political developments indicate a subtle yet significant transformation in the logic of political governance, although Japan has maintained its status as a consolidated liberal democracy in the postwar era. This situation has emerged through unique phenomena, including greater political power of the prime minister and his cabinet, which has been described as "presidentialization" of the prime minister. There has also been a frequent use of cabinet decisions that bind government ministries, while at the same time there have been fewer opportunities for deliberations in the National Diet. There has been a neutralization of judicial interventions (Krauss and Nyblade 2005; Kamikawa 2018). In the absence of amendments to the constitution, there have been changes in the realm of both political and administrative activities (Kamikawa 2018). The analysis of these patterns suggests that autocratic elements, particularly those related to media control and elite coordination, are not confined to authoritarian systems but can become embedded within democratic frameworks.

This study posits that the conceptual boundary between democratic and authoritarian governance is becoming increasingly indistinct. The presence of features characteristics of modern autocracies can be observed within democratic institutions, even in the absence of a formal regime change. The study draws on recent theoretical work, including Guriev and Treisman's (2019) concept of Informational Autocracy and Yang's (2024) model of Autocracy 2.0. Utilizing these frameworks, the study explores the potential for internal transformation in democratic systems. Japan serves as the primary case study, with Turkey serving as a comparative reference point. The analysis examines how advanced democracies can incrementally adopt autocratic logic under the pretexts of efficiency, stability, or crisis management (Carroll 2021). Japan exemplifies a more subtle, technocratic trajectory of transformation, whereas Turkey illustrates a more overt and accelerated erosion of democratic governance, particularly following the 2017 constitutional amendments and the consolidation of executive power (Sakurai 2018).

To explore the dynamics between democracy and autocracy, this study poses the following research questions:

1. How do features characteristic of modern autocracies, particularly information control and technocratic governance, manifest and become institutionalized within established democracies such as Japan?
2. How do these developments compare with the trajectory of more overtly transformed democratic systems such as Turkey, thereby complicating conventional distinctions between democratic and authoritarian rule?

By situating Japan and, by comparison, Turkey within this broader theoretical framework, the chapter aims to contribute to ongoing debates on democratic backsliding and the evolving nature of political authority in the digital age. It offers transferable insights into how democratic systems might be susceptible to similar forms of internal transformation.

2 Methodology

This chapter employs a qualitative case study approach to investigate the subtle manifestations of autocratic drift within a consolidated democracy. Japan has been identified as a "least likely" case for autocratic tendencies. This suggests that the long-standing consolidation of its democratic institutions, its relatively high political stability, and the absence of overt populist upheaval have contributed to the unanticipated emergence of such features. The examination of such cases is imperative, as it facilitates the identification of subtle transformations in governance that might otherwise be overlooked in contexts where democratic backsliding is more pronounced or overtly coercive (Ekiert 2023; Little and Meng 2024). The strength of a case study that focuses on the least likely outcome lies in its potential to reveal the underlying mechanisms of democratic erosion, even when formal institutions remain largely intact.

To broaden the analysis and facilitate comparative reflection, Turkey is included as a secondary reference case. In contrast to Japan, Turkey offers a more evident illustration of democratic deconsolidation. Significant constitutional revisions have been observed to coincide with a rise in executive personalization and the suppression of dissenting media, indicating a concurrent democratic decline (Scheppele 2018). Incorporating Turkey into an analysis facilitates a comparative perspective, thereby enabling the contextualization of the Japanese case. This is not to claim equivalence, but rather to illustrate a spectrum of autocratic tendencies that may evolve within diverse institutional and cultural environments. Moreover, the author's prior research on Turkish politics and human rights legislative systems provides a further rationale for including Turkey as a comparative case (Sakurai 2018, 2019).

The analysis is primarily grounded in the conceptual frameworks of Yang's (2024) Autocracy 2.0 and Guriev and Treisman's (2019) Informational Autocracy. These frameworks function as the primary analytical lenses through which empirical developments in Japan and Turkey are examined. This approach enables a comprehensive evaluation of two distinct contemporary patterns in executive centralization, governance transparency, digital infrastructure development, and public discourse. The observed patterns are situated within the theoretical constructs of information control, technocratic populism (Bickerton and Accetti 2017), and predictive governance.

3 Theoretical Frameworks

Contemporary contributions to the discipline of political science have advanced the typology of regimes, transcending the conventional binary distinction between democracy and autocracy. As posited by Levitsky and Way (2010, 2020), the notion of "competitive authoritarianism" is utilized to denote hybrid regimes that preserve the appearance of democratic institutions while systematically undermining them through the excision of media control, legal harassment, and electoral bias. In accordance with this theory, scholars differentiate between "electoral autocracies" and "closed autocracies," thereby highlighting the diversity of authoritarian forms and mechanisms (Lueders 2022; Schmid 2025).

In their theory of Informational Autocracy, Guriev and Treisman (2019) shift attention from overt coercion to the manipulation of the information environment. Contemporary autocrats employ state-controlled media, selective transparency, and disinformation to shape public opinion, secure legitimacy, and reduce the need for violence, thereby concealing the extent of repression. Other research emphasizes institutional mechanisms for authoritarian stability, including elite coordination, resource allocation, and bureaucratic management (Bernhard et al. 2020). A further strand of research examines the personalization of power, where authority concentrates on a single political leader, weakening institutional constraints (Frantz 2018). While this can enhance short-term decisiveness, it heightens long-term risks related to succession, policy continuity, and resilience, leaving regimes more exposed to crises (Frantz and Kendall-Taylor 2016; Esen and Gümüşçü 2016).

Yang (2024) introduces the concept of "Autocracy 2.0," which captures the transformation of authoritarian governance in the digital information era. In this study, Yang employs China as a paradigmatic example to illustrate Autocracy 2.0, a model in which state power is sustained through a strategic integration of economic incentives, aspirational narratives, and technologically enabled administration. This dynamic stands in marked contrast to the more overtly coercive and information-scarce environments typically associated with "Autocracy 1.0," a conventional conceptualization of autocracy (Yang 2024).

The concept of Autocracy 2.0 Yang proposed may be the subject to critique: A foundational critique asserts that, despite technological advancements, autocracies encounter challenges in making credible commitments to citizens, elites, and bureaucrats. As Acemoglu and Robinson (2005) argue, the absence of political oversight can erode public confidence, given that authoritarian leaders are often unable to guarantee the security of property rights or the continuity of certain privileges. This has the effect of undermining long-term cooperation and rendering the regime valuable to elite defection or popular unrest. Moreover, akin to other autocratic models, Autocracy 2.0 faces persistent problems of information asymmetry and principal–agent dynamics. The absence of free elections, independent media, and civil society has been demonstrated to limit the regime's ability to obtain accurate, timely information, creating incentives for lower-level officials to distort reports. This, in turn, results in flawed decision-making and resource misallocation (Guriev and Treisman 2022).

Another line of critique concerns deficits in legitimacy. In the absence of mechanisms for meaningful participation or contestation, the concept of Autocracy 2.0 relies on performance or coercion to generate legitimacy. However, both of these are considered unstable foundations for long-term rule. While measures such as surveillance and economic management may temporarily suppress any form of opposition, there is a risk that they may lead to public disapproval or fail to address the underlying discontent, particularly if economic growth slows or public expectations rise. Consequently, despite its innovative features, Autocracy 2.0 remains subject to the structural constraints that have historically undermined authoritarian regimes. These constraints pertain to the domains of credible commitment, information aggregation, and legitimacy (Kolstad 2023).

A defining feature of Autocracy 2.0 is its reliance on AI-integrated surveillance and algorithmic systems for monitoring, prediction, and behavioral manipulation (Beraja et al. 2023b). In contradiction to the blunt instruments of secret police and mass repression utilized by earlier autocracies, contemporary authoritarianism is increasingly dependent on digital infrastructure and data-driven governance to manage dissent and influence public behavior (Roberts 2018). Nevertheless, digital dependency introduces structural vulnerabilities. The centralized and technologically advanced nature of Autocracy 2.0 leaves it vulnerable to systemic disruptions such as cyberattacks, technical failures, or sabotage.

It is important to note that the features associated with Autocracy 2.0 are not confined to formally authoritarian regimes. Elements such as executive centralization, digital surveillance, and the marginalization of deliberative processes are increasingly evident in democratic systems, often justified in the name of efficiency, stability, or crisis response (Walker 2016). As in Table 1, the conceptual factors that structure the autocracies of versions 1.0 and 2.0 can be summarized as follows:

Table 1: Ideal-Type Comparison: Autocracy 1.0 Versus Autocracy 2.0

Dimension	Autocracy 1.0	Autocracy 2.0
Legitimacy Basis	Ideology, coercion	Performance, technocratic governance
Media Control	State monopoly, censorship	Regulatory capture, media cooptation
Civil Society	Repressed	Tolerated but constrained
Elections	Absent or overtly manipulated	Regular; legitimacy via electoral success
Opposition	Crushed through violence	Delegitimized via legal and discursive means
Public Image	Strongman rule	Managerial competence, national renewal
International Strategy	Isolation or anti-Western alignment	Strategic engagement, image management

Source: Author.

4 Mechanisms of Autocratic Drift in Democracies

Although autocracy has traditionally been viewed as being external to democratic systems, recent developments suggest a significant shift in this perception. The study explores this shift in perception in the backdrop of increasingly AI-driven authoritarian mechanisms, particularly to enable information control, technocratic centralization, and surveillance. These elements are ordinarily introduced in a gradual manner, often justified in terms of efficiency, crisis management, or modernization. Utilizing the Autocracy 2.0 framework, this section examines three interconnected pathways through which democratic institutions may undergo autocratic drift: information control, elite coordination via technocratic populism, and predictive governance through surveillance technologies.

4.1 Information Control

A salient indication of democratic deterioration is the manipulation of the information environment. In contrast to the overt bans and state monopolies that typified classical forms of censorship, contemporary democracies have been observed to deploy more subtle and decentralized forms of information control. These include the use of algorithmic content moderation by private social media platforms, indirect governmental pressure on the media, and domestic or international regulatory mechanisms that selectively penalize dissenting voices (King et al. 2017; Roberts 2018). The result of this process is a form of "soft censorship" that formally reserves freedom of speech while, in reality, constraining it.

China offers a paradigmatic example of Informational Autocracy, where the state employs strategies such as the purchase of the elite's silence, the censorship of private media, and the broadcasting of propaganda, as opposed to outright suppression (Guriev and Treisman 2019). By restricting criticism to specific forms, the regime is able to gauge public sentiment while simultaneously overwhelming dissent with state-sponsored messaging and coordinated online activity (Guriev and Treisman 2019). This model has been demonstrated to be effective in preserving regime legitimacy without resorting to overt violence. Contemporary authoritarian regimes have adopted a more discreet and less brutal approach to repression, often succeeding in garnering support while maintaining a veil of secrecy.

While liberal democracies are characterized by formally pluralistic frameworks, there is increasing evidence of similar dynamics occurring through media capture, regulatory threats, and algorithmic content curation (Levitsky and Ziblatt 2018). These practices empower governments to influence public opinion and marginalize opposition narratives, thereby achieving information control without violating legal norms in a formal sense.

4.2 Elite Coordination via Technocratic Populism

The contemporary concept of Autocracy 2.0 signifies a deviation from the traditional paradigm of loyalty, which is rooted in the principle of fear, to a novel model of loyalty that is founded on the basis of performance. In authoritarian systems such as China, local officials are frequently promoted based on economic metrics, including GDP growth within the jurisdiction. This system evokes parallel with a meritocratic tournament (Beraja et al. 2023a). The study hypothesizes that this engenders bureaucratic efficiency while concomitantly reducing the necessity for overt repression, insofar as personnel advancement is now contingent upon regime objectives (Li and Zhou 2005).

Within democratic contexts, a parallel logic emerges through what has been described as technocratic populism. In this paradigm, executive leadership increasingly bypasses conventional deliberative institutions such as legislatures, favoring instead decision-making via expert commissions, task forces, or executive decrees. This tendency was particularly pronounced during the course of the 2020 to 2022 COVID-19 pandemic, when emergency powers were invoked to centralize authority and implement sweeping policies with limited oversight (Harari 2024). Although such actions were often justified by public health imperatives, they reflected a broader shift toward performance-based legitimacy, where effectiveness rather than electoral accountability becomes the primary source of political authority. If this phenomenon is not addressed, it has the capacity to compromise the institutional balance and pluralism that are fundamental to liberal democratic governance.

4.3 Predictive Governance Through Surveillance Technologies

The advent of digital surveillance, particularly with the integration of artificial intelligence (hereinafter "AI"), has further transformed the landscape of governance in both authoritarian and democratic systems (Zuboff 2019). In high-capacity autocracies such as China, the deployment of advanced technologies, including AI and facial recognition, is utilized for the purpose of monitoring citizens, suppressing unrest, and stimulating further innovation (Beraja et al. 2023b). These instruments have been demonstrated to facilitate the establishment of a high level of autocracy, whereby the state is able to perpetuate perverse surveillance without resorting to comprehensive repression (Beraja et al. 2023b).

Furthermore, elements of this surveillance architecture have been adopted by democratic states. The implementation of data-sharing agreements, behavioral analytics, and contact-tracing systems, initially adopted during the pandemic of 2020, has resulted in the extension of the state's reach into the private sphere. While these technologies were initially justified as provisional measures to address public health crises, their ongoing utilization gives rise to concerns regarding long-term implications for civil liberty. The legacy of pandemic governance offers a particularly instructive perspective on this issue. During the crisis, restrictions on movement, mandates on behavior, and the deployment of digital surveillance were largely accepted but may now persist as standard instruments of state control, resulting in a blurring of the lines between emergencies and normal governance (Harari 2024).

The rapid development of AI-integrated surveillance tools poses an even greater challenge. Governments now possess the capability to monitor citizens' movements, associate behavior with ideological dispositions, and even target individuals deemed undesirable (Cabestan 2020). Within the paradigm of the military–industrial complex, there is a conspicuous absence of robust ethical oversight in the AI sector, thereby engendering the risk of opaque and potentially harmful algorithmic interventions. This issue is not merely hypothetical; the opacity of AI systems renders them particularly challenging to audit or contest, thereby reinforcing asymmetries of power balance between the state and the governed (Beraja et al. 2023a).

5 Case Study in the Informational Turn and Executive Power

This section conducts a detailed examination of two case studies from two distinctive types of states within Japan and Turkey. The case studies are situated within the theoretical framework of contemporary autocracies, with particular emphasis on the role of information control and executive power in these systems.

5.1 Japan as a Case Study: Under Shinzo Abe

Japan under Shinzo Abe's second premiership (2012–2020) offers a compelling case study of democratic transformation within the conceptual framework of Autocracy 2.0. Japan has been regarded as a consolidated liberal democracy with a long-standing parliamentary system and, as such, has historically been viewed as institutionally stable and normatively aligned with Western democratic standards. Postwar governance has been characterized by a powerful technocratic bureaucracy and a party system dominated by the Liberal Democratic Party (hereinafter "LDP"), which has retained power almost continuously since 1955. This continuity, while contributing to political stability, has also resulted in the entrenchment of elite networks and reduced the dynamism of democratic competition. Abe's tenure did not disrupt these legacies but rather intensified them, namely, advancing executive centralization, marginalizing deliberative pluralism, and expanding information control, not through dramatic authoritarian rupture but through incremental, technocratic realignment (Ida 2020).

(1) Familial Lineage and Political Cultivation

Abe's political identity and capacity were inextricably linked to his hereditary status as a third-generation politician. His grandfather, Nobusuke Kishi, served as prime minister from 1957 to 1960 and was instrumental in realigning Japan's postwar trajectory toward a pro-American, anti-communist orientation. This laid the ideological and institutional foundation upon which Abe would later build (Johnson et al. 2000). His father, Shintaro Abe, held the post of foreign minister and was long seen as a future prime minister before his untimely death. These familial legacies provided both symbolic recognition and tangible resources, including access to established political networks, campaign infrastructure, bureaucratic channels, and diplomatic knowledge. The mother of Shinzo Abe, Yoko Abe, played a vital role in maintaining the family's political stature, albeit one that was less visible (Abe 2022). Consequently, Abe's political development was not solely individual but embedded in a political culture that emphasized loyalty, elite continuity, and hereditary succession.

(2) Electoral Success and Support Ecosystem

Abe consolidated his position by leveraging this inherited advantage, achieving a series of electoral victories that further consolidated the LDP's legislative dominance. From 2012 to 2020, Abe guided the party to six successive national election victories, thereby enabling an unparalleled accumulation of executive power unprecedented in postwar Japan (Ida 2020). Nevertheless, these triumphs cannot be solely attributable to policy appeal or ideological coherence. Abe was supported by a robust ecosystem of political support, comprising religious affiliations, media alignment, and organizational discipline. The relationship between the LDP and the former Unification Church (now the Family Federation for World Peace and Unification) was previously the subject of little scrutiny.

However, following the assassination of Abe in July 2022, the public became concerned about the latent religious-political entanglements that had quietly bolstered electoral mobilization (Sneider 2022; McLaughlin 2023). Moreover, the LDP's long-standing alliance with Komeito, supported by Soka Gakkai as a religious group, furnished a disciplined voter base, particularly in urban districts. The strategic alliance provided two key benefits. First, it offered electoral insurance, thereby ensuring that key reforms could be passed even in the face of public opposition. Second, it provided legislative consistency, thus enabling the passage of key reforms. Such networks function as informal yet effective instruments of regime consolidation, thereby reinforcing the infrastructural power of the executive while retaining democratic appearances.

(3) Information and Bureaucracy Control

A hallmark of Abe's governance was the strategic implementation of information control. While Japan has maintained formal media pluralism, Abe's administration has subtly restructured the media environment through both institutional and informal mechanisms. As Ida (2020) argued, loyalists were appointed to key positions within Japan Broadcasting Corporation (Nippon Hōsō Kyōkai), NHK the national broadcasting corporation, and relevant public agencies. Furthermore, the press club system, a legacy of postwar corporatism that curtails access for freelance and foreign reporters, was leveraged to limit access to dissenting voices. The enactment of the Act on the Protection of Specially Designated Secrets 2013 further restricted the scope of investigative journalism by criminalizing the unauthorized disclosure of classified information, thereby chilling press freedom (Repeta 2014). Moreover, in 2021, legislation pertaining to national security through economic means was enacted, which introduces ambiguity that has the potential to constrain the scope of investigative journalism. These developments reflect patterns associated with Informational Autocracy (Guriev and Treisman 2019), characterized by the use of strategic communication, regulatory pressures, and targeted enforcement in lieu of overt censorship. Consequently, Japan's press freedom ranking is notably the lowest among G7 countries, and Japan is ranked 66th out of 180 countries by the World Freedom Press index (Reporters Without Borders [RSF] 2025a).

The scope of control was furthermore extended to the administrative bureaucracy, which was traditionally regarded as a bastion of technocratic autonomy. The establishment of the Cabinet Bureau of Personnel Affairs has been identified as a significant development in the context of the Prime Minister's Office. This provides unprecedented authority over top-level appointments, centralizing personnel decisions that had historically been diffused across various ministries (Yakushiji 2020). This centralization of personnel decisions is a notable aspect of the shift in governmental structure. This enabled the cultivation of bureaucratic loyalty, as career officials increasingly aligned their interpretations of law and policy with perceived executive preferences, a phenomenon referred to by Japanese commentators as "reading the air" (i.e., aligning behavior with unspoken executive expectations). In some instances, this incentive structure resulted in document falsification and the degradation of public accountability, thereby undermining the principles of transparency and neutrality that had anchored postwar governance.

(4) Political Controversies and International Affairs

Despite an outward appearance of technocratic control, the Abe administration was significantly affected by political scandals that highlighted the vulnerabilities inherent in concentrated executive authority. The Morimoto Gakuen and Kakei Gakuen cases, which involved allegations of preferential treatment in educational policy and national land transactions, prompted concerns about the improper use of political influence and the impact of personal relationships on policymaking (Yakushiji 2020). It has been reported that Akie Abe, the wife of Shinzo Abe, was involved in the matter under discussion. This has been identified as a factor that has served to further blur the distinction between private interest and public responsibilities. This dynamic, in turn, contributed to the exacerbation of prevailing public mistrust. These events served to exacerbate the prevailing political polarization. Supporters of Abe interpreted these events as politically motivated attacks, while critics saw them as indicative of institutional decline.

In contrast to these domestic challenges, Abe achieved notable prominence in foreign affairs. He advanced Japan's strategic profile by formulating the "Free and Open Indo-Pacific" vision, managing complex diplomatic relations with China, Russia, and South Korea, and reinforcing national security alliances with the United States (Kitaoka 2021). His diplomatic approach, characterized by direct engagement and rhetorical precision, diverged from the traditionally scripted style of Japanese leaders. This combination of assertive international diplomacy and concentrated domestic political control illustrates the paradoxes of performance-based legitimacy within the framework of Autocracy 2.0.

(5) Governance Style and Democratic Erosion

Abe's governance style reached its most pronounced expression in the state's response to the pandemic, which reflected technocratic decision-making under crisis conditions. Instead of invoking formal emergency powers, the administration relied on nonbinding advisories and "requests" for voluntary self-restraint, mechanisms described as "soft compulsion" (Ejima 2000). This strategy maintained legal formalities while subtly reshaping behavioral norms, thereby encouraging compliance through social and normative pressure rather than direct legal coercion. In this manner, the administration exhibited a manifestation of executive authority that curtailed deliberative engagement while augmenting control through social conditioning.

When viewed in its totality, Abe's Japan demonstrates the capacity of a mature democracy to undergo substantial institutional change without experiencing formal regime collapse or amendments to the constitution. It is evident that Abe administration recalibrated domestic governance with a view to prioritizing executive efficiency over accountability. This recalibration was achieved through a number of means, including consolidation of elite power, the orchestration of media narratives, the subordination of the bureaucracy, and the management of political discourse (Ida 2020; Yakushiji 2020). In this particular context, the distinction between procedural democracy and substantive democracy becomes particularly salient. Despite electoral processes remaining competitive and legal institutions being maintained, the substantive dimensions of contestation, transparency, and pluralism were progressively diminished.

Abe's political legacy exemplifies the core logic of Autocracy 2.0: charismatic leadership functioning within democratic institutions to centralize authority, neutralize opposition, and maintain legitimacy through performance and symbolic alignment rather than through participatory governance. His career serves both as a model and a cautionary example, illustrating how democratic tools can be repurposed to enable technocratic insulation and elite control, all while preserving the outward structure of democratic rule (Carroll 2021).

5.2 Turkey as a Case Study: Under Recep Tayyip Erdoğan

Turkey under President Recep Tayyip Erdoğan and the Justice and Development Party (hereinafter "AKP") illustrates a more pronounced and rapid trajectory toward features associated with Autocracy 2.0. While Turkey was once regarded as a model of democratic consolidation, especially during its early 2000s EU accession efforts, this trajectory reversed sharply in the 2010s. The 2017 constitutional referendum marked a turning point, transitioning the country from a parliamentary to a presidential system of government (Sakurai 2018). This eliminated the role of prime minister and expanded the president's authority to appoint ministers, issue decrees, and dissolve parliament (Yılmaz and Bashirov 2018). Although the referendum passed, the narrow margin exposed a deeply polarized electorate. The failed 2016 coup attempt further accelerated executive consolidation, thereby enabling Erdoğan to purge political opponents, reengineer institutional structures, and bring the judiciary and civil service under direct presidential control (Esen and Gümüşçü 2021).

(1) Technocratic Centralization and Populist Insulation

Erdoğan's leadership is marked by personalism, party centralization, and the erosion of checks and balances. As Esen and Gümüşçü (2016) argue, internal dissent within the AKP has been marginalized, thereby effectively transforming the party into an extension of the president's will. Major state institutions, encompassing the judiciary, regulatory bodies, and the military, have undergone large-scale purges, with key positions being filled by loyalists (Tansel 2018). This process was intensified following the 2016 coup attempt, which was attributed to the Gülen movement, a religious network that had previously enjoyed a close relationship with the AKP. The subsequent crackdown on Gülenists served as a justification for broad purges across the state apparatus and the education sector, where thousands of academics and teachers were dismissed or replaced. This consolidation of ideological control over educational content and institutions is a salient feature of the post-coup environment.

Concurrently, pro-government religious organizations such as Diyanet have gained prominence, reinforcing a narrative that intertwines nationalism with conservative Islamic values. While these measures have been presented as a means of promoting national stability and cohesion, concerns have been raised regarding pluralism and institutional independence. The government presents itself as pragmatic and technocratic, claiming legitimacy through service delivery and state capacity. Megaprojects such as bridges, airports, mosques, and hospitals are promoted not merely as infrastructure achievements but indeed as symbols of national resurgence under Erdoğan and the AKP. However, it is important to note that such initiatives are often planned and executed without the necessary parliamentary or public debate. This phenomenon has been shown to exacerbate the shift away from participatory democracy and toward insulated executive rule (Yılmaz and Bashirov 2018). This transformation is indicative of the logic of Autocracy 2.0, in which legitimacy is increasingly derived from narratives of competence and effectiveness rather than democratic deliberation.

(2) Media Consolidation and Digital Surveillance

Turkey has established one of the most extensive and sophisticated systems of information control among contemporary electoral autocracies. It has been reported that over 90% of media outlets are now owned by pro-government conglomerates, thus creating an environment in which opposition perspectives are systematically excluded (Yılmaz and Bashirov 2018). Independent journalists encounter obstacles such as arrest, intimidation, and prosecution, often on vague charges related to terrorism or "disinformation." Turkey has consistently received unfavorable ranking in global press freedom indices, as reported by Freedom House (2023) and RSF (2025b).

The concept of information control is applicable to digital domains as well. It is evident that a number of social media platforms are subject to monitoring and that thousands of websites have been blocked or removed. The technology industry is subject to two interrelated obligations. First, the storage of data must be conducted within the local jurisdiction. Second, compliance with restrictive content regulations is mandatory. The 2022 package of amendments, collectively referred to as the "disinformation law," grants authorities substantial powers to criminalize online speech under loosely defined security criteria (Yurtlu and Yıldız 2023). State-sponsored troll armies are mobilized to harass critics, thereby promoting official narratives, and sowing confusion online. This dual strategy of censorship and propaganda aligns with Guriev and Treisman's (2019) model of Informational Autocracy. Turkey's approach is not characterized by the suppression of information; rather, it employs a strategy of overwhelming dissent through the utilization of narrative dominance, manufactured consent, and strategic ambiguity. This approach has been demonstrated to erode public trust and effectively restrict the domain for oppositional discourse.

(3) Electoral Hegemony and Symbolic Legitimacy

Despite its authoritarian tendencies, Erdoğan's regime continues to stage regular elections. These contests, however, are neither free nor fair in a liberal democratic sense. The opposition faces legal constraints, financial disadvantages, and near-total exclusion from mainstream media, which is largely controlled by pro-government interests (Esen and Gümüşçü

2016). In 2019, the annulment of the opposition's victory in the Istanbul mayoral race revealed the regime's willingness to override unfavorable outcomes. Yet elections remain crucial to the regime's legitimacy. Erdoğan and the AKP frame their repeated victories as the embodiment of the "national will," equating opposition with subversion. This narrative is reinforced by loyalist media, religious institutions, and a state-controlled education system that promotes conservative, nationalist values while discouraging liberal or oppositional perspectives. Meanwhile, the military, which was once a secular guardian of the republic, has been brought under firm civilian control through purges and restructuring following the 2016 coup attempt. The regime also claims legitimacy through performance. Infrastructure projects, early economic growth, and assertive foreign policy are presented as signs of competent rule. Despite the ongoing economic crisis, the government of Erdoğan has managed to maintain its support by appealing to nationalist sentiments and highlighting external threats. In this model, the performance of the leader, rather than civil participation, is the defining factor of democratic success.

(4) The Hollowing of Institutions and Rule of Law

The Turkish case illustrates how democratic institutions can be employed to consolidate executive power and reduce institutional autonomy. The judiciary, which was once semiautonomous, now operates under the influence of the executive branch of the government. It routinely endorses presidential policies and prosecuting those who voice dissent (Tahiroglu 2020). Judges are dismissed for political disloyalty, and courts are used to legitimize controversial decrees (Esen and Gümüşçü 2021). Although parliament has maintained its formal integrity, its capacity to function as an effective oversight has been significantly eroded. Concurrently, civil society and academia face increasing constraints. NGOs are subject to surveillance and arbitrary audits, while universities have been stripped of institutional autonomy.

In the aftermath of the 2016 coup attempt, a comprehensive purge of entire faculties was initiated, and the appointment of university rectors was transferred directly to the president. These developments have resulted in the erosion of the deliberative infrastructure of Turkish democracy, replacing pluralism with executive conformity. The Turkish case demonstrates a fundamental paradox of Autocracy 2.0, whereby formal institutions remain largely unaltered in terms of their formal structure, yet their functional autonomy appears to have undergone significant changes. The operations of courts, legislatures, and elections are elements of a democratic façade serve to mask underlying processes of authoritarian consolidation. This phenomenon of institutional hollowing enables the regime to exercise repression without necessitating a formal rupture with the prevailing political order.

(5) Erdoğanism and the Logic of Autocracy 2.0

The consolidation of Erdoğan's rule has produced a political formula frequently termed "Erdoğanism" (Yilmaz 2025). The term under consideration reflects the principal political rules of Erdoğan, which combine his respected values of Islamic conservatism, nationalist populism, and centralized executive authority. This synthesis has enabled the regime to unify diverse constituencies while building an ideological barrier against dissent. The unsuccessful 2016 coup d'état provided a pivotal moment that enabled the government to portray opposition forces as existential threats and to legitimize extensive legal and constitutional reforms.

In the domain of foreign policy, Erdoğan meticulously cultivates an image of strength and independence, frequently positioning himself in apparent tension with traditional allies. Recent military incursions by Turkey into Syria, in addition to confrontations with the EU, and tensions within NATO are being used to rally domestic support and reinforce the regime's self-image as a guardian of Turkish sovereignty. In contrast to institutionalism and rule-of-law–based multilateralism exhibited by Abe's diplomatic approach, Erdoğan's international posture emphasizes strategic confrontation and nationalist symbolism.

In essence, the prevailing political climate in Turkey, as orchestrated by President Erdoğan, can be characterized as a manifestation of an assertive and polarized form of Autocracy 2.0. The government sustains its authority through media alignment, centralized bureaucratic control, electoral system advantages, and populist appeal, while retaining the façade of democratic governance (Bavbek and Kennedy 2024). Japan's model has been characterized by an emphasis on technocratic insulation, while Turkey's trajectory has been marked by the emergence of coercive, performative, and scrutinized dimensions of democratic backsliding. It is evident that both of these phenomena illustrate the adaptive nature of authoritarianism in the twenty-first century, wherein democratic forms are retained not to preserve liberal values but, rather, to legitimize executive rule.

6 Comparative Analysis of Japan Under Abe and Turkey Under Erdoğan

A comparative analysis of Japan under Abe and Turkey under Erdoğan reveals two distinct trajectories toward Autocracy 2.0, shaped by divergent historical and institutional contexts, yet converging in their outcomes. Both leaders maintained the façade of democratic institutions, including competitive elections, functional legislatures, and operational judicial systems, while concurrently eroding the autonomy of these institutions through the expansion of executive power, information control, and the promotion of performance-based legitimacy (Ida 2020; Esen and Gümüşçü 2021). The approaches adopted by these states reflect differing calibrations of Informational Autocracy, which have been adapted to suit domestic conditions.

Abe's consolidation of power unfolded gradually within Japan's stable parliamentary democracy, where overt authoritarianism would have provoked institutional and societal backlash. The governance model that emerged was characterized by a reliance on technocratic credibility, the continuity of elites, and a strategy of indirect media control. The attainment of informational dominance was achieved through a combination of selective appointments, bureaucratic loyalty, and subtle disincentives for dissent, rather than through repression. In contrast to the dismantling media pluralism, the Abe administration cultivated an environment of soft censorship and self-restraint. This was exemplified by the reinforcement of the press club system and the passage of the Act on the Protection of Specially Designated Secrets 2013 (Ida 2020; Repeta 2014). An often-overlooked dimension of Abe's strategy was his resonance with digitally mobilized right-wing nationalists. Although he did not formally advocate rhetoric, his symbolic actions, including visits to the Yasukuni Shrine and constitutional reinterpretations, established ideological congruence with the revisionist, and anti-neighboring countries' online discourse. This tacit alignment enhanced his digital visibility and helped delegitimize critics, contributing to the erosion of pluralistic debate and bolstering ambient support in the information ecosystem.

In contrast, Erdoğan's post-2016 coup trajectory marked a break from institutional norms, characterized by constitutional overhaul, judicial purges, and direct coercion. The Erdoğan administration has reshaped Turkey's political structure through the implementation of emergency decrees, widespread dismissals, and an expansion of presidential power, which was formally established in the 2017 constitutional referendum (Esen and Gümüşçü 2016; Bashirov and Yilmaz 2020). The dismantling of bureaucratic autonomy was not achieved by subtle incentives; rather, it was accomplished through explicit replacement of officials, thereby erasing internal constraints on executive authority. The disparities in media governance were equally pronounced.

A rigorous examination of the cases of Japan and Turkey utilizing the Autocracy 2.0 framework can elucidate a fundamental principle of Autocracy 2.0. Democratic backsliding in the twenty-first century frequently occurs through the strategic appropriation and repurposing of democratic institutions, rather than through military coups or the suspension of constitutions. Electoral processes, judicial bodies, and legislative institutions persist in their current form, yet their capacity to guarantee accountability, pluralism, and the facilitation of contestation is progressively diminishing (Walker 2016; Guriev and Treisman 2019). Despite the variability in the pace and subtlety of these processes, a discernible parallelism emerges in their aggregate trajectory.

In the context of Japan, Abe's approach entailed a focus on bureaucratic consolidation, technocratic legitimacy, and a systematic weakening of oversight mechanisms. The administration of the prime minister has been observed to have reduced the autonomy of public broadcasters and legislative review bodies, thereby cultivating a political climate characterized by deference and diffuse nationalism. In lieu of outright suppression, the government opted for incentivizing self-restraint and obscuring the distinction between civic compliance and ideological alignment.

Erdoğan's model was characterized by a more direct approach, involving institutional purges, expanded emergency powers, and legal repression, resulting in the transformation of Turkey's political system into a competitive authoritarian regime (Sakurai 2018). The dismantling of media pluralism, the erosion of judicial independence, and the enlistment of religious institutions to support regime narratives are indicative of a systematic and deliberate attempt to manipulate public opinion. Elections were maintained, though institutional changes and political conditions increasingly favored incumbents and constrained open competition.

Yet, in both cases, the core mechanisms of Autocracy 2.0 were present: control over information flows, insulation of elites from accountability, and appeals to national performance as substitutes for participatory legitimacy. These mechanisms enable contemporary autocrats to consolidate power without relinquishing democratic legitimacy. The implications for liberal democracies are grave. The notion of institutional form as a guarantee of democratic function is a fallacy. Even robust systems are vulnerable to gradual erosion when checks and balances are weakened, the media is co-opted or degraded, and civic engagement declines. In an era where algorithmic curation may shape public opinion, and populist rhetoric polarizes the electorate, the threshold for democratic breakdown has become more diffuse but no less dangerous (Levitsky and Way 2010; Bermeo 2016).

To counteract this trend, vigilance must go beyond protecting electoral procedures. It requires sustaining independent media ecosystems, ensuring judicial integrity, empowering civil society, and reinforcing a political culture of transparency and dissent. Scholars must continue to trace how democratic language, institutions, and rituals can be instrumentalized to justify illiberal outcomes.

As Wood (2022) argues, the emergence of technocratic and populist modes of governance, although ostensibly in opposition, shares a tendency to devalue contestation, transparency, and shared epistemic standards. They become, in his words, "false friends of democracy": pragmatic, expedient, and deeply illiberal when examined through the lens of democratic substance. Moreover, Autocracy 2.0 should not be understood as a static endpoint. As Yang (2024) argues, its trajectory is contingent upon the stability of elite cohesion and the robustness of technological infrastructure.

Japan and Turkey are frequently regarded as two discrete instances on a continuum of democratic erosion, exhibiting divergent methodologies yet aligning in their underlying rationales. The trajectories of these states offer a cautionary tale for the global community, suggesting that the erosion of democracy today is less a matter of revolution than of recalibration.

7 Conclusion

This study contributes to the analysis of politics in Japan and Turkey by applying the Autocracy 2.0 framework to examine both its theoretical implications and empirical manifestations. The principal findings may be summarized in three concluding observations. First, contemporary democratic erosion is characterized less by abrupt regime breakdown than by the strategic adaptation and repurposing of existing institutional forms. The expansion of executive discretion, the marginalization of legislative oversight, and the neutralization of judicial intervention collectively diminish democratic contestation while preserving the procedural façade of democracy.

Second, a defining feature of Autocracy 2.0 is the management and control of information flows, increasingly enabled by digital infrastructures and AI. Although these technologies are often portrayed as politically neutral, they facilitate elite insulation, narrative orchestration, and the substitution of public deliberation with algorithmic governance. In doing so, they gradually erode the epistemic foundations on which democratic life depends.

Third, the resilience of democracy under these conditions requires more than formal institutional safeguards. Democratic vitality is contingent on active civic participation, a pluralistic and independent media environment, and an inclusive public sphere capable of scrutinizing technocratic authority. Without the renewal of these democratic agencies, societies become vulnerable to the gradual internal transformation of democracy into an instrument of elite governance.

Future research would benefit from comparative extensions to additional regions, cross-regional analyses, and the incorporation of citizen-level perspectives. These directions would enhance the explanatory capacity and empirical robustness of the Autocracy 2.0 framework. Addressing these dimensions remains an essential task for future scholarship.

Acknowledgments

The author gratefully acknowledges David Yang for his online presentation at Tokyo College in the University of Tokyo on June 8, 2025, which served as a key inspiration for the development of this chapter.

Bibliography

Abe, Yoko. 2022. *Destiny: Talking About Shinzo Abe, Shintaro Abe and Nobusuke Kishi* [in Japanese]. Bungeishunju.

Acemoglu, Daron, and James A. Robinson. 2005. *Economic Origins of Dictatorship and Democracy*. Cambridge University Press.

Bashirov, Galib and Yilmaz, Ihsan. 2020. "The Rise of Transactionalism in International Relations: evidence from Turkey's relations with the European Union." Deakin University. Journal contribution. https://hdl.handle.net/10536/DRO/DU:30133669.

Bavbek, N. Yasemin, and Michael D. Kennedy. 2024. "Articulations of StrongMen: A Knowledge Cultural Sociology of Recognizing Autocratic Practices in Russian, Turkish, and Global Regimes." *American Behavioral Scientist* 68 (13): 1721–41. https://doi.org/10.1177/00027642241268221.

Beraja, Martin, Andrew Kao, David Y. Yang, and Noam Yuchtman. 2023a. "AI-Tocracy." *Quarterly Journal of Economics* 138 (3): 1349–402. https://doi.org/10.1093/qje/qjad012.

Beraja, Martin, David Y. Yang, and Noam Yuchtman. 2023b. "Data-Intensive Innovation and the State: Evidence from AI Firms in China." *Review of Economic Studies* 90 (4): 1701–23. https://doi.org/10.1093/restud/rdac056.

Bermeo, Nancy. 2016. "On Democratic Backsliding." *Journal of Democracy* 27 (1): 5–19. https://doi.org/10.1353/jod.2016.0012.

Bernhard, Michael, Amanda B. Edgell, and Staffan I. Lindberg. 2020. "Institutionalising Electoral Uncertainty and Authoritarian Regime Survival." *European Journal of Political Research* 59 (2): 465–87. https://doi.org/10.1111/1475-6765.12355.

Besley, Timothy, and Masayuki Kudamatsu. 2007. *Making Autocracy Work*. Suntory and Toyota International Centres for Economics and Related Disciplines. http://eprints.lse.ac.uk/id/eprint/3764.

Bickerton, Christopher, and Carlo Invernizzi Accetti. 2017. "Populism and Technocracy: Opposites or Complements?" *Critical Review of International Social and Political Philosophy* 20 (2): 186–206. https://doi.org/10.1080/13698230.2014.995504.

Bogaards, Matthijs. 2022. "Autocracy in Democracy's Mirror." *Loop*, July 11. https://theloop.ecpr.eu/autocracy-in-democracys-mirror/.

Cabestan, Jean-Pierre. 2020. "The State and Digital Society in China: Big Brother Xi Is Watching You!" In *Political and Social Control in China*, edited by Chien-wen Kou and Benjamin Hillman. ANU Press.

Carroll, Myles. 2021. "Passive Revolution in Japan: The Restoration of Hegemony Under Abe?" *Critical Sociology* 48 (1): 109–25. https://doi.org/10.1177/08969205211013884.

"Ejima, Akiko. 2020. Japan's Soft State of Emergency: Social Pressure Instead of Legal Penalty." VerfBlog, May 13, 2020. https://verfassungsblog.de/japans-soft-state-of-emergency-social-pressure-instead-of-legal-penalty/. https://doi.org/10.17176/20200513-133638-0.

Ekiert, Grzegorz. 2023. *Democracy and Authoritarianism in the 21st Century: A Sketch*. Ash Institute for Democratic Governance and Innovation.

Esen, Berk, and Şebnem Gümüşçü. 2016. "Rising Competitive Authoritarianism in Turkey." *Third World Quarterly* 37 (9): 1581–606. https://doi.org/10.1080/01436597.2015.1135732.

Esen, Berk, and Şebnem Gümüşçü. 2021. "Why Did Turkish Democracy Collapse? A Political Economy Account of AKP's Authoritarianism." *Party Politics* 27 (1): 47–60. https://doi.org/10.1177/1354068820923722.

Frantz, Erica, and Andrea Kendall-Taylor. 2016. "Pathways to Democratization in Personalist Dictatorships." *Democratization* 24 (1): 20–40. https://doi.org/10.1080/13510347.2015.1131977.

Frantz, Erica. 2018. *Authoritalianism*. Oxford University Press (Translated Japanese by Uetani, Naokatsu. Kohei Imai, and Ryo Nakai, *Authoritarianism: The history and transformation of dictatorship*. Hakusuisha. 2021)

Freedom House. 2023. *Freedom in the World 2023: Marking 50 Years in the Struggle for Democracy*. Freedom House. https://freedomhouse.org/report/freedom-world/2023/marking-50-years.

Guriev, Sergei. 2024. "Autocracy in the 21st Century." *Tocqueville Review* 45 (1): 61–71. https://doi.org/10.3138/ttr.45.1.61.

Guriev, Sergei, and Daniel Treisman. 2019. "Informational Autocrats." *Journal of Economic Perspectives* 33 (4): 100–27. DOI:10.1257/jep.33.4.100

Guriev, Sergei, and Daniel Treisman. 2022. *Spin Dictators: The Changing Face of Tyranny in the 21st Century*. Princeton University Press.

Harari, Yuval Noah. 2024. *Nexus: A Brief History of Information Networks from the Stone Age to AI*. Random House.

Ida, Michihiro. 2020. "Analysis of the Second Abe Administration Evaluation." *Review of Economics & Political Science* 88 (5–6): 1–20. [in Japanese]. http://hdl.handle.net/10291/21042.

Johnson, Chalmers, Norman A. Schlei, and Michael Schaller. 2000. "The CIA and Japanese Politics." *Asian Perspective* 24 (4): 79–103. https://doi.org/10.1353/apr.2000.0005.

Kamikawa, Ryunoshin. 2018. "An Institutional Analysis of 'Abe Strong, Many Weak (2).' " *Osaka Law Review* 67 (6): 63–92. [in Japanese]. https://doi.org/10.18910/87058.

Kelemen, R. Daniel. 2020. "The European Union's Authoritarian Equilibrium." *Journal of European Public Policy* 27 (3): 481–99. https://doi.org/10.1080/13501763.2020.1712455.

King, Gary, Jennifer Pan, and Margaret E. Roberts. 2017. "How the Chinese Government Fabricates Social Media Posts for Strategic Distraction, Not Engaged Argument." *American Political Science Review* 111 (3): 484–501. https://doi.org/10.1017/S0003055417000144.

Kitaoka, Shinichi. 2021. "The Legacy of Prime Minister Abe Shinzo: Diplomacy and Security." *Asia-Pacific Review* 28 (1): 7–21. https://doi.org/10.1080/13439006.2021.1921355.

Kolstad, Ivar. 2023. "Legitimising Autocracy: Re-Framing the Analysis of Corporate Relations to Undemocratic Regimes." *Contemporary Politics* 30 (3): 294–315. https://doi.org/10.1080/13569775.2023.2271657.

Krauss, Ellis S., and Benjamin Nyblade. 2005. " 'Presidentialization' in Japan? The Prime Minister, Media and Elections in Japan." *British Journal of Political Science* 35 (2): 357–68. http://www.jstor.org/stable/4092356.

Levitsky, Steven, and Lucan A. Way. 2010. *Competitive Authoritarianism: Hybrid Regimes After the Cold War*. Cambridge University Press.

Levitsky, Steven, and Lucan A. Way. 2020. "The New Competitive Authoritarianism." *Journal of Democracy* 31 (1): 51–65. https://doi.org/10.1353/jod.2020.0004.

Levitsky, Steven, and Daniel Ziblatt. 2018. *How Democracies Die*. Crown.

Li, Hongbin, and Li-An Zhou. 2005. "Political Turnover and Economic Performance: The Incentive Role of Personnel Control in China." *Journal of Public Economics* 89 (9–10): 1743–62. https://doi.org/10.1016/j.jpubeco.2004.06.009.

Lipscy, Phillip Y. 2023. *Japan: The Harbinger State*. Cornell University Press.

Little, Andrew T., and Anne Meng. 2024. "Measuring Democratic Backsliding." *PS: Political Science & Politics* 57 (2): 149–61. https://doi.org/10.1017/S104909652300063X.

Lueders, Hans. 2022. "Electoral Responsiveness in Closed Autocracies: Evidence from Petitions in the Former German Democratic Republic." *American Political Science Review* 116 (3): 827–42. https://doi.org/10.1017/S0003055421001386.

Lührmann, Anna, and Staffan I. Lindberg. 2019. "A Third Wave of Autocratization Is Here: What Is New About It?" *Democratization* 26 (7): 1095–113. https://doi.org/10.1080/13510347.2019.1582029.

McLaughlin, Levi. 2023. "The Abe Assassination and Japan's Nexus of Religion and Politics." *Current History* 122 (845): 209–16. https://doi.org/10.1525/curh.2023.122.845.209.

Mulgan, Aurelia George. 2022. "The Role of the Prime Minister in Japan." In *The Oxford Handbook of Japanese Politics*, edited by Robert J. Pekkanen and Saadia M. Pekkanen. Oxford University Press.

Repeta, Lawrence. 2014. "Japan's 2013 State Secrets Law: The Abe Administration's National Security Agenda." *Asia Pacific Journal: Japan Focus* 12 (10): 4086. https://apjjf.org/2014/12/10/lawrence-repeta/4086/article.

Repeta, Lawrence. 2021. "Emergency Powers: Constitutional Authority in the Japanese Diet." *East Asia Forum Quarterly* 13 (3): 30–32. https://search.informit.org/doi/epdf/10.3316/INFORMIT.114512573789215 or the journal: https://search.informit.org/toc/eafq/13/3

Roberts, Margaret E. 2018. *Censored: Distraction and Diversion Inside China's Great Firewall*. Princeton University Press.

RSF (Reporters Without Borders). 2025a. "Japan." https://rsf.org/en/country/japan.

RSF (Reporters Without Borders). 2025b. "Türkiye." https://rsf.org/en/country-t%C3%BCrkiye.

Sakurai, Yukio. 2018. "Turkey's Possible Future Directions After the 2017 Referendum: Autocracy or Democracy?" *International Journal of Interdisciplinary Civic and Political Studies* 13 (1): 33–45. https://doi.org/10.18848/2327-0071/CGP/v13i01/33-45.

Sakurai, Yukio. 2019. "Turkish Politics and Human Rights Law: Focusing on Transformation." *International Journal of Interdisciplinary Global Studies* 14 (2): 1–25. https://doi.org/10.18848/2324-755X/CGP/v14i02/1-25.

Sakurai, Yukio. 2021. "Possible Challenges to the Welfare State in a Post-COVID-19 Society: An Illustration from a Citizen's Perspective." *International Journal of Interdisciplinary Civic and Political Studies* 16 (2): 21–35. https://doi.org/10.18848/2327-0071/CGP/v16i02/21-35.

Sakurai, Yukio. 2022. "Shinzo Abe's Politics in Japan: Characteristics and Implications." *Political Reflection Magazine* 8 (4): 27–32. https://politicalreflectionmagazine.com/vol-8-no-4/.

Scartozzi, Chiara K. 2017. "Hereditary Politics in Japan: A Family Business." *Diplomat*, February 9. https://thediplomat.com/2017/02/hereditary-politics-in-japan-a-family-business/.

Scheppele, Kim Lane. 2018. "Autocratic Legalism." *University of Chicago Law Review* 85 (2): 545–84. https://chicagounbound.uchicago.edu/uclrev/vol85/iss2/2.

Schmid, Jonas Willibald. 2025. "Electoral Autocracies, Hybrid Regimes, and Multiparty Autocracies: Same, Same but Different?" *Democratization* 32 (6): 1565–88. https://doi.org/10.1080/13510347.2025.2476183.

Schumpeter, Joseph A. (1942) 2006. *Capitalism, Socialism & Democracy*. Routledge.

Slobodian, Quinn. 2021. *Globalists: The End of Empire and the Birth of Neoliberalism*. Harvard University Press.

Sneider, Daniel. 2022. "Cause to Fear What Comes After Abe's Death." *Asia Times*, July 11. https://asiatimes.com/2022/07/cause-to-fear-what-comes-after-abes-death/.

Tahiroglu, Merve. 2020. "How Turkey's Leaders Dismantled the Rule of Law." *Fletcher Forum of World Affairs* 44 (1): 67–96. https://www.jstor.org/stable/48599281.

Tansel, Cemal Burak. 2018. "Authoritarian Neoliberalism and Regime Change in Turkey." *South European Society and Politics* 23 (2): 197–217. https://doi.org/10.1080/13608746.2018.1479945.

V-Dem. 2025. *Democracy Report 2025*. V-Dem. https://www.v-dem.net/publications/democracy-reports/.

Walker, Christopher. 2016. "The Authoritarian Threat: The Hijacking of 'Soft Power.' " *Journal of Democracy* 27 (1): 49–63. Accessed March 28, 2026. https://www.journalofdemocracy.org/articles/the-authoritarian-threat-the-hijacking-of-soft-power/

Wood, Matthew. 2022. "The Political Ideas Underpinning Political Distrust: Analysing Four Types of Anti-Politics." *Representation* 58 (1): 27–48. https://doi.org/10.1080/00344893.2021.1954076.

Yakushiji, Katsuyuki. 2020. "Abe's 'Anything Goes' Administration Destroys Democracy: An Independent Administrative Agency Bowing Down to 'Abe the Strongest.'" *Toyo Keizai Online*, March 7. [in Japanese]. https://toyokeizai.net/articles/-/333304.

Yang, David Y. 2024. "China: Autocracy 2.0." NBER Working Paper No. 32993. National Bureau of Economic Research. https://doi.org/10.3386/w32993.

Yilmaz, Ihsan and Galib Bashirov. 2018. "The AKP after 15 years: emergence of Erdoganism in Turkey." Third World Quarterly, Taylor & Francis Journals, vol. 39(9): 1812-1830. DOI: 10.1080/01436597.2018.1447371.

Yilmaz, Ihsan. 2025. "Erdoğanism: The Established Hegemony in Turkey's Political Arena." SSRN, February 1. https://ssrn.com/abstract=5063947.

Yurtlu, Fatih, and Orkun Yıldız. 2023. "Disinformation Activities on Social Media Platforms and Responsibility in the Context of Criminal Law: A Case Review on the Twitter Platform." *İstanbul Ticaret Üniversitesi Sosyal Bilimler Dergisi* 22 (47): 789–804. https://doi.org/10.46928/iticusbe.1148409.

Zuboff, Shoshana. 2019. *The Age of Surveillance Capitalism*. Public Affairs.

CHAPTER 3

Shinzo Abe's Politics in Japan: Characteristics and Implications

Abstract:

This essay examines the political characteristics of former Japanese Prime Minister Shinzo Abe and analyzes the implications of his sudden death for Japan's political landscape. Focusing on hereditary politics, centralized power, control over state institutions and bureaucracy, economic policy, and diplomacy and national security, the paper highlights both Abe's political effectiveness and the controversies surrounding his leadership style. It argues that Abe's death created a leadership vacuum within the Liberal Democratic Party, contributing to political uncertainty and potential instability in a period of heightened domestic and international challenges

Keywords: Shinzo Abe; Japanese politics; political leadership; Abenomics; national security and diplomacy

1 Introduction

On July 8, 2022, former Prime Minister Shinzo Abe (1954–2022) was shot-killed by a gunman while giving a speech in support of a candidate for the House of Councilors election in Nara prefecture, Japan. This incident was an exceptional event in terms of security in Japan and gave a big shock to the Japanese people. An article appeared that commented this event on the same ground as the assassination cases in the United States, such as John F. Kennedy (JFK) case in 1963 (Lane 2022). Certainly, there are many puzzling points in this assassination case, but limited information on the event is available at this stage and nobody identifies the whole story.

In any case, Abe, who served as the longest-serving prime minister in postwar Japan, has passed away. No Japanese prime minister is as divided in opinion as Abe. Because Abe's politics had diverse aspects that seemed to be both positive and negative, Japan's national opinion has been divided. Abe's negative aspect can be assumed to include political methods that had not been seen in Japan's politics (Yakushiji 2020). This commentary summarizes some of Abe's political characteristics based on domestic and foreign materials on Abe and discusses implications of his sudden death to Japan.

2 Characteristics of Abe's Politics

2.1 Hereditary Politics and Family Business

In Japan, politicians are often a group of people who ascended office through hereditary succession, but some are ex-bureaucrats, representatives of trade unions or some industry groups, celebrities (in entertainment, sports, etc.), and former local parliament members (Scartozzi 2017). Hereditary succession is a system that places the highest priority on blood ties and does not necessarily emphasize on the abilities of politicians. In hereditary succession, politicians can inherit the support groups and supporters of the single-seat constituency system. In general, this method brings the interest of maintaining vested interests for both supporters and politicians, but it creates a weak point that prevents new entrants into the political arena and, thus, progress in reform.

Abe was a typical hereditary succession politician. The father of Abe was former Foreign Minister Shintaro Abe (1924–1991), his grandfather was former Prime Minister Nobusuke Kishi (1896–1987), and his great-uncle was former Prime Minister Eisaku Sato (1901–1975). It is said that Abe most respected his grandfather Nobusuke Kishi, who was a pro-US politician in postwar Japan (Johnson et al. 2000), through Abe's mother and Kishi's daughter Yoko's orientation (Abe 2022). Abe's profession was part of family business, but he was capable. Abe was first elected to the House of Representatives in 1993. After serving as deputy chief cabinet secretary, secretary-general of the Liberal Democratic Party (LDP), and chief cabinet secretary, Abe served prime minister from 2006 to 2007 and from 2012 to 2020 for eight years and eight months (total 3,188 days).

2.2 Power of Control

Abe had institutional power of control to the parties concerned in his politics.

(1) Politicians

Abe was so strong that he won six national elections as president of the LDP. Through his election victory, he secured a firm position in the LDP. Abe was called "Abe the strongest." Abe's politics were said to be characterized by his friends' cabinet. Because Abe appointed his friendly politicians to be ministers in his cabinet. In contrast, Abe tended to treat politicians he didn't like as cold as possible. Abe tended to shy away from people who disagreed with him and avoid discussions. Consequently, LDP politicians have come to agree with Abe's views and refrain from openly opposing him. This tendency to divide has taken the same attitude not only to politicians but also to the people. This sounds like Donald Trump's political approach. In fact, Abe had a close personal relationship with Trump.

(2) State Institutions

A distinctive feature of Abe's politics was the appointment of his supporters to heads of major state institutions, some of which required the consent of the National Diet. The state institutions are the Bank of Japan, Cabinet Legislation Bureau, Nuclear Regulatory Commission, Japan Broadcasting Corporation, and so on (Kamikawa 2018ab). The arbitrariness of his personnel appointment was often criticized by the opposition and mass media, but he took advantage of the power of the coalition-ruling parties, which held a majority in the National Diet, to force his way. Consequently, major state institutions might have lost neutrality.

(3) National Bureaucrats

Abe was powerful to control national bureaucrats. This is due to a change of the personnel system for national bureaucrats. Cabinet of Japan has collectively administered executive personnel affairs of each ministry and agency through the Cabinet Personnel Management Agency since 2014 at Abe administration. With this system, each ministry or public agency is under control of the cabinet and the prime minister can behave like a president (Toda 2015; Kamikawa 2018ab). Consequently, national bureaucrats began to read between the lines, interpreting laws in favor of Abe, and even falsifying official documents. Some issues were argued in the National Diet. Abe's politics was led by Prime Minister's Office, namely Abe and his close staff, and the LDP must follow his decisions. Therefore, Komeito, one of the leading coalition parties, has power to influence on Abe outside the LDP.

(4) Mass Media and Public Opinion

The mass media and public opinion were divided between those who supported Abe and those who criticized him. Abe's supporters are conservative, but some of them have nationalistic ideas and are called "*net-uyoku*" (nationalist supporters in SNS). Abe's cabinet office controlled public opinion by using mass media and journalists who supported Abe.

2.3 Monetary, Fiscal, and Economic Policy

Abe promoted the so-called Abenomics, which comprise the three arrows of "bold monetary policy," "flexible fiscal policy," and "economic growth strategy to stimulate private investment." In the Abe's second office, the Bank of Japan has changed its policy to quantitative easing with a 2% inflation target as a countermeasure against deflation, and this policy is still being maintained even in the current era of inflation. Apart from the real economy, stock prices on the Tokyo Stock Exchange remained high, giving the impression that the Japanese economy was doing well. Abe's economic policy relied on neoliberalism although he himself had conservative moral and ethics mind.

The analysis based on the December 2014 national poll was as follows: (a) The individual evaluation that had the strongest correlation with the overall evaluation was the economic stimulus evaluation. (b) Gender was a social attribute variable for overall evaluation, and males were a factor that enhances evaluation. (c) The recognition of the economic situation of the country stipulated the evaluation of the Abe administration rather than the recognition of the economic situation itself (Ida 2020). Experts, however, criticized Abenomics not to have reached the goals after years.

2.4 Diplomacy and National Security

Diplomacy and national security are two essential agenda for Abe's politics. Shinichi Kitaoka (2021) notes

> *three particularly significant achievements by the Abe administration in the fields of diplomacy and [national] security, which are: (i) the 2015 Legislation for Peace and Security (Ministry of Foreign Affairs of Japan [MOFA] of Japan 2015); (ii) Prime Minister Abe's statement marking the 70th anniversary of the end of World War II (Prime Minister of Japan and His Cabinet 2015); and (iii) his 2016 initiative for pursuing a Free and Open Indo-Pacific. ("FOIP," MOFA of Japan 2022)*

Abe, known by world political leaders, could make dialogues with foreign leaders by his words. This was rare for Japanese politicians to do so. Abe respected universal values such as the rule of law, democracy, and human rights and frequently expressed these values in his speech. As for national security, Abe had a strong wish to amend the constitution for Japan to have military forces for effective defense, keeping strong ties with the United States. For this purpose, he paved a way to take necessary steps such that Article 9 of the Constitution has been reinterpreted to allow for collective self-defense but had not reached the goal.

2.5 Political Implications of Abe's Sudden Death

As reviewed above, Abe was a powerful politician tactfully to take leadership in his prime minister's office and was influential with the LDP politicians and the people even after he left the office. What political implications of Abe's sudden death can be expected?

First, Abe has no children, and Abe's spouse Akie announced no possibility to run the national election at Yamaguchi prefecture. Abe's relative may succeed to the lawmaker position under Abe's mother Yoko's initiative.

Second, the LDP comprises several groups and Abe's group was conservative and the biggest in scale. It is unclear who will take over Abe's position in this group. Abe's followers are suffering from pressures caused from political issues. Namely, one is the issue related to the former Unification Church that supported many LDP politicians in elections while engaging in antisocial activities, and the other is the bribery suspect case related to the Tokyo Olympics/Paralympics 2020. Both issues were discovered soon after Abe was gone.

Third, the vacuum of the presence of Abe may make Japan's political power less powerful and change the balance of politics in Japan (Sneider 2022). As social environments surrounding Japan become severer in interior, diplomacy, and national security, it is apparent that Japan needs a capable political leader. Abe was sometimes criticized in his political methods, but he was capable to behave as the national leader, involving his team and advisors, and make dialogues with foreign leaders to determine the way. Therefore, it can be said that Japan will suffer from the vacuum of political leadership for the time being.

3 Conclusion

This commentary reviewed former Prime Minister Shinzo Abe's characteristics of politics based on materials on Abe and discussed implications of his sudden death to Japan. Abe was a typical hereditary succession politician but was capable tactfully to take leadership in his Prime Minister's Office in interior, diplomacy, and national security. Particularly, Abe's three achievements in diplomacy and national security were worth remembering. However, the opposition, part of mass media, and the people criticized him because he did not respect constitutionalism that much and behaved like a president. Two political issues are ongoing after he is gone, which will make voice of criticism bigger to the LDP. The political implication of Abe's sudden death is a political turbulence caused from uncertainty as to "who will take over Abe's political position." If this is not clarified, Japan will suffer from instability of politics. If a gunman (and his possible supporters, just in case) should have attempted such political turbulence, this can be assumed to be a terrorist attack to damage Japan politics.

Bibliography

Abe, Yoko. 2022. *Destiny: Talking About Shinzo Abe, Shintaro Abe and Nobusuke Kishi* [in Japanese]. Bungeishunju.

Ida, Michihiro. 2020. "Analysis of the Second Abe Administration Evaluation." *Review of Economics & Political Science* 88 (5–6): 1–20. [in Japanese]. http://hdl.handle.net/10291/21042.

Johnson, Chalmers, Norman A. Schlei, and Michael Schaller. 2000. "The CIA and Japanese Politics." *Asian Perspective* 24 (4): 79–103. http://www.jstor.org/stable/42705308.

Kamikawa, Ryunoshin. 2018a. "An Institutional Analysis of 'Abe Strong, Many Weak' (1)." *Osaka Law Review* 67 (5): 17–45. [in Japanese]. https://doi.org/10.18910/87043.

Kamikawa, Ryunoshin. 2018b. "An Institutional Analysis of 'Abe Strong, Many Weak' (2)." *Osaka Law Review* 67 (6): 63–92. [in Japanese]. https://doi.org/10.18910/87058.

Kitaoka, Shinichi. 2021. "The Legacy of Prime Minister Abe Shinzo: Diplomacy and Security." *Asia-Pacific Review* 28 (1): 7–21. https://doi.org/10.1080/13439006.2021.1921355.

Lane, Charles. 2022. "The Abe Assassination Reminds Us That Individuals Make History." *Washington Post*, July 13. https://www.washingtonpost.com/opinions/2022/07/13/shinzo-abe-assassination-shapes-history/.

MOFA (Ministry of Foreign Affairs) of Japan. 2015. *Japan's Legislation for Peace and Security*. MOFA of Japan. https://www.mofa.go.jp/fp/nsp/page1we_000084.html.

MOFA (Ministry of Foreign Affairs) of Japan. 2022. *Free and Open Indo-Pacific*. MOFA of Japan. https://www.mofa.go.jp/policy/page25e_000278.html.

Prime Minister of Japan and His Cabinet. 2015. "Statement by Prime Minister Shinzo Abe." August 14, 2015. https://japan.kantei.go.jp/97_abe/statement/201508/0814statement.html.

Scartozzi, Chiara K. 2017. "Hereditary Politics in Japan: A Family Business." *Diplomat*, February 9. https://thediplomat.com/2017/02/hereditary-politics-in-japan-a-family-business/.

Sneider, Daniel. 2022. "Cause to Fear What Comes After Abe's Death." *Asia Times*, July 11. https://asiatimes.com/2022/07/cause-to-fear-what-comes-after-abes-death/.

Toda, Koji. 2015. "A Study of Cabinet Personnel Management Agency." *Economic Review of Japan University of Economics* 45 (1): 53–68. [in Japanese]. https://jue.repo.nii.ac.jp/?action=pages_view_main&active_action=repository_view_main_item_detail&item_id=1503&item_no=1&page_id=4&block_id=80.

Yakushiji, Katsuyuki. 2020. "Abe's 'Anything Goes' Administration Destroys Democracy: An Independent Administrative Agency Bowing Down to 'Abe the Strongest.' " *Toyo Keizai Online*, March 7. [in Japanese]. https://toyokeizai.net/articles/-/333304.

CHAPTER 4

Turkey's Possible Future Directions After the 2017 Referendum: Autocracy or Democracy?

Abstract

After the 2017 referendum and the constitutional amendments that will take effect in 2018, Turkey's new presidential system may concentrate governing power in the president, and thus, checks and balances of power may not function well. This new system can be regarded as competitive authoritarianism, or authoritarianism, in one sense, or populism in another, since strong political leadership by the president is supported by half the nation, while the other half oppose this direction. Turkey thus has considerable political and social division among its people. Two possible directions are theoretically considered: (1) an autocracy or a dictatorship led by the president and (2) a democracy inspired by international dialogue between Turkey and other states. The first might result in greater division between Islamism and secularism, and, in the worst case, might lead to Turkey becoming a failed state, losing credibility among the United States and European states. The second direction would entail a balance of internal and external political interests that maintains a respect for universal values, including freedom of the press. This might result in a soft-landing emphasizing consensus-building that reduces divisions among the people. In terms of Turkey's best interests, the latter direction might be considered preferable for ensuring human rights and stability of the state. Guidance through dialogue thus might be provided to Turkey by international society to encourage implementation of the latter direction. Two feasible counter-ideas are offered, one related to EU membership accession and the other to the UN Human Rights Council, to facilitate Turkey proceeding to the latter direction. This chapter focuses on the

2017 referendum and analyzes recent Turkish politics and likely prospects. Literature research and interviews with experts are used for the purpose of clarifying three research questions, i.e., how the constitutional amendments will affect Turkey and its politics, how Turkish politics and society will develop as a result of the constitutional amendments, and what future directions are preferred by the Turkish people? Two possible directions and counter-policy ideas for Turkey are theoretically drawn out, followed by a conclusion.

Keywords: Turkey, Referendum, Amendments to the Constitution, Division Among the People

1 Introduction

Amendments to the constitution of the Republic of Turkey were approved through a referendum held on April 16, 2017. These amendments committed to replacing the parliamentary cabinet system with an executive presidential system that would change the governing principles of Turkey. This was an important event not only for citizens of Turkey but for all institutions related to Turkey at large. Turkey is an important nation-state from a geopolitical perspective and in international politics, as a border nation-state between Europe and the Middle East and North Africa (MENA). In fact, the Eurasia Group (2017) identified Turkey as the top political risk in 2016 and 2017, writing

> *[y]et, though most of these provisions won't go into effect until the next election in 2019, victory will embolden Erdogan to act as a de facto executive president and continue to overstep his formal powers throughout 2017. An empowered, post-referendum Erdogan will double down on his preferred policies, aggravating political, economic, and security risks.*

Turkey is now in a position to have its economy function as a part of the EU region, based on the EU-Turkey Customs Union, and the country's national security as a part of NATO. However, in the areas of politics and migration, the trends in Turkey differ greatly from those in the EU. Turkey thus has a serious dilemma with the EU and MENA, with respect to economics, politics, and migration, and with NATO, Russia, Iran, and China, with regard to national security. Facing such challenges, Turkey is no doubt in a position of importance for scholars to analyze from an academic perspective.

The following three research questions will be considered:

1. How amendments to the constitution will affect Turkey and its politics.
2. Turkey's politics and society at present and after the amendments to the constitution.
3. Future directions preferred by the Turkish people.

In the section "Referendum on April 16, 2017," we will review how the referendum was implemented and what the election results indicated. In the section "Amendments to the Constitution," we will clarify how the amendments to the constitution will affect Turkey and when this would occur. We will also examine the main results of interviews conducted with Turkish citizens by a US research agency in 2014 and 2015, as well as interviews by the author in 2018, giving us insight into the mindsets of local people. Possible implications will then be addressed in the section "What Do Turkish Citizens Think About the Direction of Turkey?" In the section "Turkish Politics and Society," we will argue about Turkish politics and society from theoretical points of views, particularly the transformation of Turkish politics and society once under the control of the AKP administration. Then, we will address mainly three issues: forms of democracy, populism, and division among the people. Possible future directions for Turkey will be addressed in the "Possible Future Directions" section. And, finally, in the "Conclusion" section, we will deduce that Turkey's future direction might preferably entail a balance of internal and external political interests that maintains a respect for universal values to a reasonable extent, particularly freedom of the press, and guidance via diplomatic dialogue should be provided to Turkey by members of international society to encourage implementation of this direction.

2 Methodology

Research mainly included literature research and select interviews with experts. This literature research encompasses approximately fifty academic books, articles, and website resources, mainly in Japanese and English, collected and reviewed between 2016 and 2018. These sources were retrieved through research in the field of political science and Turkish Studies, using "Turkey," "democracy," and "amendments to constitution" as keywords, and following academic criteria acceptable to the Japan Association for Comparative Politics and The Japan Association of International Relations. Conference materials are also referenced, including those from "The Fifth International Conference on Eurasian Politics and Society (IEPAS 2018)," which was held in April, 2018 in Istanbul, Turkey.

Interviews were conducted with fifteen experts in Istanbul (April 2018) and Tokyo (2017–2018). These experts are attached to businesses, research institutes, universities, and public agencies. The selection criteria for the experts included a long career with local businesses, public agencies, or academic societies. The interview process was as follows. After making an appointment to meet individually with experts, interviews were conducted in experts' offices in line with questionnaires prepared prior to the interviews. Summary records were then written as minutes in Japanese.

3 Referendum on April 16, 2017

According to an official report published by the Supreme Electoral Council of Turkey (*Yüksek Seçim Kurulu*) on April 27, 2017, a total of 48.94 million Turkish citizens voted (i.e. 85.43%), and 25.16 million (51.41%) voted in favor of amending the constitution, while 23.78 million (48.5%) voted in opposition. The gap between the citizens supporting and opposing the amendments was only 1.38 million voters (2.82%) out of the 48.94 million that voted, apparently providing no clear consensus on future prospects, including governing principles.

In the referendum campaign, the necessity of strong political leadership and steady security control against possible terrorism by the Kurdistan Workers' Party (*Kürdistan İşçi Partisi*, hereunder "PKK") and others was emphasized, but no detailed information on an executive presidential system was provided to the public for discussion. In fact, some local research showed that the majority of citizens support the ruling party, i.e., the Justice and Development Party (*Adalet ve Kalkınma Partisi*, hereunder "AKP"), indicating that the amendments proposal in the referendum was supported largely due to general trust of President Recep Tayyip Erdoğan (hereunder "Erdoğan") and a wish to be a "more powerful Turkey," and did not necessarily indicate support for the executive presidential system itself.[1] This was due to Erdoğan and the AKP's skillful control of public opinion, mainly by focusing attention on potential enemy or security risks inside and outside Turkey and not deeply considering the essence of an executive presidential system. The Turkish mass media seemed to entirely support Erdoğan and the AKP.

The election results indicated that there were considerable gaps by area between those supporting and opposing the amendments proposal. In general, conservative areas, i.e., mainly the inland, eastern, and southern regions of Turkey, strongly supported the AKP, and the western regions, including Izmir and major cities such as Istanbul and Ankara, did not support the AKP as much. In fact, a complicated phenomenon occurred in these eastern and southern regions, where many Kurds live, namely, division between those supporting and opposing the amendments proposal. This was partly because citizens in eastern and southern regions were similarly split into those supporting and not supporting the Nationalist Movement Party (*Milliyetçi Hareket Partisi*, hereunder "MHP"), which opposed the AKP as the result of a sudden change in the political stance of the party's leader, Devlet Bahçeli, who came to support the AKP.

It was also assumed that citizens in major cities had more opportunities than those in local villages to receive information on what an executive presidential system meant. Related to this event, after the referendum, ten mayors, duly elected through local elections in major cities, including Istanbul and Ankara, were personally requested by Erdoğan to resign, and this order was assumed to have been made in order for the city administration to tighten the AKP's political grip on local areas for the next general/presidential election. But this action raised serious questions concerning the legal authority and intentions of the president in a democratic state.

Another notable event was the significant contribution to the referendum made by Turkish nationals living abroad, particularly those in Europe. Turkey's Ministry of Foreign Affairs estimates that over 6.0 million Turkish nationals live abroad (5.5 million in Western Europe) and that over 3.0 million have voting rights.[2] Those in Germany represent the fourth-largest voting area, following Istanbul, Izmir, and Ankara.

---

[1] Refers to data on an exit poll the day after the constitutional referendum provided by IPSOS (April 21, 2017), available online on November 1, 2025, https://www.ipsos.com/en/turkish-referendum.

[2] Refers to "Turkish Citizens Living Abroad," published online by the Ministry of Foreign Affairs, Turkey, available online on November 1, 2025, https://www.mfa.gov.tr/the-expatriate-turkish-citizens.en.mfa.

In the referendum, 1.41 million Turks living abroad voted (i.e. 47.0%), and 0.78 million (59.9%) voted in favor of the AKP, which was higher than the 51.41% of all voters in favor of the AKP. In 2012, the Grand National Assembly of Turkey (*Türkiye Büyük Millet Meclisi*, hereunder "Assembly") passed an AKP-initiated bill granting voting rights to Turkish nationals living abroad (Baser 2017; Korkmaz 2017). This measure eventually led to the success of the referendum, and both Erdoğan's and the AKP's aim to amend the constitution. Voters outside Turkey faced some political and ethnic friction from local citizens in host states where they lived. Many of the overseas Turks had dual nationalities, and the host state and its citizens wondered whether they identified with the host state or Turkey and also why they largely supported Erdoğan and the AKP, which were considered by many Europeans to be undemocratic symbols.

The last point concerns the question of a fair election. A statement by the European Election Observation Unit and other organizations, including the Organization for Security and Co-operation in Europe (OSCE), implied that election activities were prioritized to favor the AKP, as Turkey was in a declared state of emergency since the abortive coup of July 2016.[3] Numerous anti-AKP journalists were purged and imprisoned, and no freedom of the press was guaranteed. In addition, important information on amendments to the constitution was not properly shown to the people before the referendum.

4 Amendments to the Constitution

How will the amendments to the constitution affect Turkey, and when would this occur?

Bill No. 6771 amending the constitution comprises eighteen articles, all making requests associated with legal procedures incurred in the amendments of the constitution, laws, and administrative rules and regulations

---

[3] Refers to the "OSCE/ODIHR Final Report on Turkey's Constitutional Referendum Recommends Reviewing Legal Framework to Secure Fundamental Rights and Freedoms," available online on November 1, 2025, https://www.osce.org/odihr/elections/turkey/311721?download=true.

in the Assembly and related ministries of the government.[4] It is thus expected that the official inauguration of the revised constitution, laws, and administrative rules and regulations will become effective after the next general election of the Assembly and the presidential election, originally planned for November 2019 but eventually rescheduled for June 24, 2018. However, de facto amendments could possibly be implemented by the president item by item even before the next general/presidential election. The main amendments to the constitution can be categorized as follows:

1. An executive presidential system would replace the parliamentary cabinet system. The position of prime minister would be abolished, and vice presidents would be newly appointed. The president may also lead the political party. In fact, Erdoğan became the head of the AKP again in May 2017.

2. Greater legal power would be given to the president, who could nominate and dismiss any cabinet member, submit the government's annual budget to the Assembly, dissolve the Assembly, and exert influence on higher judicial posts through the appointment of members of the Supreme Board of Judges and Prosecutors (*Hakimler ve Savcılar Yüksek Kurulu*). While the Assembly's legal right to dismiss the president is to be prescribed in the revised constitution, conducting a dismissal procedure in the Assembly would be practically impossible as long as the AKP occupies the majority.

3. The general election and the presidential election are held on the same day every five years. The term of the presidency in the revised constitution after the next general and presidential co-elections will be a maximum of two terms for a total of ten years. In the presidential election, political parties that obtain more than 5% of the total number of effective votes alone or with other political parties in the previous election, or at least 100,000 voters, may field candidates.

4. The number of Assembly seats will be increased from 550 to 600 seats, and the age requirement for candidates for lawmakers in the Assembly will be lowered from 25 to 18.

---

[4] Refers to Council of Europe "European Commission for Democracy Through Law (Venice Commission) Turkey Law No. 6771 Amending the Constitution 23 February 2017," available online January 7, 2026. https://www.coe.int/en/web/venice-commission/-/cdl-ref-2017-018-e

5 What Do Turkish Citizens Think About the Future Direction of Turkey?

What do Turkish citizens think about the future direction of Turkey? In the declared state of emergency since the abortive coup in July 2016, the collection of unbiased public opinions has been nearly impossible, but the results of interviews of Turkish citizens by a US research agency conducted in 2014 and 2015 are available and can be summarized as follows (Pew Research Center 2014, 2015).[5]

A majority (51% in 2014 and 54% in 2015) of citizens were dissatisfied with the direction of the government, while 49% in 2014 and 44% in 2015 of the respondents were satisfied with the direction of the government. In 2015, 77% of the respondents who expressed dissatisfaction with the direction of the government supported the largest opposition party, the Republican People's Party (*Cumhuriyet Halk Partisi*, hereunder "CHP"). Of the citizens who were satisfied with the direction of the government, 78% in 2014 and 79% in 2015 supported the ruling AKP. The main complaints in 2015 were high inflation, crime, disparity between rich and poor, and unemployment. A majority (52% in 2015) of the respondents said that their children's generation would be more economically painful. In 2014, 50% of the respondents said that the economy was good, while 46% said that the economy was bad. In sum,

> *as with views of the country's direction overall, the public has been divided over the state of the economy in recent years. Prior to 2011, however, economic ratings were dismal, especially following the 2008–2009 worldwide financial crisis. Furthermore, AKP supporters, rural Turks, and more devout Muslims are generally happier with current economic conditions. (Pew Research Center 2014, 5)*

A favorable view of Erdoğan declined year by year from 62% in 2013 to 51% in 2014 and to 39% in 2015, while an unfavorable view of Erdoğan steadily increased from 34% in 2013 to 44% in 2014 and to 51% in 2015. The confidence target for the army was a majority (55% in 2014 and 52% in 2015), but the police, justice, religious leaders, and media were all less than half in 2015. A majority (56% in 2015) of the respon-

---

[5] These face-to-face interviews were held with approximately 1,000 Turkish adults aged 18 and older. They were conducted in Turkish from April to May 2014 and April to May 2015, respectively.

dents said that a "democratic government" was preferable to a "strong leader." In 2014, an overwhelming majority (69%) said that Islam played a large role in the political life of Turkey, while only 26% said that it played a small role. In 2002, prior to Erdoğan's election as prime minister, the public was split: 45% said that Islam played a large role, while 43% said just the opposite.

A majority of citizens responded that Turkey should be respected by foreign countries (54% in 2015) and that it was desirable to achieve accession to the EU (53% in 2014 and 55% in 2015). Support for both NATO and the United States was low, i.e., 19% in 2014 and 20% in 2015, and most felt that Turkey should not be complicit in NATO and US-led military action. The overwhelming majority (80% in 2015) responded that it was better not to increase refugee acceptance.

Although the Turkish economy had basically improved and society had become more stable since the AKP took office, problems such as a rise in commodity prices, crime, disparity between the rich and the poor, and unemployment remained unsettled. There was dissatisfaction with the situation, and the majority of Turkish citizens felt uneasy about the Turkey's future. Yet it is assumed that over the long term, the lives of AKP supporters improved, particularly supporters prior to 2002, when the AKP took office, and those supporters were relatively satisfied with the situation. Those people are assumed to be Muslims with not much formal education and limited future prospects.

Meanwhile, it is reasonable to question why Erdoğan and the ruling AKP were largely supported in recent elections, including the 2017 referendum, even though the foregoing research clearly indicates that the initial favorable view of Erdoğan had sharply declined from 2013 to 2015. In fact, the results of the general election indicated a sharp decline of AKP support in June 2015 but a recovery in November 2015. After that, the abortive coup attempt occurred, and then a state of emergency was declared in July 2016 and has been in force to date, being extended each time for three-month periods.

Since the 2015 survey, the following changes seem to have occurred. First, trust in the military plummeted due to the failed military coup attempt. In the past, the Turkish military had played a significant role in Turkish society, much like judicial institutions, and intervened in Turkish politics during military coups in 1960 and 1980, and a military coup threat in 1971. This directed Turkish politics toward a Kemalism orientation that strictly complied with the constitution. However, the situation has changed, and Turkish citizens today have shown no willingness to support military intervention in the country's politics. Additionally, the military is now under AKP control. Second, the expectation for EU accession has declined due to EU integration and migration troubles. Turkey still maintains a governmental policy for EU accession, but in practice, it has no prospect of succeeding. Third, the proportion of the population desirous of a strong leader rather than a democratic government might have risen, and support for Erdoğan might have recovered to some extent due to the continual terrorism in 2016.

In 2018, the Turkish economy has become rather unstable; in particular, the country's currency, the Turkish *lira*, has weakened considerably against the US dollar and euro.[6] This is one of the reasons why Erdoğan rescheduled the earlier general/presidential elections for June 24, 2018, and formed a political alliance with the MHP. The economic situation in Turkey has become unclear again, and this could negatively influence the minds of Turkish citizens. But Turkish citizens are generally afraid of government crackdowns, which occurred in severe forms after the Gezi Park protests in 2013 and the abortive coup attempt in 2016, and thus citizens now hesitate to express their own political opinions in public (Interviews with the author, Istanbul 2018). In fact, many Turkish citizens might have negative views of Erdoğan and the AKP but reluctantly support the AKP because no other political party is seen as trustworthy or capable of taking office (Interviews with the author, Istanbul 2018).

6 Turkish Politics and Society

Does Turkey have a working democracy, and if it does, what form of democracy does Turkey have now? Under the constitution, a rule of law is applied in Turkey, and the country has a working democracy. But after the referendum and the amendments to the constitution that will follow, it is expected that the new presidential system may concentrate governing power in the president, and checks and balances of power may not function well. This is considered to be competitive authoritarianism in one sense or populism in another.

---

[6] The Turkish *lira*/US dollar exchange rate has sharply declined over the years from 0.5574 on May 3, 2013, to 0.2420 on May 3, 2018, and 0.0238 on October 31, 2025, according to Bloomberg online, https://www.bloomberg.com/quote/TRYUSD:CUR.

A competitive authoritarianism is rising in Turkey (Baser and Ozturk 2017, 260), which means "although elections are regularly held and are generally free of massive fraud, incumbents routinely abuse state resources, deny the opposition adequate media coverage, harass opposition candidates and their supporters, and in some cases manipulate electoral results." In other words, democracy works in appearance but not in substance under the bias of the government, particularly in the electoral, media, legislative, and judicial arenas (Levitsky and Way 2002, 2010). This is pointed out for the electoral arena and media in this chapter in the foregoing section "Referendum on April 16, 2017" and for the legislative and judicial arenas in the section "Amendments to the Constitution" and was common in 2015 election circles. Claims have been made that "elections are no longer fair, civil liberties are being systematically violated, and the playing field is highly skewed in favor of the ruling AKP. The June 2015 election results and their aftermath further confirm that Turkey has evolved into a competitive authoritarian regime" (Esen and Gümüşçü 2017a, 1582–84). A competitive authoritarian regime is a hybrid regime that could be found mainly in developing states after the Cold War (Morline 2008). A hybrid regime refers to a political situation that basically adopts democratic principles such as elections and referendums but contains authoritarian characteristics, including human rights violations. A hybrid regime thus has a feature of combining democracy and authoritarianism and also the vagueness of official and unofficial institutions mixing within one regime. Turkey is assumed to be a hybrid regime.

According to a report prepared by the World Justice Project,[7] Turkey fell two ranks, from 99 in 2016 to 101 in 2017 (118 in 2025), in the Rule of Law Index, and left many questioning the effectiveness and fairness of the rule of law in Turkey. It is assumed to be political common sense in the contemporary world that presidential systems need checks and balances of power, particularly in the judicial arena, as demonstrated by the examples of Brazil and Indonesia (Hazama 2017). Turkey's political trends defy common sense. In fact, it seems that judicial attitudes changed and became more sympathetic to the president and the AKP since 2014 (Özbudun 2015). The competitive authoritarianism government may simply transform to authoritarianism after the revised constitution becomes

---

[7.] Refers to "World Justice Project Rule of Law Index," available online on November 1, 2025, https://worldjusticeproject.org/rule-of-law-index/country/2025/T%C3%BCrkiye.

effective with a president having enlarged powers (Baser and Ozturk 2017), or even before the revised constitution is adopted, during which a de facto authoritarianism could be assumed to be implemented. In such a case, Turkey's present and future relies on the decisions of one man, the president, and no political balance to hedge the risk.

Are Erdoğan and the AKP populists? This is a simple but fundamental question. The answer may differ, depending on how "populist" or "populism" is defined. The terms "populist" and "populism" are widely used and are "notoriously vague terms" (Canovan 1999, 3). There are largely two major definitions of populism. One is a political style that directly appeals to the public beyond established institutions, including party systems and parliament. This concept of populism refers mainly to a method or strategy of a political leader. The other definition is a political movement that criticizes established politics and political elites from the standpoint of citizens. This concept of populism refers mainly to a political movement of citizens. It is not always certain which of the two definitions is correct, and the one does not deny the other (Mizushima 2016; Deiwiks 2009). It might be better to understand populism as implying either of the two—political styles of leaders or political movements of citizens—but a political movement of citizens tends to be more focused than a political style of leaders in the contemporary world. Margaret Canovan (1999, 3) asserted: "Populism in modern democratic societies is best seen as an appeal to "the people" against both the established structure of power and the dominant ideas and values of society. This structural feature in turn dictates populism's characteristic legitimating framework, political style and mood."

We will now examine whether those two definitions are applicable to Turkey, mainly to Erdoğan and the AKP. Erdoğan and AKP politicians appeal directly to their supporters, as well as potential supporters, and do not direct their appeals to the opposition. Other than direct appeals, the AKP has a well-organized party supporters' network in residential districts, where mostly lower-middle class families reside.[8] The AKP usually takes care of those citizens by having AKP staff, sometimes municipality staff, visit each apartment and directly offer some support for a better life. In return, a vote in support of the AKP is personally suggested. The

---

[8] This human network is widely recognized locally in Turkey, although written documentation in English appears limited. During the author's business assignment in Istanbul (2011–2014), the author learned about such networks through regular conversations with the author's company driver, a committed supporter of the AKP and district-level organizer within the party. He frequently described President Erdoğan as a national hero and expressed personal pride in having three children—the number publicly encouraged by Erdoğan.

AKP must continue to provide some benefit with specific citizens at large; otherwise support for the AKP will erode. This is a kind of de facto social distribution system, separate from the public welfare system, such as taxation or the social security system. As long as this mechanism works for the AKP, it is believed that AKP supporters would naturally support the AKP. In light of these observations, we can deduce that Erdoğan and the AKP are not always typical populists in the sense of political style.

Movements by citizens to criticize established politics and political elites have occasionally occurred, like the Gezi Park protests in 2013, but not frequently. It seems that the supporters of Erdoğan and the AKP may naturally accept any views provided by Erdoğan and the AKP, while they often criticize westernized Turkish citizens or the rich. At the same time, those who oppose Erdoğan and the AKP criticize Erdoğan and the AKP for their established conservative politics and political elite status. In Turkey, "citizens" are not united as one, but are clearly divided into two, i.e. pro-Erdoğan and anti-Erdoğan. There is no common ground for citizens to stand on to share the same anti-elitist feelings. From the viewpoint of citizens, Erdoğan and the AKP are not always a party of typical populists. In conclusion, it is thus assumed that Erdoğan and the AKP are not always typical populists, although they may partly act as populists that fit into the two accepted aforementioned definitions of "populism" and "populist."

But Erdoğan's political behaviors are so unique that it is practically difficult to compare him with political leaders of other nation-states. In fact, Erdoğan's political leadership has become stronger after each political crisis, first in 2007 and then in 2013 and 2016 (Türk 2018). In fact, a new word, "Erdoğanism," has come into usage. The integral pieces of Erdoğanism are composed of political Islam, authoritarianism, and Turkish nationalism (Cagaptay and Aktas 2017). This could partly explain Erdoğan's unique political style and philosophy and his strong character and powerful political leadership, but not fully. It is assumed that Erdoğanism means that Turkish citizens rely on one man, President Erdoğan, as an autocrat or dictator. If this should happen, Erdoğanism would have a similar status to Kemalism, or even replace Kemalism in the future, depending on how Erdoğanism performs and how Turkish citizens accept and appreciate it.

A neo-populism discussion may come from the political economic side. Turkey currently has limited economic development capability, but Erdoğan and the AKP have favored an extraordinary monetary policy to keep the economy active—a policy that sometimes risks excessive activation of the market. This is done to obtain utmost political support from the market and citizens but has led to the privatization of national assets, even sometimes by violating rule of law (Kaynak 2016). The AKP's initial economic policy was successful from 2002 to 2011 with vital liberalization of the Turkish economy during a period of possible accession to the EU and a wide liquidity relaxation boom (Akan 2011). But the situation with the economy has entirely changed. Erdoğan and the AKP have kept the country operating in almost the same manner as before. It might be partly because some economics technocrat politicians such as Ali Babacan, former minister and vice prime minister from 2002 to 2015, left the cabinet. In effect, the risk to the political economy is that it might overrun its fair capability.

Looking at society in and the citizens of Turkey, the strong political leadership of the president is fully supported by half the population, but the other half opposes this direction. Turkey has considerable division among the citizens in terms of political and social orientation. The current division among the citizens in politics is between those who are pro-Erdoğan and others who are anti-Erdoğan. Erdoğan has a charismatic speaking ability, and he can understand ordinary citizens' minds by speaking the same words that they do (Cagaptay 2017). This is the reason why Erdoğan is highly appreciated by pro-Erdoğan supporters. However, he has little mind to communicate with those who do not give him their support. Therefore, his political attitude leaves the division of the people in a serious, unsolved state.

Traditionally, Turkey has had various divisions in society—between Islamism and secularism, Sunni and Alavi, Turkish and Kurdish, and rightists and leftists—in addition to gaps in lifestyle and the economy by area. Turkey has a wide variety of cultures, religions, and people within one nation-state. Mustafa Kemal Atatürk (hereunder "Kemal") has been a national symbol of the integration of Turkey and the Turkish since the republic of Turkey was established in 1923, but Erdoğan does not respect traditional ways and looks at the Islamic way of thinking as a personal belief,[9] which may greatly influence Turkish citizens not only in the social and political fields but also in the arts and cultural ones.[10]

It seems that Turkey is turning the corner in the "transformation" from a strict secularist society to a society that is a balance between secularist

---

[9] This refers to Erdoğan's widely cited remark at the Muslim Arab Youth Association Conference in 1996, in which he stated that "democracy can never be a goal; rather, it can only be considered a useful tool to transform a secular-democratic society into an Islamic one." The speech is available in Turkish with English subtitles on YouTube: "Recep Tayyip Erdoğan on Democracy – English Subtitles," accessed November 1, 2025, https://www.youtube.com/watch?v=oQ-Zqn8-wF0.

[10] This refers to several ongoing developments in Turkey, including educational reforms that increase the emphasis on Islamic instruction in primary schools and the demolition of the symbolic Atatürk Cultural Center (AKM), which was replaced by a new opera house and an adjoining mosque.

and Islamist (Keyman and Gümüşçü 2014, 48). And thus, establishments that have protected secularism, such as the military and the judiciary, have been powered down, while AKP and Muslim entrepreneurs have powered up. In other words, the tutelary democracy, which had been initiated mainly by the military and judiciary, is entirely over (Baser and Ozturk 2017; Scotti 2017). Thus, a slight but steady change in the balance between secularism and Islamism is occurring, with a more Islamic orientation under the current constitutional framework (Naito 2017).

A fair public opinion theater in Turkey has not been properly established nor ever fully dismantled by the AKP.[11] This theater could contribute to building some consensus within society and narrowing gaps of understanding in various respects. This is the basic foundation of democracy. Without this mechanism, it is hard for citizens to understand the situation properly and to exchange views freely in public. Many citizens do not trust mass media under AKP control and rely largely on social media (Bulut and Yoruk 2017). Turkey is ranked 155th out of 180 states in the 2017 (154th out of 179 in the 2025) World Press Freedom Index,[12] four spots down from the 151st ranking recorded in 2016. In such a situation, counter-democracy activities (Rosanvallon 2006) by the citizens may eventually occur, as in the Gezi Park protests in 2013,[13] or in even more radical ways. On the other hand, the Turkish government maintains strict authoritarian control over Turkish citizens who may protest against the government, and many suspects related to the Fetullahçı Terror Organization (*Fetullahçı Terör Örgütü*, hereunder "FETÖ") were detained, captured, and labeled as terrorists under a state of emergency.[14] This situation, including many possible suspected cases of human rights violations, would be a malfunction of a proper democracy, tasked with respecting public opinion and the views of both the majority and the

---

[11.] Refers to the article "Turkish Media Group Bought by Pro-Government Conglomerate," published by the *New York Times*, dated March 21, 2018, as an example. Available online on November 1, 2025, https://www.nytimes.com/2018/03/21/world/europe/turkey-media-erdogan-dogan.html.

[12.] Refers to the World Press Freedom Index published by Reporters Without Borders, available online on November 1, 2025, https://rsf.org/en/ranking.

[13.] Refers to a unique analysis of the Gezi Park protests, which referred to them as "an initiative of various wage-earning class fractions led by service-sector employees and the educated youth" (Gürcan and Peker 2015, 338–39).

[14.] Refers to Press Release "No: 38, 8 February 2018, Press Release Regarding the Resolution of the European Parliament Entitled 'Current Situation of Human Rights in Turkey'," published online by the Ministry of Foreign Affairs, Turkey, available on January 7, 2026. http://www.mfa.gov.tr/no_-38_-ap-nin-turkiyede-mevcut-insan-haklari-durumu-baslikli-karari_en.en.mfa.

minority regardless of class, leading to certain frustrations or unjust feelings being shared by the citizens.

7 Possible Future Directions

In line with the aforementioned arguments, the following two directions are theoretically drawn out.[15] One is an autocracy or dictatorship led by President Erdoğan. This might result in greater division between pro-Erdoğan and anti-Erdoğan supporters and also between Islamism and secularism in Turkey. A greater division of the citizens would lead to an unstable society, damaging the trust and legitimacy of the nation-state. The integrity of Turkey has been maintained so far by the dignity of Turkey's founder, Kemal, but the state's integrity must be founded on equality of the citizens. A greater division of the citizens might break down this particular value of equality. In the worst case, it might lead to Turkey becoming a failed state, losing national trust from the US and European states, as occurred during the multiple sovereign defaults in the past.

Turkey largely relies on the US for national security through the NATO framework and on European states for economic prosperity through the EU-Turkey Customs Union. Thus, diplomatic relations between Turkey and the United States, as well as with European states, are vital. If those are significantly damaged, political turmoil could result as a typical political risk (Bremmer and Keat 2010; Eurasia Group 2016, 2017). Without doing anything in particular, Turkey's future would naturally be in line with this direction. In this direction, Turkey may have another option to maintain diplomatic ties with Russia, Iran, and China, instead of the United States and the European states, as a theoretical concept. However, in practice, this new attempt has not matured much, and Turkey seems to be using this diplomatic alliance mainly to demonstrate an alternative and subsequently gain more negotiating power with the United States and European states (Sheibani 2018). Thus, this diplomatic option is not feasible in the short and middle terms, but in the longer term, Turkey might have such an option.

---

[15] Refers to another research project made by Alaranta (2016), which provides a future-oriented analysis in the form of three scenarios: (1) an authoritarian Islamist state; (2) a consolidated liberal democracy; and (3) the dissolution of the Turkish state.

The second direction would entail a balance of internal and external political interests that maintains a respect for universal values to a reasonable extent, particularly freedom of the press. This might result in a possible soft-landing emphasizing consensus-building that reduces divisions among the citizens. Consequently, society would be kept reasonably stable, and diplomacy would be maintained to ensure the frameworks of NATO and the EU-Turkey Customs Union. Even if conflict occurs in Turkey, a solution through a democratic process may be challenging. Counter-democracy activities by some of the citizens would not lead to a catastrophic event and might be considered healthy public expressions as long as they remain within a democratic framework. This scenario relies on the political intention to minimize risk in politics and society, and it would be feasible to materialize if Erdoğan and the AKP clearly choose to take this course of action. Guidance through dialogue could possibly be provided to Turkey by international society to encourage implementation of the latter direction.

Two ideas would appear to be feasible. The first involves the use of the EU framework. Turkey's EU membership accession is a practicable process to encourage Turkey to meet the "Copenhagen criteria," including political, economic, administrative, and institutional capacity requirements.[16] This might be an ideal course for Turkey to naturally continue to the second scenario, but its negotiation process seems to be unofficially stopped. An alternative idea would be for the EU to offer Turkey a new status of EU-associated membership.[17] This would not be full membership but would be better than being an EU candidate for nearly two decades. Theoretically, it is understood that EU core members such as France and Germany, in the center of the European continent, and the United Kingdom and Turkey, as peripheral areas in the north and south, may make sense as a formation of balance in the greater EU concept. One serious issue is public opinion in the EU and United Kingdom/Turkey, and whether people in those states would accept such a new formation. Another pending issue is how the United Kingdom will withdraw from the EU and the legal status the United Kingdom will maintain in the EU after withdrawal. Once the UK issue is

---

[16] Refers to European Commission "Accession Criteria," published online, available on November 1, 2025, https://ec.europa.eu/neighbourhood-enlargement/policy/glossary/terms/accession-criteria_en.

[17] This concept was proposed by German Chancellor Angela Merkel as a form of "privileged partnership" (*privilegierte Partnerschaft*). Although the idea was previously unpersuasive when applied solely to Turkey, the prospect may now hold greater diplomatic relevance, as both the United Kingdom and Turkey share a similar non-member legal status vis-à-vis the European Union.

clarified, Turkey might be able to seek a similar status, which would also be some criteria lower than that of the Copenhagen criteria.

This might lead Turkey to a second idea, the United Nations framework, and that is one in which the UN Human Rights Council considers Turkey to be in violation of human rights within its territory and its surrounding areas, including North Iraq and Northwest Syria. At the time of the third cycle of the Universal Periodic Review (UPR) in 2020, when Turkey is peer-reviewed and there is interactive dialogue with UN member states,[18] the UN Human Rights Council could publicly announce that UN member states have reached a consensus that Turkey needs to demonstrate more respect for international human rights laws. This announcement itself would have no enforcement power in a purely legal context but would be immediately heard by all UN member states and would thus force Turkey to react to any action taken by a foreign state or NGO. Nowadays, questioning the reputation of a national government can immediately affect the movement of stocks, currency exchange markets, and country risk ratings. This would thus create an opportunity for Turkey to improve its attitude toward international human rights laws and the opinions of international society and could indirectly lead Turkey in the second direction. This is a part of soft law, which could prove its effectiveness based on the dignity of the UN and the values of international human rights laws.

8 Conclusion

Following the 2017 constitutional referendum and the amendments scheduled to take effect in 2018, Turkey's new presidential system is expected to concentrate governing authority in the presidency, raising concerns that mechanisms of checks and balances will not function effectively. As a result, competitive authoritarianism has become increasingly evident. Although democratic procedures formally remain in place, substantive democratic practices have weakened due to government bias across electoral, legislative, and judicial arenas as well as significant constraints on the media. Under such conditions, a competitive authoritarian regime may evolve into full authoritarianism after—and potentially even before—the revised constitutional framework becomes fully operational. These devel-

---

[18.] Refers to the United Nations Office of the High Commissioner for Human Rights (OHCHR), *Universal Periodic Review – Türkiye*, official records from the first cycle (2010) and the second cycle (2015). Published online and accessed November 1, 2025, https://www.ohchr.org/en/hr-bodies/upr/tr-index.

opments suggest the possibility that Turkey may continue shifting toward a more overtly autocratic or dictatorial model of governance.

From a theoretical perspective, Erdoğan and the Justice and Development Party (AKP) do not fit neatly into conventional definitions of populism. While certain elements of Erdoğan's leadership style and the AKP's political mobilization reflect characteristics associated with populism, Erdoğan's political behavior exhibits a degree of idiosyncrasy that complicates direct comparison with leaders of other states. Erdoğan's authority consolidated further following successive political crises—most notably, in 2007, 2013, and 2016—thereby contributing to the use of the term Erdoğanism to describe his mode of governance. The core components of Erdoğanism combine political Islam, authoritarian governance, and Turkish nationalism. In this formulation, Erdoğanism implies a system in which political authority is highly personalized, grounded in reliance on a single leader.

With respect to society and the citizenry, Erdoğan's leadership continues to divide public opinion sharply. Approximately half of the population supports his political direction, while the other half remains opposed. This polarization is reflected in survey data collected by a US research agency in 2014 and 2015, as well as in interviews conducted by the author in 2018. Erdoğan's political approach has therefore contributed to a persistent societal division that remains unresolved.

For the future well-being of Turkey and its citizens, it is desirable that Turkey pursue a political trajectory that balances domestic and international interests while maintaining reasonable respect for universal values—particularly freedom of the press—as a foundation for state stability and human rights. Respect for the democratic choices of Turkish citizens remains fundamental. At the same time, constructive diplomatic engagement by the international community could help encourage Turkey to reinforce democratic norms and human rights protections. Two potential avenues merit consideration: renewed dialogue regarding EU accession and engagement through mechanisms of the UN Human Rights Council. These channels, while indirect, may offer feasible means of supporting Turkey in pursuing a political direction conducive to both national stability and the welfare of its citizens.

Acknowledgments

The author wishes to acknowledge the 5th World Congress Middle Eastern Studies (WOCMES 2018), held July 16–20, 2018, in Seville,

Spain, for the stimulation to draft this chapter, and Michael Hassett for his constructive review and edit of the draft.

Bibliography

Akan, Taner. 2011. "The Political Economy of Turkish Conservative Democracy as a Governmental Strategy of Industrial Relations Between Islamism, Neoliberalism and Social Democracy." *Economic and Industrial Democracy* 33 (2): 317–49. https://doi.org/10.1177/0143831X11411328.

Alaranta, Toni. 2016. "Turkey's Political Direction: Authoritarianism, Liberal Democracy or Dissolution?" *The Finnish Institute of International Affairs Working Paper* 90: 1–22. Accessed January 7, 2026. https://fiia.fi/en/publication/turkeys-political-direction.

Baser, Bahar. 2017. "Turkey's Diaspora Engagement Policy Under the Justice and Development Party." International Migration Institute, University of Oxford. Accessed August 1, 2018. Accessed January 7, 2026. https://www.migrationinstitute.org/blog/turkey2019s-diaspora-engagement-policy-under-the-justice-and-development-party.

Baser, Bahar, and Ahmet Erdi Ozturk. 2017. *Authoritarian Politics in Turkey: Elections, Resistance and the AKP.* I.B. Tauris.

Bremmer, Ian, and Preston Keat. 2010. *The Fat Tail.* Reprint ed. Oxford University Press.

Bulut, Ergin, and Erdem Yoruk. 2017. "Digital Populism: Trolls and Political Polarization of Twitter in Turkey." *International Journal of Communication* 11: 4093–117. Accessed August 1, 2018. http://ijoc.org/index.php/ijoc/article/view/6702/2158.

Cagaptay, Soner. 2017. *The New Sultan: Erdogan and the Crisis of Modern Turkey.* I.B. Tauris.

Cagaptay, Soner, and Oya Rose Aktas. 2017. "How Erdoganism Is Killing Turkish Democracy: The End of Political Opposition." *Foreign Affairs,* July 7. Accessed August 1, 2018. https://www.foreignaffairs.com/articles/turkey/2017-07-07/how-erdoganism-killing-turkish-democracy.

Canovan, Margaret. 1999. "Trust the People! Populism and Two Faces of Democracy." *Political Studies* 47 (1): 2–16. https://doi.org/10.1111/1467-9248.00184.

Deiwiks, Christa. 2009. "Populism." *Living Reviews in Democracy* 1: 1–9. Accessed January 7, 2026. chrome-extension://efaidnbmnnnibpca-jpcglclefindmkaj/https://ethz.ch/content/dam/ethz/special-interest/gess/cis/

cis-dam/CIS_DAM_2015/WorkingPapers/Living_Reviews_Democracy/ Deiwiks.PDF

Esen, Berk, and Şebnem Gümüşçü. 2017a. "Rising Competitive Authoritarianism in Turkey." *Third World Quarterly* 37 (9): 1581–606. https:// doi.org/10.1080/01436597.2015.1135732.

Esen, Berk, and Şebnem Gümüşçü. 2017b. "A Small Yes for Presidentialism: The Turkish Constitutional Referendum of April 2017." *South European Society and Politics* 22 (3): 303–26. https://doi.org/10.1080/13 608746.2017.1384341.

Eurasia Group. 2016. "Top Risks 2016." Accessed August 1, 2018. https://www.eurasiagroup.net/issues/top-risks-2016.

Eurasia Group. 2017. "Top Risks 2017." Accessed August 1, 2018. https://www.eurasiagroup.net/issues/top-risks-2017.

Gürcan, Efe Can, and Efe Peker. 2015. "A Class Analytic Approach to the Gezi Park Events: Challenging the 'Middle Class' Myth." *Capital & Class* 39 (2): 321–43. https://doi.org/10.1177/0309816815584015.

Hazama, Yasushi. 2017. "Transition to Presidential System in Turkey." *Middle East Cooperation Center News* 5: 8–16. [in Japanese].

Kaynak, Akif Bahadır. 2016. "Rise of Neo-Populism and the Decline of European Agenda in Turkey." *BUJSS* 9 (1): 173–86. Accessed January 7, 2026. https://dergipark.org.tr/en/pub/bujss/article/297310.

Keyman, E. Fuat, and Şebnem Gümüşçü. 2014. *Democracy, Identity, and Foreign Policy in Turkey: Hegemony Through Transformation*. Palgrave Macmillan.

Korkmaz, Emre Eren. 2017. "How Might the Turkish Referendum Outcome Affect Turkey's Policies Towards Refugees and Migrants?" International Migration Institute, University of Oxford. Accessed January 7, 2026. https://www.migrationinstitute.org/blog/how-might -the-turkish-referendum-outcome-affect-turkey2019s-policies -towards-refugees-and-migrants.

Levitsky, Steven, and Lucan A. Way. 2002. "The Rise of Competitive Authoritarianism." *Journal of Democracy* 13 (2): 51–65. Accessed January 7, 2026. https://www.journalofdemocracy.org/articles/elections-without-democracy-the-rise-of-competitive-authoritarianism/.

Levitsky, Steven, and Lucan A. Way. 2010. *Competitive Authoritarianism: Hybrid Regimes after the Cold War*. Problems of International Politics. Cambridge University Press.

Mizushima, Jiro. 2016. *What Is Populism? Is It an Enemy against Democracy, or a Hope for the Reform?* [in Japanese]. Chuo-Koron-Shinsha.

Morline, Leonardo. 2008. "Hybrid Regimes or Regimes in Transition?" *FRIDE Working Paper* 70: 1–18. Accessed January 7, 2026. chrome-extension://efaidnbmnnnibpcajpcglclefindmkaj/https://repository.uobaghdad.edu.iq/file/publication/pdf/0b3e82c2-d9a9-429b-aaa2-2f9131dea567.pdf.

Naito, Masanori. 2017. "Grasp the Common People's Heart with 'Islamic Justice': The Politics of Turkish President Erdogan." *Synodos*, May 29. [in Japanese]. Accessed August 1, 2018. Synodos Opinion. May 29. [in Japanese]. Accessed January 7, 2026. https://synodos.jp/opinion/international/19809/.

Özbudun, Ergun. 2015. "Turkey's Judiciary and the Drift Toward Competitive Authoritarianism." *Italian Journal of International Affairs* 50 (2): 42–55. https://doi.org/10.1080/03932729.2015.1020651.

Pew Research Center. 2014. "Turks Divided on Erdogan and the Country's Direction: About Half Support Gezi Park Protests." July 30. Accessed August 1, 2018. http://www.pewglobal.org/2014/07/30/turks-divided-on-erdogan-and-the-countrys-direction/.

Pew Research Center. 2015. "Deep Divisions in Turkey as Election Nears—But Turks Share Negative Views of Foreign Powers." October 15. Accessed August 1, 2018. http://www.pewglobal.org/2015/10/15/deep-divisions-in-turkey-as-election-nears/.

Rosanvallon, Pierre. 2006. *Counter-Democracy: Politics in an Age of Distrust*. The Seeley Lectures. Translated by Masaki Shimazaki. Iwanami Shoten.

Scotti, Valentina Rita. 2017. "Presidentialism in Turkey: A First Appraisal of 2017 Constitutional Reform." *DPCE Online* 30 (2). Accessed August 1, 2018. http://www.dpceonline.it/index.php/dpceonline/article/view/388.

Sheibani, Mohammad Reza. 2018. "Iran-Russia Alliance Should Become a Model for Solving Regional Crises." *Valdai*, October 4. Accessed August 1, 2018. http://valdaiclub.com/a/highlights/iran-russia-alliance-should-become-a-model-for-sol/.

Türk, H. Bahadir. 2018. "'Populism as a Medium of Mass Mobilization': The Case of Recep Tayyip Erdoğan." *International Area Studies Review* 21 (2): 1–19. https://doi.org/10.1177/2233865918761111.

ART II

National Independence, Sovereignty, and Citizen Well-Being

CHAPTER 5

The Evolution of Japan's Limited Sovereignty: From the Era of Unequal Treaties to the Japan–US Alliance

Abstract

This chapter examines the evolution of Japan's limited sovereignty across two distinct historical periods: the nineteenth-century era of unequal treaties and the post–World War II era shaped by the Japan–US alliance. In the earlier period, treaties imposed by Western powers curtailed Japan's jurisdictional and tariff autonomy. Paradoxically, these constraints catalyzed rapid modernization and a national drive to restore sovereign equality. In contrast, the postwar period introduced a different model of limited sovereignty: one characterized by strategic dependence through the Japan–US Security Treaty and the Status of Forces Agreement (SOFA). These legal arrangements grant the United States significant military rights on Japanese territory, including base maintenance and jurisdictional authority, raising ongoing concerns about Japan's territorial and legal autonomy. Further tensions arise from the opaque operation of the Japan–US Security Consultative Committee, whose limited transparency and perceived imbalance in representation have prompted criticism regarding undue US influence. Evolving regional security dynamics and potential shifts in US foreign policy further complicate Japan's sovereignty posture. Additionally, growing secrecy surrounding national security and the technical nature of defense policy hinder public deliberation and raise broader questions about democratic accountability. Employing an interdisciplinary framework that draws from international law, political science, and history, this study analyzes the legal instruments and socio-political contexts that shaped these two periods. By comparing externally imposed and internally accepted constraints on sovereignty, the chapter contributes to a deeper understanding of how nations negotiate autonomy within global power structures. This analysis, grounded in a comprehensive review of English and Japanese scholarship, offers a nuanced perspective on Japan's evolving relationship with limited sovereignty and its implications for democratic governance and strategic positioning in East Asia.

Keywords: Autonomy, Sovereignty, Unequal Treaties, Japan–US Security Treaty, Japan–US Status of Forces Agreement (SOFA), Japan–US Security Consultative Committee

1 Introduction

National sovereignty, nation-building, reconstruction, and national consciousness are key concepts for understanding the formation and evolution of modern states. These elements are closely interrelated, shaping both the development of state institutions and the construction of national identity. Among them, national sovereignty occupies a central place, referring to a state's supreme authority to govern its internal affairs without external interference (Odaka 1984). It is grounded in the classical doctrine that a state consists of three fundamental components: a defined territory, a permanent population, and sovereign authority (Odaka 1984).

Japan's nineteenth-century experience with unequal treaties, imposed by Western imperial powers, directly challenged its territorial integrity, legal autonomy, and economic independence. The post–World War II era of limited sovereignty, while also constraining national autonomy, arose from a significantly different historical and geopolitical context. Shaped by the Cold War and Japan's continued security dependence on the US, this era's constraints focused primarily on defense and foreign policy, notably formalized through the Japan–U.S. Security Treaty and related agreements (Ministry of Foreign Affairs of Japan 2025).

These two distinct cases of limited sovereignty in Japan offer valuable insights into how states navigate within a system of unequal power. The concept itself reflects complex international dynamics. Formally recognized sovereign states frequently encounter constraints on their autonomy, arising from diverse internal and external sources, including economic dependence, military alliances, political pressure, and participation in international organizations. Japan's experience is not unique. Throughout history, numerous states have experienced limitations on their sovereignty.

The purpose of this chapter is to analyze the complex and enduring issue of Japan's limited sovereignty as it has manifested across two critical historical periods: the nineteenth-century era of unequal treaties and the post–World War II period of constrained sovereignty under the Japan–US alliance. By examining how Japan has navigated these externally imposed and internally accepted limitations, the chapter explores their implications for the country's international standing, domestic policy, and evolving national identity.

Examining the legal instruments and agreements defining these periods, and analyzing their socio-political contexts, this study offers a nuanced understanding of sovereignty's multifaceted nature and the challenges of balancing power, security, and autonomy. Specifically, this chapter explores Japan's adaptations to limited sovereignty, demonstrating how constraints have been transformed into opportunities for growth, influence, and national identity. This analysis offers a novel, comparative perspective on the evolution of sovereignty.

2 Theoretical Background

In political theory, sovereignty is defined as the ultimate authority within a political community to make binding decisions and maintain internal order. As one of the most contested and multifaceted concepts in political science and international law, sovereignty intersects with the broader ideas of statehood, governance, independence, and democracy (Tagami 1962; Britannica, n.d.). Stephen Krasner (1999) provides a foundational typology by identifying four distinct yet overlapping dimensions of sovereignty: international legal sovereignty (formal recognition by other states), Westphalian sovereignty (non-intervention and territorial autonomy), domestic sovereignty (the ability to control internal affairs), and interdependence sovereignty (regulation of cross-border flows). This framework allows for a more nuanced understanding of how sovereignty operates in practice and under constraints.

In the case of Japan, international legal sovereignty and Westphalian sovereignty are of particular relevance, as they highlight the complex tensions between formal recognition and external pressures that limit Japan's autonomous decision-making. While domestic and interdependence sovereignty are less directly applicable to the primary argument, they provide important contextual background for assessing the evolving nature of sovereignty in a globalized and interdependent world.

Within the field of international relations, sovereignty is frequently constrained by asymmetrical power dynamics, strategic alliances, and institutional dependencies. This phenomenon—commonly referred to as *limited sovereignty*—describes situations in which states, despite formal recognition and legal independence, face restrictions on their ability to exercise sovereign powers fully. These constraints can affect critical areas such as defense, foreign policy, economic governance, and domestic legal autonomy (Loughlin 2017).

Importantly, *limited sovereignty* is distinct from the status of unrecognized states, which lack international legal standing, or collapsed states, which suffer from institutional breakdown and ineffective governance (Krasner 2004). In this chapter, *limited sovereignty* refers specifically to states that hold international legal sovereignty but experience partial limitations due to historical, geopolitical, or institutional factors.

The concept of *limited sovereignty* is evident in both historical and contemporary contexts. During the Cold War, the Brezhnev Doctrine asserted the Soviet Union's right to intervene in other socialist countries. This doctrine severely restricted the sovereignty of Eastern European nations. In another setting, many developing states continue to face limitations on their economic sovereignty. These constraints often stem from structural dependence on international financial institutions such as the International Monetary Fund (IMF) and the World Bank.

A further example can be seen in the case of European Union (EU) member states. Although these states retain formal sovereignty, they participate in a form of pooled or shared sovereignty. Legislative and regulatory powers are transferred to supranational institutions to enable collective policymaking and implementation. These examples show that sovereignty is not an absolute or unchanging condition but instead, that it is shaped by historical, geopolitical, and institutional factors. As a result, sovereignty remains a flexible and context-dependent concept, with significant consequences for national interests, policy autonomy, and domestic governance (Krasner 2001).

3 Methodology

This study examines Japan's experience of limited sovereignty across two distinct historical periods: the prewar era of unequal treaties and the postwar era shaped by the Japan–US alliance. Each period is analyzed through its legal instruments and agreements that defined sovereignty constraints, as well as its broader socio-political context, including prevailing global power dynamics. A comparative analysis follows, highlighting the enduring implications for Japan's political development, foreign relations, and domestic governance. The conclusion synthesizes the key findings.

The central research question guiding this study is as follows: *How have externally imposed and internally accepted constraints on sovereignty in two key historical periods—Japan's prewar era of unequal treaties and the postwar U.-Japan alliance—shaped the trajectory of Japan's political autonomy and international positioning?* This question drives comparative inquiry and underpins the selection of sources, analytical framework, and interpretive lens.

An interdisciplinary approach is employed, drawing on insights from international law, political science, history, and sociology. This framework enables a multifaceted examination of the evolution and consequences of Japan's limited sovereignty. A comprehensive literature review was conducted using both English and Japanese sources, incorporating scholarly works, legal texts, historical archives, and contemporary policy analyses. This methodological integration allows for a nuanced analysis that situates legal constraints within their broader historical and political contexts.

The research process focused on key terms such as "Japan–US Security Treaty," "limited sovereignty," and "unequal treaties," complemented by related concepts, including "extraterritoriality," "Japan–US Status of Forces Agreement (SOFA)," "Japan–US Security Consultative Committee," and "tariff autonomy." Searches were conducted through major academic databases and repositories, including Google Scholar, the University of Tokyo Library, and the National Diet Library of Japan, to identify relevant journal articles, books, government documents, and legal databases.

Unlike previous studies that examine the nineteenth-century and postwar sovereignty limitations in isolation, this study adopts a comparative framework that analyzes both periods through the shared lens of limited sovereignty. The analysis differentiates these periods by the nature of the constraints—legal, economic, or military—and by whether these limitations were externally imposed or internally accepted.

While theoretical and contextual challenges are acknowledged, this comparative approach is crucial for understanding the contemporary manifestations of constrained sovereignty. It highlights how the legacies of nineteenth-century arrangements continue to shape present-day debates on Japan's autonomy. Moreover, it points to the possibility of future sovereignty challenges, suggesting that evolving geopolitical and institutional dynamics may again test Japan's capacity for independent decision-making.

4 The Unequal Treaties and Their Impact on Japan

4.1 Extraterritoriality and Tariff Restrictions

The mid-nineteenth century marked a watershed moment in Japanese history. The nation's long-standing policy of seclusion (*sakoku)* was abruptly ended by the arrival of Western imperial powers. Admiral Matthew C. Perry's (1794–1858) forceful entry into Edo Bay in July 1853 with four armed ships, including two steam-powered vessels, followed by his second visit with nine armed ships, including three steam-powered vessels, signaled the end of Japan's self-imposed isolation and the beginning of its engagement with the modern world. However, this engagement was far from equal.

Confronted with the overwhelming military and technological superiority of Western powers, such as the armed steam-powered vessels equipped with many cannons, Japan was compelled to enter into a series of treaties that significantly compromised its sovereignty. These treaties, beginning with the 1854 Treaty of Kanagawa with the US (Office of The Historian 1853) and extending to the commercial treaties of 1858, became known as "unequal treaties." These agreements not only facilitated foreign trade in Japanese ports but also established extraterritoriality and imposed substantial limitations on Japan's tariff autonomy, thus severely restricting its sovereignty.

During the nineteenth-century age of imperialism, international law categorized the world, according to a Western-defined "standard of civilization," classifying nations as "civilized," "semi-civilized," and "uncivilized" (Mälksoo 2017; Shahabuddin 2019). While these terms are now recognized as inappropriate and discriminatory, they were historically used to categorize states. "Civilized" denoted sovereign states, "semi-civilized" designated states with limited sovereignty, and "uncivilized" referred to colonies. European nations and the US were deemed "civilized," while Japan, under the then -prevailing Eurocentric legal framework, was classified as "semi-civilized" (Sakurai 2023).

The prevailing legal principle held that "civilized" nations possessed the right to apply their laws extraterritorially. This meant that their citizens would not be subject to legal systems deemed "semi-civilized," such as traditional Japanese trials lacking legal representation, or punishments considered brutal, like torture. This historical legal reasoning stemmed from the perceived absence of European-style legal systems in Japan (Sakurai 2023). Japan's acceptance of extraterritoriality for "civilized" peoples (i.e., the application of, for example, English law outside of England) was coupled with the renunciation of tariff autonomy in treaties with foreign powers, including the US, the Netherlands, Russia, Great Britain, and France.

The implications of extraterritoriality and the loss of tariff autonomy imposed by the unequal treaties were profound. Extraterritoriality, a legal principle granting foreign nationals' immunity from local laws, meant that foreigners residing in Japan were subject to the jurisdiction of their own consular courts, not Japanese law. This provision undermined Japan's legal sovereignty and created a situation of legal asymmetry, where foreigners enjoyed privileges and immunities not afforded to Japanese citizens. This system effectively established foreign enclaves within Japan, where Westerners operated outside Japanese legal authority, further eroding Japan's control over its territory and population.

The loss of tariff autonomy, which prevented Japan from establishing its own import and export tariffs, had equally profound economic effects. Japan was unable to protect its nascent domestic industries from competition with cheaper foreign goods. For instance, within the textile sector, Japanese silk and cotton producers experienced diminished competitiveness against British and American imports. This constraint hampered industrial development, fostered economic dependence on Western powers, and restricted the government's revenue generation capacity, thereby further limiting its fiscal sovereignty.

4.2 The Tokugawa Shogunate's Initial Response

During the 1850s and 1860s, Japan was governed by the Tokugawa Shogunate, a hereditary ruling system headed by a Shogun (the supreme military and political leader) from the Tokugawa family, which had held power since 1603 (Sakurai 2023). A defining characteristic of the Tokugawa Shogunate was its policy of national seclusion, implemented between 1633 and 1854. This policy restricted foreign interaction to limited, authorized trade with Dutch merchants at the designated enclave of Dejima in Nagasaki.

Consequently, even high-ranking officials within the Tokugawa Shogunate possessed limited knowledge of foreign countries and lacked knowledge of modern legal systems and international law when treaty negotiations were being held. Indeed, it was not until discussions with Townsend Harris, the American consul-general, in 1857 that they gained a rudimentary understanding of international legal principles.

Recognizing this deficiency, the Tokugawa Shogunate dispatched two young officials, Amane Nishi (1829–1897) and Masamichi Tsuda (1829–1903), to the Netherlands in the early summer of 1863 to study modern law (Nagao 1979; Sakurai 2023). There, they dedicated themselves to learning Dutch until 1865, attending twice-weekly lectures at the residence of Leiden University Professor Simon Fisseling (1818–1888). Their studies encompassed five key areas: natural law (primarily civil law), international law, constitutional law, economics, and statistics.

Upon their return, these two officials served as advisers to the last Shogun, Yoshinobu Tokugawa, and subsequently published treatises on law. However, the immediate impact of these publications was limited due to the subsequent collapse of the Tokugawa Shogunate. In 1867, Yoshinobu Tokugawa relinquished his position as Shogun and pledged allegiance to the emperor. The following year, the Meiji Restoration restructured governance, centralizing authority under imperial rule. In 1869, the emperor was transferred from Kyoto to Tokyo, marking a symbolic shift in power.

4.3 The Struggle for Treaty Revision by the New Government

A primary objective for the leaders of Japan in the newly established government was the rapid transformation of the country into an internationally recognized modern sovereign state (Sakurai 2023). This objective provided a strong impetus for modernization undergirded by the establishment of a modern legal system and the adoption of a parliamentary system. To inform this process, the Iwakura Mission was established. This was headed by Tomomi Iwakura (1825–1883) and involved a comprehensive round-the-world tour between November 1871 and September 1873.

The aim of this mission was to research various nations to identify suitable models for Japan's modernization, in addition to conducting official diplomatic visits on behalf of the new government. The Iwakura Mission, a delegation of approximately 150 officials, undertook a diplomatic tour of 12 countries, including the US, Great Britain, France, Russia, Germany, Austria, and Italy. The mission engaged in discussions with the leaders of these countries, meticulously documenting their diplomatic activities and observations. The mission submitted detailed reports to the Japanese government, providing a comprehensive account of their experiences and observations (Japan Center for Asian Historical Records 2018).

Following the tour, Iwakura concluded that Germany, as a rising imperial power, offered the most suitable model for a modernizing Japan. The mission members were particularly impressed by Chancellor Otto von Bismarck (1815–1898) and the seemingly harmonious relationship between the Kaiser and the Chancellor, viewing Germany as a potential blueprint for a future Japanese empire. This admiration for Germany significantly influenced the drafting of the 1889 Constitution, the 1898 Civil Code, and other legal instruments, which drew heavily from German legal principles (Sakurai 2023).

However, the Japanese government strategically adopted a diversified approach to modernization, drawing inspiration from various nations. For example, railway and road infrastructure, along with the postal system, were modeled after British examples; law, medical science, and military organization drew heavily from Germany; engineering and shipbuilding techniques were adopted from Scotland; and the bureaucratic system and administrative law were inspired by France. This diversified approach to modernization reflects a deliberate Japanese policy to avoid over-reliance on any single foreign power, driven by a paramount concern for national independence and preventing potential domination.

4.4 Reclaiming Autonomy After 57 Years

To achieve modernization and recognition as a "civilized" nation by Western-defined international legal standards, Japan implemented substantial reforms, including the establishment of a modern legal system and a parliamentary system, alongside concurrent militarization and industrialization efforts. Subsequently, the Japanese government initiated a systematic process of treaty revision negotiations with the US, Great Britain, and other relevant nations.

This long-term effort gradually led to revisions in the late nineteenth and early twentieth centuries. Through diplomatic efforts, coupled with Japan's demonstrable progress in modernization and its growing military strength, the Western powers eventually agreed to treaty revision. The abolition of extraterritoriality in 1899 significantly restored Japan's jurisdictional sovereignty. The restoration of full tariff autonomy in 1911 further liberated Japan from the economic constraints imposed by the treaties, enabling independent economic policymaking.

This treaty revision process became intertwined with broader projects of nation-building and modernization, even as Japan simultaneously emerged as an imperial power, extending its rule over neighboring territories, including Taiwan (1895) and the Korean Peninsula (1910). These achievements marked a turning point in Japanese history, signifying the restoration of national sovereignty and paving the way for Japan's emergence as a major power. The period of significant limitations on sovereignty that Japan experienced as a result of the unequal treaties has been commonly viewed as a powerful catalyst for national transformation.

Japan's experience of unequal treatment by Western powers fostered a strong desire to overcome externally imposed limitations. Nationalistic sentiment, along with the practical need to revise unequal treaties, became a key driver of Japan's modernization. This is reflected in the country's rapid industrialization, military expansion, and social reforms. Diplomacy alone did not lead to treaty revision. Japan was also forced to engage in costly wars and large-scale national mobilization to gain recognition from Western powers. It sought to be acknowledged as a "civilized" nation under the standards of international law at the time.

The pursuit of treaty revision came at significant military and financial cost. Japan fought two major wars: against China (1894–1895) and Russia (1904–1905), resulting in over 100,000 deaths. The expenses far exceeded Japan's annual national budget. The Russo-Japanese War alone cost approximately ten times the annual budget and left the country burdened with long-term debt. War debt repayment began in 1906 and continued until 1986. The legacy of unequal treaties is complex. While they initially constrained Japan's sovereignty and development, they also—paradoxically—spurred its transformation into a modern, powerful state (Shahabuddin 2019).

5 The Era of Limited Sovereignty After the War

5.1 The Postwar Occupation Context

Japan's defeat in World War II and subsequent seven-year occupation between 1945 and 1952 by the Allied forces, primarily the US under the Supreme Commander for the Allied Powers (SCAP), General Douglas MacArthur (1880–1964), marked a profound nadir in its national sovereignty (Nishi 2005). The period of occupation, which lasted from September 1945 to April 1952, was initially characterized by stringent demilitarization and democratization policies. Under the direction of the SCAP, Japan underwent a fundamental transformation, with sweeping reforms reshaping its political, economic, and social landscape (Nishi 2005).

These reforms encompassed substantial amendments to the Constitution, with the objective of establishing a pacifist and democratic framework; restructuring the education system, aimed at dismantling militaristic ideologies and promoting democratic values; reforming the agricultural land ownership system, aimed at redistributing land and empowering farmers; legalizing and promoting trade unions, aimed at empowering workers; and reforming the family system, aimed at challenging traditional patriarchal structures. These reforms aimed to reshape Japanese society and establish the foundations for a democratic and peaceful nation. However, some scholars, such as Helen Mears ([1948] 2015), have argued that these reforms, particularly given the numerous strictures imposed on Japan, also reflected a degree of retribution for wartime actions.

A key element of continuity between the pre- and postwar periods was the retention of the existing Japanese bureaucracy. This bureaucracy, with its established structures and expertise, was deemed essential by the US occupation forces to ensure the smooth administration of the country during the transition and to facilitate the implementation of the extensive reform programs. The bureaucracy played a crucial role in supporting the US occupation and the implementation of its transformative agenda.

The emergence of the Cold War and escalating tensions between the US and the Soviet Union profoundly impacted the strategic landscape in the Far East. The US, increasingly concerned about the spread of communism, particularly after the Chinese Revolution of 1949 and the Korean War (1950–1953), began to view Japan not as a defeated enemy but as a vital strategic partner in its containment policy. This geopolitical shift led to a reassessment of US occupation policy, paving the way for the eventual restoration of Japanese sovereignty.

5.2 Treaty of San Francisco and the Japan–U.S. Security Treaty

On 8 September 1951, the Treaty of San Francisco of 1951 formally restored Japan's sovereignty, marking the official conclusion of the Allied occupation in 1952 (Tanaka, n.d.). However, this restoration of formal independence was inextricably linked to the simultaneous signing of the Treaty of Mutual Cooperation and Security between the United States and Japan of 1951. This bilateral agreement, focused on the stationing of U.S. Forces Japan (USFJ) for the maintenance of international peace and security in the Far East, became the foundation for Japan's postwar security policy (Office of The Historian 1952).

The treaty provided Japan with a crucial security guarantee, particularly in the volatile context of the Cold War but also imposed significant constraints on Japan's military autonomy (Office of The Historian 1952). Article 9 (Renunciation of War) of the Constitution, heavily influenced by the occupation authorities and renouncing war as an instrument of national policy, coupled with the security treaty, constitutionally restricted Japan's ability to develop a fully independent and robust military capability. While the treaty was instrumental in providing security, it simultaneously constrained Japan's defense policy autonomy.

The 1960 revision of the Japan–U.S. Security Treaty marked a pivotal moment in its evolution, signifying a shift toward a more equitable partnership. Key changes included a clear US commitment to defend Japan (Article V), requiring prior US consultation with Japan before deploying forces from Japanese bases for operations outside of Japan, and a revised Status of Forces Agreement (SOFA) clarifying the legal status of US forces. These revisions strengthened Japan's security, increased reciprocity in the alliance, and solidified the treaty as the cornerstone of Japan's defense policy, shaping its security posture and its relationship with the US for decades to come.

While the treaty has been subject to various interpretations and debates over the decades, it is evident that the postwar security arrangement with the US has been instrumental in providing crucial stability for Japan, facilitating its remarkable economic resurgence. This stability, while requiring adjustments in Japan's defense posture, has allowed the nation to focus on economic development and cultivate its diplomatic influence. This long-term continuity underscores the enduring impact of the initial postwar settlement on Japan's sovereignty and its place in the international system (Green and Cronin 1999; Green 2010; Oros, n.d.).

5.3 The Japan–U.S. Status of Forces Agreement (SOFA)

The SOFA, a pivotal legal instrument accompanying the Security Treaty, further delineated the practical implications of the security arrangement and codified the limitations on Japan's territorial and legal sovereignty (Aketagawa 1999, 2017; Ministry of Foreign Affairs of Japan 2024a). The SOFA delineates the legal status and operational modalities of the US military within Japan, thereby granting the US military the right to maintain bases and facilities throughout the country. This right constitutes a significant encroachment on Japan's territorial integrity, extending beyond mere physical presence.

For instance, the US air base at Yokota, among others, influences Japan's management of the greater Tokyo airspace, raising questions about the nation's capacity to independently manage its air traffic and security (Yabe 2017). These restrictions, while not explicitly codified in Japanese law, appear to stem from de facto arrangements during the occupation, later formalized as a "temporary measure" in the 1952 agreement based on the SOFA (The Mainichi 2019; Yoshida 2016). The restoration of control over the Yokota airspace has been a subject of ongoing discussion in the Diet; however, substantive progress toward this objective has yet to be resolved.

Furthermore, the agreement addressed complex jurisdictional issues, particularly concerning criminal jurisdiction, frequently granting exemptions from Japanese law in specific circumstances to US military personnel and civilian employees associated with the military. This provision has been a persistent source of tension and legal debate, raising questions about the extent of Japan's legal sovereignty and its ability to exercise full control over its territory and the individuals within it. Notably, incidents involving US military personnel, even those deemed unlawful, have frequently remained unresolved under Japanese law, intensifying public concern about the limitations imposed by the SOFA (Office of The Historian 1957a, 1957b).

The agreement also delineated various administrative aspects of the US military presence, including entry and exit procedures, customs regulations, taxation, and claims for damages arising from US military activities. These provisions, while arguably necessary for the practical functioning of the alliance, further solidified the limitations on Japan's sovereign control and underscored the complex legal and administrative framework underpinning the constrained nature of its sovereignty (Fujiu 2024). A notable aspect of the SOFA is the grant of authority to the US to establish and maintain bases across Japan without explicit limitations, which grants a substantial degree of influence on the US and potentially compromises local autonomy and land use rights (Yabe 2017).

5.4 The Japan–U.S. Security Consultative Committee

The Japan–U.S. Security Consultative Committee, established in accordance with the SOFA, serves as the primary forum for bilateral discussions regarding the US military presence in Japan (Yoshida 2016). Comprised of representatives from both governments, this committee is entrusted with the responsibility of addressing operational issues, resolving disputes, and ensuring the seamless functioning of the security arrangement. The Committee's contribution to security policies has been the subject of considerable recognition. However, the committee's deliberations and transparency have been subject to scrutiny, with a key point of contention related to the Committee's composition (Yoshida 2016).

The Japanese delegation comprises high-ranking government officials from ministries under the purview of the Director-General of the North American Affairs Bureau at the Japanese Ministry of Foreign Affairs. In contrast, the US delegation consists of US military officers and the Minister at the US Embassy in Japan, led by the Deputy Commander of USFJ. Consequently, the Joint Committee's deliberations and resolutions are not conducted through official diplomatic channels between the Ministry of Foreign Affairs of Japan and the US Embassy in Japan (Department of State). This raises concerns regarding the level of diplomatic oversight and the potential for military considerations to supersede broader political and diplomatic concerns.

Critics contend that the committee's closed proceedings impede transparency. The minutes of the Joint Committee have not been made public since 1952, except for eighty-four pieces of joint statements accessible on the Ministry of Foreign Affairs website (The Diet 2022; Ministry of Foreign Affairs of Japan 2024a). This is due to the 1960 Committee's agreement that the official minutes of the Committee are considered official documents concerning both governments and are not published unless agreed by both parties. Therefore, the Japanese public is largely uninformed regarding the specifics of discussions and agreements that considerably impact their lives and national security.

During a Diet debate, Katsuya Okada, a member of the Diet and former foreign minister, commented:

> I consider the agreement reached between a director at the Ministry of Foreign Affairs and the deputy commander of the U.S. Forces Japan to be highly inappropriate. This is because it overrides the 2001 Information Disclosure Act and the 2009 Public Records Management Act, which were enacted by the Diet. (The Diet 2022)

These legal instruments establish a framework that enables citizens to access government-held information and ensures the proper management of public records. The absence of transparency, in conjunction with the perceived imbalance in influence between the two parties, gives rise to concerns regarding Japan's capacity to effectively assert its national interests.

It has been argued that significant policy matters pertaining to the US military presence in Japan are determined through non-transparent processes, thereby circumventing public scrutiny and democratic accountability. Consequently, while the Committee plays a vital role within the alliance framework, it also represents a potential channel for US influence over Japanese defense and security policy. This underscores the subtle, yet substantial, constraints imposed on Japan's sovereignty within the alliance framework. Yoshida (2016) suggests that the Japan–U.S. Security Consultative Committee operates outside the purview of the Japanese Constitution. If substantiated, this would constitute a serious infringement on Japanese sovereignty.

5.5 Complexities of Limited Sovereignty

While postwar security arrangements with the US facilitated Japan's economic prioritization and subsequent growth, they also constrained aspects of its sovereignty, thus impacting Japan's autonomy. The following four examples illustrate typical disputes arising from this dynamic:

1. The 1957 Girard incident: A US soldier killed a Japanese woman while on duty at a U.S. Army firing range, sparking a jurisdictional dispute under the SOFA. While the US initially asserted jurisdiction, subsequent negotiations within the Japan–U.S. Committee led to the US agreeing to allow Japan to prosecute. Girard was ultimately tried and convicted in a Japanese court, receiving a suspended sentence (Office of The Historian 1957a, 1957b).

2. The 1959 Sunagawa case: Seven individuals were prosecuted for violating laws related to the Japan–U.S. Security Treaty by entering a US military base during a protest. The Tokyo District Court acquitted them, citing the unconstitutionality of the US military presence under Article 9 of the Constitution of Japan. However, the Supreme Court reversed this decision, ultimately convicting the defendants (Courts of Japan, n.d.). In doing so, the Supreme Court invoked the "act of state doctrine," arguing that highly political matters, such as the Security Treaty, are not subject to judicial review, thereby avoiding a direct constitutional ruling. Declassified US documents, which were revealed in 2008 in the US, suggested prior informal discussions between the Chief Justice and the US Ambassador (The Asahi Shimbun 2024a).

3. The 1995 Okinawa Minor Rape Incident: This incident underscored the limitations of Japanese criminal jurisdiction under the SOFA, igniting public outrage and large-scale protests. The US initially resisted handing over the suspects to Japanese authorities prior to indictment, citing provisions within the SOFA that, at the time, allowed US military personnel suspected of crimes to remain in US custody. This stance further fueled criticism of the agreement. The case intensified calls for revising the SOFA to grant Japan greater judicial control, specifically regarding the custody and prosecution of US military personnel accused of committing crimes on Japanese soil (Guinto 2024).

4. The Futenma Base Relocation Issue: While the necessity of relocating the Futenma airbase is generally acknowledged due to safety and noise concerns, the ongoing debate surrounding the proposed relocation site in Henoko underscores a significant discord between local and national interests (The Asahi Shimbun 2024b). The substantial financial burden associated with the Henoko construction project, coupled with persistent environmental concerns—particu-

larly regarding the impact on the delicate marine ecosystem—and the complex interplay between national security imperatives and the desire for regional autonomy, highlights the multifaceted challenges inherent in attempting to reconcile national defense policies with the aspirations and concerns of local communities.

The publication of *Ryukyu Shimpo* (2004) found that USFJ facilities and areas numbered 135, occupying 0.27% of Japanese territory. The prefectures hosting the largest number of these facilities and areas, in descending order, were Okinawa (Area share in the prefecture: 10.43%), Hokkaido (0.41%), Kanagawa (0.89%), Nagasaki (0.11%), and Hiroshima (0.06%), demonstrating the disproportionate concentration in Okinawa Prefecture. This concentration has led to significant local resentment and political activism. For the most current information on major USFJ facilities and areas, consult the Ministry of Defense website (Ministry of Defense of Japan 2025).

The ongoing presence of US military bases and the provisions of the SOFA have been a persistent source of domestic political debate, raising complex questions about the balance between national security, local concerns, and the extent of Japan's effective sovereignty. These debates frequently center on issues of base relocation, environmental impact, the legal status of US military personnel, and the disproportionate burden borne by Okinawa. These issues underscore the ongoing tension between the perceived benefits and the tangible constraints of Japan's security dependence, and its implications for national sovereignty, despite the apparent lack of readily available resolutions.

5.6 Current Security Situation in the Far East

In the wake of post–Cold War shifts in the international landscape, particularly the rise of China, the Japan–U.S. alliance has evolved into a more deeply cooperative partnership, with an expanded role for Japan. The Japan–U.S. security framework has shifted from a relationship of dependency to one of collaboration, influencing Japan's standing within the global community. Through strategic adaptation and sustained diplomatic efforts, Japan has progressively transformed the alliance from a potential constraint on its autonomy into a platform for regional leadership and cooperation.

The Japan–U.S. 2+2 Ministerial Meetings, a key platform for bilateral dialogue between the foreign and defense ministers, facilitate addressing evolving security challenges and pursuing shared strategic objectives. These meetings have fostered enhanced security cooperation. Furthermore, the July 1, 2014, reinterpretation of Article 9 of the Constitution, previously limiting Japan to individual self-defense, now permits collective self-defense. This shift, coupled with increased military integration, raises concerns about Japan's potential involvement in broader regional conflicts. The framework of security cooperation has expanded to encompass the Indo-Pacific region, including bilateral initiatives with Australia, India, and Vietnam.

The continued presence of US forces in South Korea still remains crucial for regional stability. A significant reduction in the US military presence could necessitate a fundamental reassessment of security strategies by all East Asian nations, including Japan. This scenario presents a considerable military and diplomatic challenge, requiring a thorough examination of potential power vacuums, regional rivalries, and the future of the Japan–U.S. alliance. Such a substantial shift highlights the inherent vulnerability of Japan's security posture under its current framework of limited sovereignty.

The recent US administration's policies, including protectionist trade measures and a reduced commitment to international alliances, have introduced potential uncertainties into the Far Eastern security landscape. Possible shifts in US foreign policy, particularly concerning military commitments and alliance configurations, are a significant concern. Such shifts could have far-reaching consequences, potentially reshaping East Asian security dynamics and destabilizing a region that has experienced relative peace since the Korean War armistice in 1953 (Ikenberry and Watanabe 2024).

From the perspective of ordinary citizens, current national security policies are increasingly difficult to understand. This is especially true in areas such as defense capability development and the deepening integration of command-and-control systems between Japanese and US forces for potential regional conflicts (Johnstone and Schoff 2024). Two main factors contribute to this complexity: limited public access to security-related information and the highly technical nature of the subject matter. As a result, understanding is confined largely to experts, and opportunities for meaningful citizen participation in national security debates and policymaking remain limited, despite the critical importance of these issues.

6 Discussion

6.1 Comparison of Japan's Limited Sovereignty: 19th Century vs. Postwar Era

Japan's prewar and postwar experiences with limited sovereignty differ significantly in their origins, nature, and consequences. These divergent historical trajectories have given rise to a range of divergent scholarly interpretations. The prewar era, marked by the imposition of unequal treaties by imperialist Western powers, represents a direct assault on Japan's sovereignty. This was legally binding and resulted in the infringement of fundamental sovereign rights. This era, characterized by economic exploitation and legal subjugation, nevertheless catalyzed a powerful drive for modernization and national self-strengthening.

Akira Irie and Kenneth Pyle emphasize that Japan's deliberate and strategic modernization was instrumental in overcoming the challenges posed by the treaties and in establishing its position as a sovereign nation in the international community (Irie 1966; Pyle 1996). Japan's experience with limited sovereignty fueled a national drive for equality with Western powers. This spurred rapid industrialization, military expansion, and legal reforms, all designed to demonstrate Japan's capacity to be a modern, "civilized" nation by Western-defined international legal standards (Pyle 1996).

Japan's pursuit of recognition and autonomy ultimately contributed to its own imperial ambitions, a complex and ultimately tragic consequence of its earlier experience with limited sovereignty. This interpretation aligns with the concept of a "reactive state" (Calder 1988), which posits that external pressure and perceived threats to national identity can lead to a heightened sense of insecurity and a desire to assert national power. This orientation also stemmed from the pragmatic and ideological motivations of political leaders to facilitate national modernization and integrate internal debates.

In contrast, the postwar era's limited sovereignty stemmed from the security alliance with the US following the seven-year occupation, a markedly distinct context. While the unequal treaties were imposed by external powers against Japan's will, the postwar security arrangements were, in a sense, chosen by Japan, albeit within the constraints of its defeat and occupation. As Mears ([1948] 2015) explores, the initial period of occupation represented a profound disruption of Japanese sovereignty, with the Allied forces, particularly the US, exerting significant control over Japan's political, economic, and social institutions.

However, the evolving Cold War context led to a shift in US policy, transforming Japan from a defeated enemy into a crucial strategic partner. The Japan–U.S. Security Treaty, while constraining Japan's military autonomy, also furnished a pivotal security umbrella that enabled Japan to prioritize economic reconstruction and development. In the postwar period, Japan's sovereignty was constrained by the ideological imperatives of the Cold War and the context of "chosen" limitations.

Rather than being characterized by direct legal restrictions on core sovereign powers as seen in the unequal treaties, this period was marked by a strategic reliance on the US for security, which, in turn, influenced Japan's foreign policy and its capacity to act independently in international affairs. The limitations were thus less explicit, more embedded in the structure of the security relationship, and arguably more beneficial in the short term, albeit potentially limiting in the long run. This viewpoint is consistent with the prevailing narrative that Japan's security dependence was solely a strategic choice rather than a constraint.

This aligns with the observations of scholars Masataka Kosaka ([1968] 2006) and Hiroshi Nakanishi (2010), who emphasized the crucial role of the US security guarantee in enabling Japan's economic revitalization. This strategy, often termed the "Yoshida Doctrine" after Prime Minister Shigeru Yoshida (1878–1967), placed significant emphasis on Japan's reliance on the US for security and strategically leveraged postwar constraints to prioritize economic growth (Kosaka [1968] 2006; Nakanishi 2010).

The nature of the imposed limitations differed significantly. The unequal treaties focused on economic and legal restrictions, directly affecting Japan's ability to regulate its own trade, administer its justice system, and participate equally in the international legal order. In contrast, the postwar limitations were oriented toward security and defense, impeding Japan's capacity to develop a fully independent military and pursue an autonomous foreign policy. This discrepancy can be attributed to the shifting priorities of the international system.

In the nineteenth century, the primary concerns were trade, legal recognition, and territorial control. In the postwar era, national security, particularly in the context of the Cold War, became the dominant concern. The Japan–US alliance became a cornerstone of US security policy in the Far East, shaping Japan's strategic options and influencing its relationships with other regional actors. This paradigm shift was codified in the

1960 conclusion of the Japan–U.S. Security Treaty, which accentuated mutual cooperation and security between the two nations.

These two periods of limited sovereignty also had distinct impacts on Japanese society (see Table 1). The unequal treaties era fostered a keen sense of national grievance and a determination to overcome imposed limitations, fueling modernization and contributing to Japan's rise as a major power (Irie 1966). Moreover, the experience of these unequal treaties shaped Japan's understanding of international relations, fostering a belief in the importance of national strength and self-reliance (Irie 1966).

The postwar period witnessed significant controversy and opposition to the Japan–U.S. Security Treaty, particularly in the 1950s and 1960s, reflecting anxieties about Japanese sovereignty. However, subsequent decades have seen greater public acceptance of the alliance's constraints. This shift is partly due to the tangible benefits from the US security umbrella, including peace and economic prosperity. From a cost-benefit perspective, Japan has strategically leveraged the alliance, deriving substantial advantages that arguably outweigh the limitations on its sovereignty. While the SOFA presents operational challenges and requires continuous dialogue, it also serves as a crucial mechanism for managing the alliance's evolving dynamics and reflects Japan's growing assertiveness.

While a utilitarian perspective offers one lens for evaluating the alliance, it risks overlooking the potential erosion of essential elements of national identity. As generational memory of wartime experiences fades, public understanding of fundamental state principles and the significance of sovereignty may diminish. Revisiting these often overlooked normative aspects and reaffirming the importance of national sovereignty for informed civic participation in the contemporary context seems imperative.

Japan's security dependence on the United States has significantly constrained its autonomy in foreign, monetary, and trade policy, while also shaping its national identity. As the postwar global order shifts from US hegemony toward a multipolar system, the ability to formulate independent policies becomes increasingly important. Such autonomy is vital for securing essential resources—including energy, food, and minerals— ensuring national stability and advancing self-determination. To navigate this transition and enhance its sovereignty, Japan must develop national strategies and cultivate human resources grounded in its own values and priorities.

Table 1: Comparison of Japan's Limited Sovereignty: Nineteenth Century vs. Postwar Era

Feature	Unequal Treaties Era (1854–1911, Treaty Revision Complete)	US Occupation/Security Treaty (1945–Ongoing)
Primary Constraint	External legal restrictions	Security dependence on the US
Source of Limitation	Western imperial powers	US occupation, Cold War
Legal Basis	Unequal Treaties	Security Treaty, SOFA
Scope of Sovereignty Affected	Legal, territorial, and economic restrictions	Military and foreign policy constraints
Key Mechanisms	Extraterritoriality, tariff restrictions	Key Mechanisms US bases, SOFA, and Security Consultative Committee arrangements
Geopolitical Context	Imperialism	Cold War and post–Cold War
Japan's Response	Modernization, military buildup, industrialization	Economic focus, alliance with US, reinterpretation of Article 9 and expansion of self-defense forces
Consequences	Modernization, great power status, shaped national identity, and foreign policy outlook	Economic prosperity, constrained military, ongoing debate on security dependence and national identity
Scholarly Views	Reactive nationalism, modernization catalyst	Strategic dependence, "chosen" limitation, debate on democratic implications of US dependence
Contemporary Issues	Legacy of unequal treaties and national identity	US policy shifts, regional security, debate on Article 9

Source: Author's compilation.

6.2 Prospect for the Future: Democratic Consensus

Japan has consistently deepened security cooperation with the US, pursuing mutual economic and strategic benefits while contributing to regional stability in the post–Cold War era (Sakurada 1997). This policy has been consistently reaffirmed by successive leaders in both countries. However, this security reliance constrains Japan's diplomatic autonomy. Specifically, it aligns Japan's foreign policy with that of the US, limits its independent military capacity, and raises questions about its territorial and legal sovereignty due to the US military presence. This dependence impacts Japan's relationships with other nations and its ability to pursue fully independent diplomatic initiatives.

Jennifer Lind (2022) has questioned the long-term implications of this reliance for Japanese democracy and public engagement with national sovereignty and foreign policy. The ongoing debate surrounding Article 9 of the Japanese constitution underscores the persistent tension between Japan's pacifist identity and aspirations for a more conventional military posture. Fundamentally, Japan, as an independent nation, must autonomously consider its present and future based on established principles of state sovereignty.

Scholars such as Jeffrey Hornung (2019) and Terashima and Kurashige (2024) argue that Japan's current security framework, rooted in the postwar era, requires re-evaluation in light of today's geopolitical realities. The future of the Japan–US alliance demands a transparent, forward-looking approach that emphasizes accountability and is strategically integrated into broader initiatives, such as the "Free and Open Indo-Pacific" (Ministry of Foreign Affairs of Japan 2024b). Japan's participation in the QUAD (Australia, India, Japan, and the United States) reflects both its alignment with US strategic priorities and its pursuit of sovereign hedging. Beyond the QUAD, Japan seeks to assert its sovereignty in navigating an increasingly volatile world order. However, its strategic autonomy remains constrained by shifting US policies and escalating regional threats.

In practice, national security matters in Japan are often shielded from public scrutiny, a situation exacerbated by the 2013 Act on the Protection of Specially Designated Secrets. This act grants broad government discretion in classifying information and imposes severe penalties for leaks, fostering public skepticism and impeding informed public discourse on national security issues. This, in turn, hinders the democratic processes that the alliance is ostensibly intended to protect. This mechanism creates a dilemma for Japanese citizens: while national defense is a crucial issue, its complexities and lack of transparency place it beyond effective public oversight.

Japan's long-standing security dependence on the United States has deeply shaped its security identity. This reliance seems to have slowed the development of a clear understanding of sovereignty and independence, especially within the education system. It has also limited public debate on these fundamental concepts. As a result, a diminished sense of sovereignty may exist in Japanese society. Many citizens appear unaware of how their country's autonomy is restricted or what that means in practice. These constraints are often accepted without reflection on their origins or consequences. As Takashi Inoguchi (1998) argues, building a strong sense of sovereignty is a vital civic duty.

Looking ahead, a key long-term challenge is how to manage potential revisions to the Japan–U.S. Security Treaty and related agreements within the existing bilateral framework. While persistent obstacles remain, there is growing recognition of the need for greater transparency and public participation in security policymaking. These elements are essential not only to maintaining the strength of the alliance but also to upholding democratic values. This need is further underscored by the recurring shifts in US foreign policy following presidential elections, which introduce uncertainty and demand that Japan remain adaptable while ensuring that its own democratic processes guide long-term strategic decisions.

A broader historical perspective—from 1854 to the present—provides critical insight into how such complexities have been addressed and how more equitable solutions might emerge. Public deliberation in both countries on the alliance's future is essential to achieving mutual benefit and lasting peace. Broad-based agreement on a fair and balanced framework enables citizens to hold governments accountable and foster democratic consensus. This consensus is vital not only to secure future prosperity but also to uphold the alliance's normative foundations. These aspirations—rooted in transparency and mutual understanding—must be cultivated across generations to ensure that security does not come at the expense of democracy.

7 Conclusion

Japan's experience of limited sovereignty has taken distinct forms in two pivotal historical periods: the externally imposed legal constraints of the unequal treaties in the nineteenth century and the internally accepted limitations of the postwar Japan–US security alliance. Both episodes profoundly shaped Japan's political autonomy and international positioning, albeit in divergent ways.

The era of unequal treaties, marked by extraterritoriality and loss of tariff autonomy, served as a catalyst for Japan's modernization. These externally imposed constraints, while initially degrading, served as a powerful drive toward national self-assertion. As scholars such as Pyle have argued, the imperative to reclaim full sovereignty galvanized industrial, legal, and military reforms, enabling Japan to emerge as a modern power capable of renegotiating its place in the international order.

By contrast, the postwar period involved a self-chosen limitation through the US alliance framework, particularly the Security Treaty and SOFA. While these arrangements ensured national security and facilitated economic recovery, they simultaneously circumscribed Japan's defense and foreign policy autonomy. This strategic dependence, though voluntary, has given rise to enduring tensions—particularly in constitutional debates over Article 9 and the future of the alliance—highlighting the complex interplay between sovereignty, security, and democratic accountability.

Taken together, these cases reveal that sovereignty is not a static or absolute concept but a historically contingent and politically negotiated condition. Japan's trajectory illustrates how externally imposed constraints can trigger efforts toward autonomy while internally accepted limitations may produce both stability and long-term dependency. The legacies of these two eras continue to shape contemporary debates on Japan's role in global affairs, including its responses to shifting geopolitical dynamics in the Asia-Pacific.

Ultimately, this study underscores that sovereignty in Japan has been both constrained and redefined through legal structures, strategic choices, and historical circumstance. By comparing these two periods, it becomes evident that Japan's political development has been forged not in the absence of sovereignty but in the ongoing struggle to reclaim, redefine, and strategically manage it in an interdependent world.

Bibliography

Aketagawa, Takeshi. 1999. *The Political History of the Japan–US Administrative Agreement: An Introduction to the Study of the Japan–US Status of Forces Agreement* [in Japanese]. Hosei University Press.

Aketagawa, Takeshi. 2017. *The Japan–U.S. Status of Forces Agreement: Its History and Present* [in Japanese]. Misuzu Shobo.

Britannica. n.d. "Sovereignty." Accessed January 8, 2026. https://www.britannica.com/topic/sovereignty.

Calder, Kent E. 1988. "Japanese Foreign Economic Policy Formation: Explaining the Reactive State." *World Politics* 40 (4): 517–41. https://doi.org/10.2307/2010317.

Courts of Japan. n.d. *Sunagawa Case, Judgment of the Supreme Court of Japan* (16 December 1959, Supreme Court, Grand Chamber). [in Japanese]. January 8, 2026. chrome-extension://efaidnbmnnnibpcajpcglclefindmkaj/https://www.courts.go.jp/assets/hanrei/hanrei-pdf-93840.pdf.

Fujiu, Satoshi. 2024. "Main Issues and Current Situation Regarding the Implementation of the Japan–U.S. Status of Forces Agreement (1/2): Summary of Issues Based on Diet Debate, etc." *The National Diet Library, Legislation and Research* 469/470: 225–50, 217–31. [in Japanese]. https://www.sangiin.go.jp/japanese/annai/chousa/rippou_chousa/backnumber/20240920.html; https://www.sangiin.go.jp/japanese/annai/chousa/rippou_chousa/backnumber/20241101.html.

Green, Michael J. 2010. "Redefining and Reaffirming the U.S.-Japan Alliance." *Asia Policy* 10 (1): 16–20.

Green, Michael J., and Patrick M. Cronin. 1999. *The US-Japan Alliance: Past, Present, and Future*. Council on Foreign Relations Press.

Guinto, Joel. 2024. "US Soldier Charged in Japan for Rape of Minor." *BBC News*, June 26. https://www.bbc.com/news/articles/cpwwdyye4vgo.

Hornung, Jeffrey W. 2019. *Managing the U.S.-Japan Alliance: An Examination of Structural Linkages in the Security Relationship*. 2nd ed. Sasakawa USA. https://spfusa.org/publications/managing-the-u-s-japan-alliance/.

Ikenberry, G. John, and Yuichi Watanabe. 2024. "A New Trump Presidency: The Implications for U.S.-Japan Relations." Online Seminar, Daiwa Anglo-Japanese Foundation, November 19. https://dajf.org.uk/event/a-new-trump-presidency-the-implications-for-us-japan-relations.

Inoguchi, Takashi. 1998. "Looking Back to Look Forward: The Westphalian, Philadelphian, and Anti-Utopian Paradigms." Presented at the International Studies Association, Columbia University, March. https://ciaotest.cc.columbia.edu/conf/int01/.

Irie, Akira. 1966. *Japanese Diplomacy: From the Meiji Restoration to the Present*. [in Japanese]. Chuokoron-Shinsha.

Japan Center for Asian Historical Records. 2018. "The Iwakura Mission: Tracking 150 People Who Crossed the Oceans." https://www.jacar.go.jp/english/iwakura_en/index.html.

Johnstone, Christopher B., and James Schoff. 2024. "A Vital Next Step for the U.S.-Japan Alliance: Command and Control Modernization." *Center for Strategic & International Studies (CSIS)*, February 1. https://www.csis.org/analysis/vital-next-step-us-japan-alliance-command-and-control-modernization.

Kosaka, Masataka. (1968) 2006. *Prime Minister Shigeru Yoshida* [in Japanese]. Chuokoron-Shinsha.

Krasner, Stephen D. 1999. *Sovereignty: Organized Hypocrisy*. Princeton University Press.

Krasner, Stephen D. 2001. "Sovereignty." *Foreign Policy* 122: 20–29. https://doi.org/10.2307/3183223.

Krasner, Stephen D. 2004. "Sharing Sovereignty: New Institutions for Collapsed and Failing States." *International Security* 29 (2): 85–120. http://www.jstor.org/stable/4137587.

Lind, Jennifer. 2022. "Japan Steps Up: How Asia's Rising Threats Convinced Tokyo to Abandon Its Defense Taboos." *Foreign Affairs*, December 23. https://www.foreignaffairs.com/japan/japan-steps.

Loughlin, Martin. 2017. "The Erosion of Sovereignty." *Netherlands Journal of Legal Philosophy* 2: 57–81. https://doi.org/10.5553/NJLP/.000048.

Mälksoo, Lauri. 2017. "Sources of International Law in the 19th Century." In *The Oxford Handbook on the Sources of International Law*, edited by Jean d'Aspremont and Samantha Besson. Oxford University Press.

Mears, Helen. (1948) 2015. *Mirror for Americans: Japan*. Translated by Nobuji Ito. [in Japanese]. Kadokawa. Originally published in 1948 by Houghton Mifflin, Boston.

Ministry of Defense of Japan. 2025. "List of Designated USFJ Facilities and Areas." https://www.mod.go.jp/en/presiding/law/usfj.html.

Ministry of Foreign Affairs of Japan. 2024a. "Japan–United States Status of Forces Agreement and Related Information." September 12. [in Japanese]. https://www.mofa.go.jp/mofaj/area/usa/sfa/kyoutei/index.html.

Ministry of Foreign Affairs of Japan. 2024b. "Diplomatic Bluebook 2024." https://www.mofa.go.jp/policy/other/bluebook/2024/pdf/en_index.html.

Ministry of Foreign Affairs of Japan. 2025. "Japan–United States Security Arrangements." January 25. https://www.mofa.go.jp/region/n-america/us/security/index.html.

Nagao, Ryuichi. 1979. "AMANE NISHI on Man and Society." The Annals of Legal Philosophy 1978: 117-141. [in Japanese]. https://doi.

org/10.11205/jalp1953.1978.117. https://www.jstage.jst.go.jp/article/jalp1953/1978/0/1978_0_117/_article/-char/en.

Nagao, R. n.d. Blog. [in Japanese]. http://ouranos2.web.fc2.com/1C_2FOLDER.html.

Nakanishi, Hiroshi. 2010. "Diplomatic Strategy of a Defeated Nation: Shigeru Yoshida's Diplomacy and His Successors." In *History of Strategic Thought in Japan and the United States*, edited by Takashi Ishizu [in Japanese]. Sairyusha.

Nishi, Toshio. 2005. *MacArthur Surrenders Nation* [in Japanese]. Chuokoron-Shinsha, Inc.

Odaka, Asao. 1984. *Introduction to Jurisprudence*. 3rd ed. [in Japanese]. Yuhikaku.

Office of the Historian (U.S.). 1853. "Milestones: 1830–1860: The United States and the Opening to Japan, 1853." https://history.state.gov/milestones/1830-1860/opening-to-japan.

Office of the Historian (U.S.). 1952. "No. 480 Memorandum by the Secretary of State and the Secretary of Defense (Lovett) to the President: Arrangements for United States Forces in Japan in the Post-Peace Treaty Period." January 18. https://history.state.gov/historicaldocuments/frus1952-54v14p2/d480.

Office of the Historian (U.S.). 1957a. "137. Memorandum from the Assistant Secretary of State for Far Eastern Affairs (Robertson) to the Secretary of State." May 20. https://history.state.gov/historicaldocuments/frus1955-57v23p1/d137.

Office of the Historian (U.S.). 1957b. "158. Draft Memorandum for the President Prepared in the Department of State: The Girard Case." May 25. https://history.state.gov/historicaldocuments/frus1955-57v23p1/d158.

Oros, Andrew. n.d. "The Revision of the US-Japan Security Treaty in 1960: Lessons for the Current Standards Alliance." National Institute for Defense Studies (NIDS) Data. January 8, 2026. chrome-extension://efaid-nbmnnnibpcajpcglclefindmkaj/https://www.nids.mod.go.jp/event/report/pdf/Anpo50th_s_07.pdf.

Pyle, Kenneth B. 1996. *The Making of Modern Japan*. 2nd ed. Wadsworth Publishing.

Ryukyu Shimpo. 2004. *The Concept of the Japan–US Status of Forces Agreement: Confidential Documents of the Ministry of Foreign Affairs: Revised Edition* [in Japanese]. Koubunken.

Sakurada, Daizo. 1997. *WP No. 07/97: For Mutual Benefit: The Japan–US Security Treaty: From a Japanese Perspective*. Centre for Strategic

Studies, Victoria University of Wellington. https://www.wgtn.ac.nz/strategic-studies/publications-and-research/publications-archive/working-papers.

Sakurai, Yukio. 2023. "International Cooperation of Asian Law Systems Beyond Diversity." *Political Reflection Magazine* 9 (3): 27–31. https://politicalreflectionmagazine.com/vol-9-no-3/.

Shahabuddin, Mohammad. 2019. "The 'Standard of Civilization' in International Law: Intellectual Perspectives from Pre-War Japan." *Leiden Journal of International Law* 32 (1): 13–32. https://doi.org/10.1017/S0922156518000559.

Tagami, Jun. 1962. "The Concept of Sovereignty." *Hitotsubashi University Research Annual Report, Law Studies* 4: 1–22. [in Japanese].

Tanaka, Akihiko. n.d. "The World and Japan Database: Security Treaty Between Japan and the United States of America." January 8, 2026. https://worldjpn.net/documents/texts/docs/19510908.T2E.html.

Terashima, Jiro, and Akira Kurashige. 2024. "Terashima Jiro's 'Japan Revitalization Initiative'—A Paradigm Shift in the Japan–US Alliance." *The Economist Online*, June 6. [in Japanese]. https://weekly-economist.mainichi.jp/articles/20240606/se1/00m/020/002000c.

The Asahi Shimbun. 2024a. "Editorial: Top Court Chief's Behavior during Sunagawa Case Crossed the Line." January 23. https://www.asahi.com/ajw/articles/15125438.

The Asahi Shimbun. 2024b. "Editorial: Forceful Way Futenma Base Is Being Relocated a National Disgrace." December 28. https://www.asahi.com/ajw/articles/15569358.

The Diet, House of Representatives, Committee of Foreign Affairs. 2022. "Diet Proceedings (Katsuya Okada vs. Yoshimasa Hayashi)." March 16. [in Japanese]. https://kokkai.ndl.go.jp/#/.

The Mainichi. 2019. "Editorial: Change Pact with US Forces to Give Japan Full Control of Tokyo Air Traffic." February 18. https://mainichi.jp/english/articles/20190218/p2a/00m/0na/011000c.

Yabe, Isao. 2017. *You Must Not Know: The Hidden Structure of Japanese Domination* [in Japanese]. Kodansha.

Yoshida, Takeshi. 2016. *Research on the Japan–U.S. Security Consultative Committee: Uncovering the Mysterious Power Structure (Postwar Rediscovery Series, no. 5)* [in Japanese]. Sogensha.

CHAPTER 6

The Impact of Third Parties on Japanese Politics and Sovereignty: Limited Sovereignty Theory and Political Party Mediation

Abstract

This chapter extends Stephen Krasner's Limited Sovereignty Theory to analyze Japan's contemporary experience of cooperative and infiltrative constraint in its relations with China. It examines how domestic political mediation and transnational policy networks channel external preferences into Japan's policymaking processes. Focusing on the Komeito Party's moderating influence within the Liberal Democratic Party (LDP)–Komeito coalition and the broader web of friendship associations and business linkages, the study demonstrates how indirect, institutionalized mechanisms promote diplomatic restraint and normative convergence. Drawing on Stewart and Yamaguchi et al., the analysis identifies a hybrid structure of influence in which pacifist ideology, coalition dependency, and economic interdependence collectively sustain Japan's cautious engagement posture toward China. The findings illustrate productive power—the shaping of actors' preferences through social and institutional relations rather than coercion—and highlight how democratic sovereignty can erode through coordination and normalization rather than overt domination. Japan's case underscores the need for renewed transparency and civic accountability to reconcile external cooperation with autonomous self-governance.

Keywords: Komeito Party, China–Japan Relations, Coalition Politics, Limited Sovereignty, Productive Power

1 Introduction

Japan's history of formal independence coupled with external structural constraint since the Meiji Restoration of 1868 positions it as an unparalleled case study in the dynamics of limited sovereignty within a major industrial democracy. The current era of great power competition has rendered the mechanics of policy autonomy particularly obscure, necessitating an investigation into the confluence of long-term alliances and emerging rival influences. The simultaneous existence of highly complicated international relations and often polarized national perspectives on domestic politics—where ideological divides concerning defense and foreign policy often obscure empirical evidence of policy compromise—creates an intellectual vacuum that demands clarification. This study is fundamentally motivated by the necessity to cut through this geopolitical complexity and domestic polarization, seeking to understand what really is happening now regarding the nation's policy autonomy from a rigorous political science perspective. This historical context conditions Japan as a critical case study for understanding the nature of limited sovereignty in a globally interconnected world.

Historically, the exercise of influence by one state over another's policymaking processes has long been recognized as an instrument of foreign policy—manifested through traditional mechanisms like cultural diplomacy and "soft power" (Nye 1990). These conventional mechanisms successfully shaped the cognitive and institutional environment within which national choices were made, often through attraction and shared values. However, in the twenty-first century, this external pressure has evolved into more complex, persistent, and insidious forms. Rather than episodic, blunt coercion or simple attraction, contemporary influence operations act as continuous pressures on agenda-setting, opinion formation, and elite incentives. Among these, the phenomenon of "sharp power" (Walker and Ludwig 2017) marks a crucial conceptual shift, departing from soft power's reliance on attraction by instead utilizing manipulation, institutional penetration, and information distortion. Sharp power systematically leverages the transparency and pluralism inherent to democratic systems, exploiting their openness to external narratives, strategic lobbying, and ideological persuasion to achieve nontransparent policy convergence.

This research applies Limited Sovereignty Theory (Krasner 2004) to Japan's complex and rapidly evolving geopolitical position, specifically refining the framework to account for non-explicit and networked constraints that operate beneath the surface of formal diplomacy. Japan's experience reveals a distinctive, interlocking dual structure of constraint. The first layer is the explicit, institutionalized security dependence on the United States, a structurally defined legacy of the postwar era established by formal treaties and known obligations. The second, more elusive layer is the emerging constraint from the People's Republic of China (PRC), which operates through an indirect, relational, and infiltrative model. To capture this subtle dynamic—which relies on leveraging shared economic interests and co-opting domestic political actors—this research introduces the conceptual refinement of Cooperative/Infiltrative Sovereignty Limitation. This is defined as a situation where external preferences are embedded within domestic policy coordination channels through institutionalized consent, mutual interest, or shared elite incentives rather than overt domination or traditional coercion. The operational efficacy of this influence mechanism hinges on the subtle transmission of external preferences through ostensibly benign engagement, making both democratic detection and political redress profoundly difficult.

The core empirical focus lies in analyzing the precise mechanism by which the PRC's indirect influence is transmitted: political party mediation within the Japanese ruling coalition. The chapter examines the distinctive role of the Komeito Party and its associated networks, which are actors positioned strategically to serve as institutional buffers that reliably moderate policy alignment and constrain more hawkish foreign policy positions, particularly concerning sensitive issues like Taiwan, Hong Kong, and human rights resolutions. These parties function as a critical transmission belt, ensuring that the necessary consensus for proactive policy actions—which might antagonize the PRC—is subtly sabotaged or diluted at the domestic coalition level, thereby serving external interests while maintaining the appearance of internal political balance. Accordingly, this chapter addresses three fundamental research questions: How does the PRC's emerging cooperative/infiltrative influence on Japanese politics differ in mechanism and effect from traditional US-mediated constraints within the framework of Limited Sovereignty Theory? How can this phenomenon be precisely conceptualized as a Cooperative/ Infiltrative Sovereignty Limitation that operates through coalition politics and elite networks? And what specific implications do these constraints have for Japan's democratic control, policy accountability, and national autonomy? The purpose of this study is, therefore, to extend Krasner's framework to network-based mechanisms, analyze China's indirect mediation through the Komeito Party, and evaluate the implications for democratic resilience, ultimately arguing that transparency-based reforms are essential to safeguard policy autonomy.

2 Methodology

This research adopts a rigorous Comparative Institutional Analysis framework, integrating insights from history, law, and political science, which is essential for analyzing a phenomenon that spans formal legal agreements, internal coalition political processes, and subtle sociocultural norms. The study draws on a diverse set of primary and secondary sources, including official Diet proceedings and legislative records, Sino-Japanese diplomatic records, party documents, public reports concerning the Komeito Party and its affiliated Soka Gakkai organization, and official PRC sources, particularly materials related to United Front Work (Brady 2017). Given the inherent opacity of influence operations, the study employs methodological triangulation, synthesizing documentary evidence, observable policy trends (such as consistent policy moderation in sensitive areas), and inferential reasoning to identify plausible mechanisms and demonstrate consistency across different strands of evidence, acknowledging that direct causal proof of covert manipulation is often unattainable in democratic contexts.

Theoretically, the model expands on Limited Sovereignty Theory (Krasner 1999) by incorporating the notion of networked sovereignty erosion, which describes how informal actors and transnational networks modify policymaking autonomy without formal legal intrusion. The analysis is further informed by Complex Interdependence (Keohane and Nye 1977) to understand nonmilitary relational power dynamics, and Power in Global Governance (Barnett and Duvall 2005) to contrast relational power with the structural power mechanisms that amplify influence through Japan's governance system. This combination allows the study to move beyond traditional focus on state-to-state coercion and analyze the subtle, indirect, and institutionalized nature of Cooperative/Infiltrative Sovereignty Limitation. Finally, the study explicitly recognizes key methodological limitations, including the scarcity of verifiable financial data, the restricted transparency of coalition negotiation processes in Japan, and the resulting potential for interpretive bias when analyzing subtle influence, ensuring analytical transparency regarding its methodological boundaries.

3 The Theoretical Structure of Limited Sovereignty and Its Application to Japan

3.1 Redefining Sovereignty Under Global Interdependence

In both international law and political theory, sovereignty denotes a state's authority to govern within its territory and to exclude external interference. However, under globalization and complex interdependence (Keohane and Nye 1977), this classical Westphalian notion has eroded. Economic interconnection, multilateral institutions, and transnational corporate influence now constrain states' policymaking capacity. Krasner (1999) systematized this reality through his Limited Sovereignty Theory, which recognizes that states may retain legal independence while losing substantive autonomy. Sovereignty is thus not absolute but conditioned—its "organized hypocrisy" reflecting the gap between formal norms and practical realities.

Building on this foundation, the present study introduces Cooperative/ Infiltrative Sovereignty Limitation: a situation in which external influence operates through ostensibly cooperative domestic channels, embedding external preferences within internal policy coordination. Such influence differs from coercive dependence because it is maintained through consent, mutual interest, or institutionalized coordination rather than overt domination. This theoretical refinement enables analysis of subtle, continuous influence patterns—especially in democratic contexts where explicit coercion is infeasible yet policy alignment emerges through soft coordination and shared elite incentives.

3.2 Japan as a Case of Passive Sovereignty

Japan exemplifies what may be termed a Passive Sovereignty Model, characterized by long-term acceptance of external coordination as a normal condition of statecraft. During the Meiji period, the Unequal Treaties restricted legal sovereignty; in the postwar period, the Japan–U.S. Security Treaty institutionalized dependency in security and diplomacy. Katzenstein (1996) notes that Japan's national security culture evolved under US tutelage, prioritizing stability and alliance maintenance over full autonomy. This structural pattern—deference to external frameworks in exchange for stability—has conditioned Japanese elites to perceive coordination as prudence rather than constraint. The post-1972 normalization of Japan–China relations added a second dimension to this structure.

Komeito, whose diplomatic outreach played a crucial role in normalization, has since been described by both Chinese and Japanese observers as maintaining a "dialogue-oriented" stance (Ehrhardt et al. 2014; Wang 2012). While such engagement contributes to regional stability, it also creates a durable interface through which external preferences may be transmitted into coalition decision-making. Accordingly, Japan's sovereignty is constrained on two complementary levels: an explicit institutional limitation via the US alliance framework, and a cooperative/infiltrative limitation arising from informal political and ideological linkages with China.

3.3 Multilateral Pressures and the Blocs of Limited Sovereignty

In the current geopolitical environment, Japan's sovereignty cannot be analyzed solely through bilateral relations but must be situated within a broader multilateral structure of bloc competition between liberal and authoritarian states. The liberal bloc (United States, Europe, Australia, Japan) promotes transparency and rule-based governance; the authoritarian bloc (China, Russia, North Korea) employs hybrid strategies combining coercion and influence operations. This context generates a geopolitical dilemma of alignment: Every policy decision risks alienating one bloc while accommodating another. Japan's ruling coalition thus faces constant pressure to maintain balance—reinforcing the utility of mediating actors such as Komeito that facilitate cautious, dialogue-oriented positions. From China's perspective, exploiting Japan's coalition structure offers a low-cost method to moderate Tokyo's alignment with the liberal bloc. Rather than overt interference, the PRC's strategy relies on cultivating long-term relationships with political, economic, and intellectual intermediaries to shape narratives and preferences from within.

3.4 Summary of Section 1

This section has reconceptualized sovereignty as a layered, networked construct rather than a unitary attribute of statehood. Japan's experience illustrates how historical dependence and coalition politics create conditions for cooperative/infiltrative sovereignty limitation. The next section analyzes these mechanisms empirically—focusing on China's strategies, the mediating role of Komeito, and the broader networks that transmit influence through Japan's ruling coalition and public discourse.

4 The Mechanism of Third-Party Influence Within Japan's Ruling Coalition

4.1 China's Strategy: From Coercion to Cooperative Soft Control

Traditional sovereignty constraints often relied on coercive force or formal institutional dependence. In contrast, China's influence on Japanese politics functions through a multidimensional approach combining strategic pressure and cooperative engagement. This aligns with what scholars describe as "sharp power"—a form of influence that manipulates information and institutions under the appearance of normal exchange (Walker and Ludwig 2017). China's strategy rests on strategic patience and institutional embedding. Instead of seeking immediate policy reversals, the PRC promotes long-term alignment by cultivating relationships with intermediaries capable of shaping discourse and incentives within Japan's policymaking system. Such methods are well-documented in studies of United Front Work (Brady 2017; Lam and Lam 2013), which describes the systematic coordination between state, party, and civil networks to promote favorable narratives abroad. In the Japanese context, this influence rarely takes the form of explicit direction. Rather, it tends to operate as agenda-setting power—guiding what topics are considered legitimate for discussion and which policy approaches are deemed "constructive." Over time, this process narrows Japan's policy space, particularly on sensitive issues such as Taiwan, human rights, and defense posture.

4.2 Political Mediation: The Komeito Party and Coalition Dynamics

Among Japan's political actors, the Komeito Party occupies a distinctive position. Rooted in the Soka Gakkai religious movement and maintaining longstanding ties with Chinese counterparts since the normalization of diplomatic relations in 1972, Komeito has consistently emphasized dialogue-based diplomacy and regional cooperation (Ehrhardt et al. 2014).

The LDP formed a coalition with Komeito in 1999 primarily to regain and sustain a legislative majority, particularly after losing its dominance in the House of Councilors. Despite ideological differences, electoral incentives and complementary geographic bases fostered a durable partnership between the two parties (Liff and Maeda 2019). Over the subsequent decades, this coalition has persisted through effective electoral coordination, pragmatic policy compromises, and mutual benefits in maintaining political stability and governance (Yakushiji 2014).

Within the LDP–Komeito coalition, Komeito functions as a moderating intermediary. Its policy positions often stress de-escalation, humanitarian perspectives, and multilateral dialogue. While these tendencies sometimes align with Beijing's preference for minimizing criticism on human rights or security issues, this alignment should not be read as evidence of external manipulation. Rather, it reflects an intersection between Komeito's pacifist ideology and China's strategic interest in constraining anti-China rhetoric. Empirical evidence—including coalition negotiations and Diet debates—suggests that on sensitive issues such as Taiwan engagement or Uyghur human rights resolutions, final policy statements tend to adopt moderated language consistent with Komeito's diplomatic caution (Naito 2025). Such outcomes illustrate how coalition dynamics can operate as mechanisms of policy moderation, translating internal ideological commitments into external diplomatic restraint.

Komeito's mediating function extends to Japan's China policy more broadly. Stewart (2020) characterizes the party's approach as a "new middle way," balancing Japan's security concerns with sustained economic and diplomatic engagement with Beijing. Rooted in pacifism and informed by Soka Gakkai's transnational networks, Komeito's discourse promotes stability and restraint in foreign affairs. Yamaguchi et al. (2022) further situate Komeito within China's "cognitive domain" influence environment, noting that Beijing engages with political actors favoring stable bilateral relations. Although no evidence indicates that Komeito operates under Chinese direction, its conciliatory stance often corresponds with China's preference for reducing friction. Reports of Chinese concern over Komeito's possible withdrawal from the ruling coalition underscore its perceived importance as a stabilizing channel in Sino-Japanese relations (Stewart 2020; Yamaguchi et al. 2022).

Analytically, Komeito's role is best understood not as an agent of external control but as an institutional buffer that facilitates indirect influence. This aligns with Barnett and Duvall's (2005) conception of productive power, whereby social relations shape actors' preferences and possibilities for action without overt coercion. Through coalition-mediated moderation, Komeito exemplifies how domestic political structures can generate outcomes that—while internally driven—nonetheless resonate with external strategic interests.

4.3 Policy Networks and Friendship Associations

The moderating role of Komeito within the ruling coalition is mirrored and reinforced by a broader web of cross-party and business networks that sustain Japan–China engagement. Beyond formal party politics, China's cooperative influence extends through long-established institutional linkages such as the Japan–China Friendship Parliamentarians' League and the Japan–China Economic Association. The Friendship League, composed of legislators from multiple parties—including key LDP and Komeito members—conducts regular exchanges with Chinese counterparts and state-affiliated organizations. While these activities constitute legitimate forms of parliamentary diplomacy, they also foster what You (2023) terms "normative convergence," as repeated interpersonal contact cultivates shared cognitive frameworks and rhetorical moderation in discussing bilateral issues. Such transnational interactions may not alter formal policy positions directly, but they subtly shape the cognitive and discursive environment in which Japan's China policy is formulated.

Economic networks contribute an equally influential layer to this environment. The Japan–China Economic Association, representing major corporations with extensive investments and supply chains in China, consistently advocates policy restraint and predictability to safeguard business stability. This economic interdependence creates structural incentives for policymakers to avoid actions that could provoke diplomatic or commercial friction. In this sense, Komeito's coalition-mediated moderation and the economic sector's preference for stability operate synergistically, embedding conciliatory tendencies within Japan's policymaking ecosystem.

Collectively, these political and economic linkages constitute what may be described as a hybrid influence network—a blend of diplomacy, lobbying, and social capital through which external preferences become normalized within domestic deliberation. The process exemplifies what Barnett and Duvall (2005) describe as productive power: the shaping of possibilities for action through social and institutional relations rather than coercive control. Following Krasner's insight, such dynamics illustrate how sovereigny erosion or constraint often proceeds through institutional adaptation and discursive normalization rather than overt subjugation. Within this framework, China's influence in Japan emerges not as direct manipulation but as a form of embedded interdependence, operating through political mediation, coalition dynamics, and transnational policy networks that collectively sustain an environment of cautious engagement.

4.4 Influence on Public Opinion and Epistemic Communities

Influence operations are not confined to elite politics. They also target the cognitive dimension of sovereignty—the public understanding of national autonomy and foreign relations. Japanese media and academic communities display a diversity of positions regarding China policy. Some liberal-leaning outlets, such as Asahi Shimbun and Mainichi Shimbun, historically emphasize the importance of maintaining dialogue and avoiding escalation. While such editorial orientations cannot be equated with foreign influence, they contribute to a discursive environment in which critical discussions of China are often framed as "hawkish" or "right-wing." Guo (2023) demonstrates that Chinese state media deploy soft-power narratives designed to normalize cooperative relationships and discredit security-oriented critiques. Comparable framing effects are occasionally observable in Japanese public discourse, where pacifist and economic arguments coincide with Beijing's diplomatic messaging.

However, causality remains inferential; media pluralism ensures that countervailing conservative voices also exist. In academia, a subset of scholars specializing in Sino-Japanese relations advocate engagement-oriented approaches, emphasizing interdependence and mutual restraint. Such views, while intellectually legitimate, can indirectly validate Chinese policy narratives. The key analytical point is not ideological bias but the structural asymmetry of knowledge production: Access to Chinese data and fieldwork is often contingent on maintaining positive relations with Chinese institutions, which can subtly shape academic discourse. Consequently, public opinion formation in Japan reflects a mix of autonomous debate and externally resonant framing. The diffusion of these narratives contributes to what the present study terms a cognitive narrowing of sovereignty—a gradual shift in the range of acceptable policy ideas.

4.5 Illustrative Cases and Mechanism Synthesis

Several observable cases illustrate how these mechanisms interact. For instance, Komeito's diplomatic missions to China, publicly documented by both parties, routinely emphasize dialogue and mutual trust. While these exchanges are standard practice, Chinese officials often highlight Komeito's role as a "stabilizing force" in bilateral relations (Wang 2012). Media coverage of sensitive topics—such as human rights resolutions or defense budget increases—frequently reports coalition negotiations resulting in moderated outcomes. The avoidance of direct confrontation or explicit criticism of China demonstrates agenda-shaping effects rather than overt interference. Taken together, these cases exemplify how Cooperative/Infiltrative Sovereignty Limitation operates through the intersection of institutional mediation within the ruling coalition, economic interdependence shaping incentive structures, and cognitive influence through public discourse. Each channel alone may appear benign, yet collectively they contribute to a structural environment where policy autonomy is constrained by the anticipation of diplomatic or economic repercussions.

4.6 Alternative Interpretations

It is important to acknowledge competing interpretations. Some analysts argue that Komeito's mediating role enhances stability by preventing policy escalation and sustaining regional peace (Ehrhardt et al. 2014). From this perspective, moderation does not represent sovereignty erosion but rather a form of strategic restraint consistent with Japan's postwar pacifist identity. Furthermore, diplomatic engagement through friendship associations can promote transparency and communication, reducing the likelihood of miscalculation. Similarly, economic interdependence, while constraining, can generate mutual deterrence against conflict. Recognizing these perspectives underscores that sovereignty limitation and stability promotion are not mutually exclusive. The analytical task is to identify when coordination ceases to be reciprocal and becomes structurally asymmetric—when mutual benefit transforms into dependency. This distinction frames the subsequent discussion of governance asymmetry in Section 3.

4.7 Summary of Section 2

This section has examined the indirect mechanisms through which the PRC influences Japan's policy environment. These include political mediation through Komeito, networked engagement via friendship and business associations, and opinion-shaping within public and academic spheres. While none of these mechanisms constitute direct coercion, their cumulative effect embeds external preferences into Japan's policymaking process, aligning with the concept of Cooperative/Infiltrative Sovereignty Limitation. The next section analyzes why these mechanisms are particularly effective in Japan by exploring the structural asymmetry between China's centralized strategy and Japan's decentralized governance framework.

5 The Structure of Amplification

5.1 China's Unified Strategic Model and Japan's Fragmented Governance

A central proposition of this study is that the effectiveness of China's cooperative and infiltrative influence is amplified by a structural asymmetry between the two states' systems of governance. The PRC operates through a highly integrated strategic apparatus in which the Communist Party, state bureaucracy, military, and United Front Work Department coordinate under unified strategic objectives. This coherence enables consistent pursuit of long-term influence goals through diplomatic, economic, and informational channels (Beckley and Brands 2023; Lam 2021). In contrast, Japan's governance is characterized by institutional pluralism and procedural fragmentation. Policymaking depends heavily on the coordinating functions of the Cabinet Secretariat and informal negotiation among ministries and coalition partners. While this pluralism supports democratic accountability, it also diffuses authority and slows unified response to external influence. Within this decentralized system, mediating actors such as the Komeito Party gain disproportionate importance as facilitators of coalition consensus.

From the perspective of institutional analysis, these actors represent nodes of connectivity—bridges linking the domestic and international dimensions of policymaking. Consequently, China's engagement with

Komeito or related organizations can indirectly affect Japan's foreign policy tone, not through command but through agenda calibration. This asymmetry—centralized coordination on one side and decentralized negotiation on the other—creates a structural environment that magnifies the efficacy of subtle influence. The phenomenon echoes Keohane and Nye's (1977) concept of "asymmetric interdependence," where power resides in the capacity to organize and sustain networks of interaction rather than in coercion alone.

5.2 The Institutional Vulnerability of Japan's Cabinet Center

Japan's Cabinet-centered system exhibits both strengths and weaknesses in managing complex coalition governance. While the Cabinet Secretariat coordinates policy formulation, its authority depends on political consensus within the ruling parties. In areas of foreign and security policy—traditionally dominated by the Ministry of Foreign Affairs and the Prime Minister's Office—Komeito's coalition role ensures that certain policies require bilateral approval within the alliance framework. This arrangement, while democratic in design, can lead to policy inertia when coalition partners hold diverging priorities. The Cabinet Secretariat's limited analytical capacity to monitor informal influence networks, combined with the absence of comprehensive transparency mechanisms (e.g., disclosure of coalition negotiation records), further weakens its ability to assess external impact. Official records such as the Annual Policy Coordination Report (Cabinet Secretariat 2022) reveal a heavy reliance on interministerial consensus and limited oversight of nongovernmental interlocutors.

As a result, decision-making often occurs within closed deliberation circles, shielded from public scrutiny. Such opacity allows subtle preference shifts to proceed without explicit recognition. Over time, this fosters what institutional theorists term path dependency—a situation in which prior coalition norms constrain future policy alternatives. Therefore, even absent direct interference, Japan's internal coordination structure can amplify external influence by institutionalizing deference to stability and continuity. This dynamic reflects Krasner's notion of domestic sovereignty erosion: when internal governance mechanisms themselves normalize responsiveness to external preferences.

5.3 Komeito's Strategic Value and Network Position

Within Japan's coalition architecture, Komeito's influence exceeds its parliamentary size. Its organizational base, rooted in the Soka Gakkai's mobilized electorate, grants it substantial bargaining leverage. In coalition politics, electoral reliability translates into policy bargaining power. China's recognition of this structural position is evident in official and semiofficial communications that describe Komeito as an important "channel of dialogue" (Wang 2012). While such recognition does not imply subordination, it reflects the mutual instrumentalization of networks: Komeito enhances its diplomatic prestige through engagement, while China benefits from a moderate interlocutor. This mutuality, however, creates asymmetric dependencies. For Japan, maintaining coalition stability often necessitates avoiding positions that would alienate Komeito or jeopardize its China engagement.

For China, the cost of maintaining this channel is minimal, consisting mainly of symbolic diplomacy and selective economic goodwill. Consequently, the coalition framework itself becomes an institutional conduit through which foreign policy moderation is internalized as coalition consensus. This process exemplifies Barnett and Duvall's "structural power"—the shaping of actors' capacities and interests through systemic configurations rather than direct coercion. The empirical implication is that sovereignty erosion in contemporary Japan is less a matter of legal constraint and more a question of institutional codependency: an internal governance structure that rewards caution and discourages autonomy in external relations.

5.4 Public Consciousness and the Diffusion of Passive Sovereignty

Beyond institutional design, societal attitudes also reinforce Cooperative/ Infiltrative Sovereignty Limitation. Japan's postwar political culture has long emphasized peaceful coexistence and international coordination as moral imperatives. These values, though normatively desirable, can unintentionally normalize external consultation as a prerequisite for legitimacy. The notion of "passive sovereignty," originally linked to Japan's postwar alliance dependence (Sakurai 2023), has evolved into a broader public disposition. Opinion surveys consistently reveal strong public support for alliance stability and economic pragmatism, often at the expense of assertive autonomy.

This mindset, shaped by decades of pacifism and economic interdependence, produces what sociologists describe as adaptive conformity—a collective preference for maintaining equilibrium rather than exercising agency. Komeito's discourse of "friendship diplomacy" and "Asian harmony" resonates with these values, presenting engagement with China as a moral extension of Japan's pacifist identity. As a result, policy restraint can appear as ethical prudence rather than constraint. This framing reduces societal sensitivity to subtle sovereignty erosion. From a constructivist perspective, such normative alignment represents a discursive reproduction of limited sovereignty: Citizens and elites alike internalize the expectation that external coordination is both necessary and virtuous. Consequently, influence operations need not rely on manipulation; they operate effectively within preexisting cultural scripts.

5.5 Alternative Perspectives on Structural Asymmetry

While this analysis emphasizes asymmetry, it is important to consider counterarguments. Some scholars argue that Japan's decentralized governance is itself a source of resilience, preventing authoritarian capture by distributing decision-making authority (Katzenstein 1996). Under this view, pluralism may dilute external influence by requiring broad consensus across institutional actors. Furthermore, China's centralized model carries internal rigidity that limits adaptability. The very coherence that facilitates influence can also produce overreach or reputational backlash, as seen in recent regional pushback against Chinese diplomacy. Thus, asymmetry does not guarantee dominance; it merely creates opportunity structures. This comparative insight refines the argument: Cooperative/ infiltrative limitation is not deterministic but contingent on domestic institutional receptivity. Japan's vulnerability arises less from external coercion than from internal structural incentives to avoid conflict and preserve coalition equilibrium. Strengthening transparency and public deliberation could mitigate these effects without undermining democratic pluralism.

5.6 Summary of Section 3

This section has analyzed how the asymmetry between China's unified strategic apparatus and Japan's fragmented governance amplifies external influence. The limited coordination capacity of Japan's Cabinet Secretariat, combined with coalition dynamics and normative pacifism, generates conditions conducive to Cooperative/Infiltrative Sovereignty Limitation.

However, these dynamics are not inevitable. Democratic pluralism and transparency reforms can offset them if consciously strengthened. The next section explores the normative and institutional consequences of this structural environment, outlining potential reforms to restore substantive sovereignty and democratic accountability.

6 Discussion

6.1 The Substantive Hollowing of Sovereignty

External influence on Japan's policy formation does not merely represent a nominal adjustment of sovereignty but entails a gradual erosion of substantive autonomy in legislation, diplomacy, and judicial reasoning. The process identified here as Cooperative/Infiltrative Sovereignty Limitation manifests when decisions that ought to reflect domestic deliberation increasingly mirror the strategic preferences of external actors. In such contexts, sovereignty is hollowed out not by legal coercion but by policy convergence born of institutional dependency. The resulting outcomes—whether moderation in human rights debates or caution in defense initiatives—cannot be dismissed as manipulation, yet they cumulatively reflect an externally conditioned decision space. This phenomenon poses a constitutional dilemma. Japan's popular sovereignty principle presupposes policymaking autonomy anchored in democratic accountability. When elite negotiations internalize external expectations, the link between the electorate's will and national policy weakens. The challenge, therefore, is to restore the transparency and pluralism that reconnect sovereign decision-making to democratic legitimacy.

6.2 Risks to Democratic Governance and Accountability

The most acute danger of limited sovereignty lies in the erosion of democratic control. Influence transmitted through coalition mediation and informal negotiation often escapes institutional oversight. Because coalition councils and party coordination meetings are rarely recorded in full, public access to deliberation processes remains minimal. This opacity generates what Levitsky and Ziblatt (2018) describe as a "twilight zone of democracy"—a condition where formal democratic procedures coexist with declining substantive accountability. Civil society and opposition parties face informational asymmetry, limiting their capacity to evaluate government actions. From a rational-choice standpoint, governing elites maximize short-term political stability and economic benefits—such as campaign cooperation or access to Chinese markets—over long-term sovereignty preservation (Watanabe 2024). These incentives foster a feedback loop: Secrecy sustains elite advantage, which in turn deepens citizen disengagement. Over time, democratic responsiveness decays into procedural minimalism, in which elections persist but genuine policy autonomy erodes.

6.3 External Projection of "Autocracy 2.0"

The identified mechanism parallels the externalization of what Yang (2024) terms Autocracy 2.0—the export of digital and cognitive control practices developed within authoritarian regimes. China's domestic governance combines centralized data management, information filtering, and opinion guidance. Elements of this model—especially narrative management and agenda calibration—appear increasingly in its external engagement strategies (Feldstein 2019; Beckley and Brands 2023). Rather than imposing censorship abroad, these practices operate through partnerships and media ecosystems in which foreign interlocutors voluntarily disseminate narratives aligned with Chinese diplomacy. In Japan, this dynamic manifests through selective access for sympathetic scholars, media collaborations, and civic exchanges that privilege stability narratives. Such practices exemplify what may be termed digital sharp power: influence that functions within the cognitive domain by shaping perception rather than coercing behavior. Traditional theories of international relations—focused on material power—struggle to capture these mechanisms. Integrating insights from communication studies and network analysis is therefore essential for understanding sovereignty in the digital age.

6.4 Comparative Models of Limited Sovereignty

Placing Japan's experience in comparative perspective clarifies both its uniqueness and generality. The U.S. Model (Explicit Limitation), for example, features dependence structured by formal treaties and transparent obligations, such as alliance frameworks and the Status of Forces Agreement. In contrast, the China Model (Cooperative/Infiltrative Sovereignty Limitation) operates through relational networks, economic incentives, and narrative alignment, where constraints are implicit and diffuse. A third case, the Australia Model (Economic Coercion/Transparency Response), involves external pressure through trade leverage combined with domestic counter-legislation, most notably the Foreign Influence Transparency Scheme Act (2018). Japan differs in that its constraints operate through low-visibility cooperation embedded within domestic institutions. Whereas Australia and the United States face overt interference or treaty-based dependence, Japan encounters embedded coordination, making detection and redress more difficult. This comparison reinforces Krasner's (1999) argument that sovereignty is context-specific. In Japan's case, formal independence masks a substantive dependence sustained by political culture, coalition structures, and cognitive norms.

6.5 The Democratic Security Dilemma

Open societies confront a paradox: The very openness that underpins democracy provides entry points for external influence. Countermeasures that centralize power or restrict information risk replicating authoritarian techniques, thereby undermining democratic legitimacy. The appropriate response is therefore transparency-based resilience, not securitized secrecy. Governments must disclose the existence of foreign lobbying or informational campaigns while preserving pluralism and open debate. This approach aligns with Grant and Grant and Keohane's (2005) conception of accountable multilateralism—balancing openness with institutional safeguards. Civil society plays a crucial role in this equilibrium. As Putnam (1993) demonstrated, dense horizontal networks foster trust and democratic self-correction. When citizens understand the mechanisms of influence and articulate informed responses, the scope for covert manipulation narrows. Strengthening civic literacy about sovereignty thus constitutes a form of democratic self-defense.

6.6 Governance Reforms for Sovereignty Preservation

Building on the preceding analysis, three complementary reforms are proposed, each seeking to enhance transparency, accountability, and civic engagement without compromising democratic openness. The first is an Academic and Foreign Influence Transparency Initiative, which would establish a voluntary, university-led system to collect and publish data on foreign funding, academic partnerships, and political exchanges—modeled on FARA principles but adapted to Japan's legal framework (Department of Foreign Affairs and Trade 2019). By locating oversight within neutral research institutions such as the Japan Institute of International Affairs, this initiative would supplement rather than politicize government monitoring. The second reform involves Legislative and Diplomatic Transparency Measures, specifically amending Diet procedures to require the disclosure of coalition coordination minutes and informal diplomatic consultations, subject to security exceptions. Public availability of such records would enable independent evaluation of policy rationale and mitigate suspicions of opaque mediation.

Finally, the third reform centers on Civic Education and Sovereignty Awareness, integrating the concept of limited sovereignty into civic education curricula and public forums. Encouraging citizens to debate the balance between cooperation and autonomy cultivates collective vigilance, and Public Opinion Forums organized through online platforms and local assemblies could function as distributed arenas of deliberation, strengthening social capital and participatory oversight. Together, these reforms operationalize democratic defense through openness: a strategy that transforms transparency itself into a safeguard of sovereignty.

7 Conclusion

This study has extended Stephen Krasner's Limited Sovereignty Theory to analyze Japan's contemporary experience of cooperative and infiltrative constraint in its relations with China. The findings demonstrate that sovereignty in democratic states may erode not through overt domination but through embedded coordination mechanisms operating within domestic institutions and discourse.

In Japan, this process manifests across three interrelated dimensions. First, political mediation within the LDP–Komeito coalition functions as a channel of indirect alignment, as Komeito's pacifist and pragmatic diplomacy moderates anti-China rhetoric and contributes to policy restraint. Second, policy networks and friendship associations—including parliamentary leagues and business organizations—amplify this moderation through sustained interpersonal and economic linkages that normalize conciliatory narratives. Third, cognitive diffusion in media and public debate reinforces these tendencies, recasting external accommodation as prudence and stability. Together, these dynamics exemplify Krasner's concept of sovereignty erosion through institutional normalization rather than coercive subjugation.

Theoretically, the chapter situates these findings within a broader typology of limited sovereignty, distinguishing between explicit, infiltrative, and transparency-responsive models. Japan's case corresponds most closely to the infiltrative type, characterized by productive power (Barnett and Duvall 2005)—where social and institutional relations shape actors' identities and policy options without direct coercion. This configuration also connects Japan's experience to global trends associated with "Autocracy 2.0," in which authoritarian states externalize influence through normative and informational channels rather than overt force.

Normatively, the analysis underscores that defending sovereignty in open societies requires governance innovation grounded in transparency, pluralism, and civic participation. The proposed measures—a transparency initiative, procedural disclosure, and sovereignty education—represent practical avenues for reinforcing democratic accountability while maintaining openness to international cooperation.

Ultimately, Japan's experience offers a broader insight: Sovereignty in the twenty-first century is not a static possession but a dynamic civic practice. It must be continually reaffirmed through institutions that align external engagement with internal accountability. Future research should therefore assess the legal feasibility of transparency legislation within Japan's constitutional framework and develop empirical methodologies to map cross-sectoral influence networks. By reframing sovereignty as a shared civic responsibility rather than a governmental monopoly, democratic states can transform interdependence from a source of vulnerability into a foundation for resilient and autonomous self-governance.

Bibliography

Barnett, Michael, and Raymond Duvall. 2005. "Power in International Politics." International Organization 59, no. 1: 39–75. http://www.jstor.org/stable/3877878.

Beckley, Michael, and H. W. Brands. 2023. "China's Threat to Global Democracy." *Journal of Democracy* 34(1): 65–79. https://www.journalofdemocracy.org/articles/chinas-threat-to-global-democracy/.

Brady, Anne-Marie. 2017. *Magic Weapons: China's Political Influence Activities Under Xi Jinping*. Woodrow Wilson Center Press. https://www.wilsoncenter.org/article/magic-weapons-chinas-political-influence-activities-under-xi-jinping

Cabinet Secretariat. 2022. *Annual Policy Coordination Report*. [in Japanese]. Government of Japan. https://www5.cao.go.jp/j-j/wp/wp-je22/index_pdf.html

Department of Foreign Affairs and Trade (Australia). 2019. "Foreign Influence Transparency Scheme." Australian Government. https://www.dfat.gov.au/international-relations/Pages/foreign-influence-transparency-scheme.

Ehrhardt, George, Axel Klein, Levi McLaughlin, and Steven R. Reed. 2014. *Kōmeitō: Politics and Religion in Japan*. University of California Press. https://muse.jhu.edu/book/79135.

Feldstein, Steven. 2019. *The Rise of Digital Repression: How Technology Is Reshaping Power, Politics, and Resistance*. Oxford University Press. https://global.oup.com/academic/product/the-rise-of-digital-repression-9780190057497?cc=jp&lang=en&.

Grant, Ruth W., and Robert O. Keohane. 2005. "Accountability and Abuses of Power in World Politics." American Political Science Review 99, no. 1: 29–43. https://doi.org/10.1017/S0003055405051476.

Guo, Dongnu. 2023. "Revealing China's Soft Power Narratives in State-Owned Media." *Chinese Journal of International Review* 5 (2). https://doi.org/10.1142/S2630531323500087.

Katzenstein, Peter J. 1996. *Cultural Norms and National Security: Police and Military in Postwar Japan*. Cornell University Press. https://www.cornellpress.cornell.edu/book/9780801483325/cultural-norms-and-national-security/#bookTabs=1.

Keohane, Robert O., and Joseph S. Nye. 1977. *Power and Interdependence: World Politics in Transition*. Little, Brown.

Krasner, Stephen D. 2004. "Sharing Sovereignty: New Institutions for Collapsed and Failing States." *International Security* 29 (2): 85–120. http://www.jstor.org/stable/4137587.

Lam, Wai-Man, and Kay Chi-Yan Lam. 2013. "China's United Front Work in Civil Society: The case of Hong Kong." *International Journal of China Studies* 4(3): 301-325. chrome-extension://efaidnbmnnnibpcajpcglclefindmkaj/https://umcms.um.edu.my/sites/institute-of-china-studies-v2/img/files/lamlam.pdf.

Levitsky, Steven, and Daniel Ziblatt. 2018. *How Democracies Die*. Crown. https://www.amazon.co.jp/-/en/How-Democracies-Die-Steven-Levitsky/dp/0525574530.

Liff, Adam P., and Ko Maeda. 2019. "Electoral Incentives, Policy Compromise, and Coalition Durability: Japan's LDP–Komeito Government in a Mixed Electoral System." *Japanese Journal of Political Science* 20 (1): 53–73. https://doi.org/10.1017/S1468109918000415.

Naito, Edo. 2025. "Communist China's Quiet Influence on Japanese Politics." *The Japan Times*, April 30. https://www.japantimes.co.jp/commentary/2025/04/30/japan/china-influence-ops-japan/.

Nye, Joseph S. 1990. "Soft Power." *Foreign Policy*, no. 80: 153–71. https://doi.org/10.2307/1148580.

Putnam, Robert D. 1993. *Making Democracy Work: Civic Traditions in Modern Italy*. Princeton University Press. https://press.princeton.edu/books/paperback/9780691037387/making-democracy-work.

Sakurai, Yukio. 2023. "The Evolution of Japan's Limited Sovereignty." *The Rest* 15 (2): 45–68.

Stewart, Devin. 2020. "Resilience and Vulnerabilities: Traits Unique to Japan." *China's Influence in Japan: Everywhere Yet Nowhere in Particular*. Center for Strategic & International Studies, July 1. https://www.jstor.org/stable/resrep25323.5.

Walker, Christopher, and Jessica Ludwig. 2017. "The Meaning of Sharp Power: How Authoritarian States Project Influence." *Journal of Democracy* 28 (4): 9–20. https://doi.org/10.1353/jod.2017.0065.

Wang, Hongxiang. 2012. "Groundbreaking Proposals for Japan–China Relations." *Soka Education* 5: 182–93.

Watanabe, Tsuneo. 2024. *The Liberal Democratic Party and Factions*. Jitsugyō no Nihon Sha.

Yakushiji, Katsuyuki. 2014. "The Komeito's Curious Journey." *The Tokyo Foundation*, April 8. https://www.tokyofoundation.org/research/detail.php?id=628.

Yamaguchi, Shinji, Masaaki Yatsuzuka, and Rira Momma. 2022. *China's Quest for Control of the Cognitive Domain and Gray Zone Situations*. National Institute for Defense Studies. https://www.nids.mod.go.jp/english/publication/chinareport/index.html.

Yang, David Y. 2024. *China: Autocracy 2.0*. NBER Working Paper No. 32993. National Bureau of Economic Research. https://www.nber.org/papers/w32993.

CHAPTER 7

The Challenges of Local Politics in Japan: Focusing on Self-Government, Political Succession, and Ethics

Abstract

This chapter examines the evolution of local politics in the postwar era, as well as the issues and challenges that have emerged, with a particular focus on the following key words: self-government, political succession, and ethics. Approximately 34,000 local politicians, comprising local governors, mayors, and local assembly members, bear responsibility for the oversight of local political management in Japan. The democratic structures that have been developed in Japan in the postwar period may now be exhibiting indications of deterioration at the local level. Demographic projections indicate that substantial reform of local political structures is necessary in the medium to long term to enhance the quality of life in Japan. This is a consequence of Japan's aging population and declining birthrate, which is leading to a downsizing of local self-governments. The emergence of capable and proficient newcomers in local politics can facilitate reform of local politics. This chapter puts forth strategies for encouraging newcomers to engage with local politics and recommends that public policy be established to facilitate this endeavor. This is an essential measure for fostering a local society where individuals can repose their hopes for the future, overcoming the hereditary succession of local politicians and ethical issues. This chapter is based on literature surveys on political science and policy studies in Japanese and English. While the scope of discussion is basically in Japan, some implications might have a global application given demographic change.

Keywords: Local Politics, Political Succession, Ethics, Self-Government, Newcomers

1 Introduction

The democratic structures that have been established and developed in Japan in the postwar period may now be exhibiting indications of deterioration at the local level (Taniguchi 2024). Indeed, the recent local elections in Japan have been characterized by a number of structural problems, including: (i) a decline in voter turnout, (ii) a significant increase in uncontested elections, (iii) the introduction of nonpreferential elections, (iv) a lack of candidates, and (v) an underrepresentation of female members and an overrepresentation of older members (Sasaki 2020). This is in part attributable to the context of a declining population and an aging population with low birth rates but is not limited to. The chapter puts forth the proposition that it is inadequate to merely anticipate that local parliaments and local governments will revitalize local democracy (Taniguchi 2024). Instead, the chapter identifies the capacity of local political actors and populations to collaborate as a pivotal factor in this process (Taniguchi 2024). This is because local politics, speaking generally, has become inactive and is no longer a subject of public interest. The question, therefore, is how this situation came about.

In Japan, approximately 34,000 individuals occupied political office as of December 31, 2023. In the context of local politics, the number of individuals occupying elected office is considerable. This encompasses 47 prefectural governors, 1,741 municipal mayors, 2,644 prefectural assembly members, and 29,135 municipal assembly members (Statistics Bureau 2024). These individuals, collectively designated as professional local politicians, bear the responsibility of overseeing local politics. In contrast, in the context of national politics, there are 713 members of the National Diet, comprising 465 members of the House of Representatives and 248 members of the House of Councilors.

The local administration system underwent significant changes before and after the 1946 revision of the Constitution of the Empire of Japan, also known as the Meiji Constitution, which was promulgated in 1889 and came into effect in 1890. The Meiji Constitution regime established the prefectural and county systems in 1890, conferring considerable administrative authority upon the Ministry of Home Affairs of Japan. This ministry was responsible for appointing local governors of all prefectures as national agents, selecting individuals from among its bureaucrats who had passed the higher civil service examination (Ministry of Internal Affairs and Communications of Japan 2024a).

The foundation of local politics is closely aligned with the local self-government system, as delineated in the Constitution of Japan and its associated legislation. Following the revision of the Meiji Constitution, the Constitution of Japan was promulgated on November 3, 1946 with the assent of the emperor and came into effect on May 3, 1947. The Constitution of Japan institutionalized a parliamentary system, democracy, and local autonomy to ensure popular sovereignty, respect for basic human rights, and pacifism. The Constitution of Japan stipulates the local self-government system in Chapter 8, Articles 92–95 as quoted below, while the details were stipulated by the Local Autonomy Act of 1947 (Ministry of Internal Affairs and Communications of Japan 2024b).

> *CHAPTER VIII. LOCAL SELF-GOVERNMENT*
>
> *Article 92.Regulations concerning organization and operations of local public entities shall be fixed by law in accordance with the principle of local autonomy.*
>
> *Article 93.The local public entities shall establish assemblies as their deliberative organs, in accordance with law. The chief executive officers of all local public entities, the members of their assemblies, and such other local officials as may be determined by law shall be elected by direct popular vote within their several communities.*
>
> *Article 94.Local public entities shall have the right to manage their property, affairs and administration and to enact their own regulations within law.*
>
> *Article 95.A special law, applicable only to one local public entity, cannot be enacted by the Diet without the consent of the majority of the voters of the local public entity concerned, obtained in accordance with law.*

The constitutional and legislative provisions pertaining to democratization were designed with the objective of conferring autonomy upon local self-governments, thereby establishing a clear separation from the national administration apparatus. This was done with the intention of devolving authority over local political matters to the autonomous public (Etoh 2020). The Ministry of Home Affairs, which had previously exercised control over local administration in accordance with the provisions of the preceding constitution, was dismantled and divided into multiple central ministries, each with a specific function (Ministry of Internal Affairs and Communications of Japan 2024a).

The Constitution of Japan, as set forth in Article 93 above, establishes an electoral system for local self-governments. This system, along with the relevant laws, provides for the election of the chiefs and local assemblies of 47 prefectures and 1,741 municipalities, which constitute the local administrative units at present. The local political system is based on a system of dual representation, whereby the local population elects both a chief executive and a council, which collectively constitutes the decision-making body, the local assembly (Sasaki 2020). This is in contrast to the unitary representative system adopted in Japan today, whereby only the members of the Diet are elected by the national population and a majority of them form the cabinet, which becomes the executive body (Sasaki 2024).

The legislative system has been established in theory with the intention of enabling local politics to perform in accordance with the principles set forth in Article 93 and relevant laws. However, in practice, local self-governments, with the exception of the Tokyo Metropolitan Government, have consistently been subject to the authority of the central government. This is evidenced by the term 30% self-government, which reflects the reality that each local government is allocated only 30% of the tax revenue required to operate (Matsuda 2003). Consequently, they are compelled to rely on local tax subsidies and grants from the central government to fund the remaining 70%. This structural deficiency can be attributed to the fact that local fiscal autonomy was constrained under the centralized administrative system that was in place in postwar Japan (Matsuda 2003). In particular, the State has curtailed the fiscal authority of local governments and set limits on the extent of local tax revenues, thereby reducing the scope for local governments to expand their financial resources autonomously and increasing their reliance on State financial support.

Eventually, the long-term care insurance system, which commenced in April 2000, has established local governments as the principal operators, thereby reinforcing the involvement of municipalities. Due to a lack of fiscal and operational autonomy, many municipalities merge with other municipalities to form larger municipalities with the aim of achieving financial and operational sustainability. The number of municipalities has consequently been reduced from over 3,000 to 1,741. This movement of municipal reformation that occurred between 2000 and 2010 is referred to as the Heisei Great Merger of Municipalities (Ministry of Internal Affairs and Communications of Japan 2024c).

The decline in the birthrate and the aging of the population have had a considerable effect on local authorities' tax revenue projections and local welfare planning. This impact will persist into the future, contingent on the continuation of demographic change. In this drastically changing social environment of Japanese society, multiple issues are being addressed at the local level. However, local politics is often obscured by the influence of central politics, which is based on the Diet and the central government. As a result, it is challenging to comprehend local politics from the perspective of local populations. Consequently, the present study will concentrate on the field of local politics in Japan, with a view to examining pertinent issues.

The objective of this chapter is to examine the evolution of local politics in Japan in the postwar era and to evaluate the issues and challenges facing local politics from a historical and ethical standpoint. This analysis will contribute to the development of potential future solutions to these issues and challenges. This chapter subsequently addresses the contemporary issues and challenges confronting local politics, their prospective ramifications, and the measures that may be implemented to address these challenges. Furthermore, recommendations are provided regarding potential policy solutions for the future.

2 Methodology

This study employs a methodology that draws upon the disciplines of political science and policy studies regarding local politics in Japan, with a particular focus on the review of literature surveys pertaining to the subject of self-government, political succession, and ethics. This is demonstrated by the review of sources in Japanese and English, as listed in the references. In light of the author's expertise in law and political science, this chapter draws upon insights from these two disciplinary perspectives. This study builds upon the author's previous research on Japanese occupational hereditary succession among politicians and medical professionals (Sakurai 2024). From the perspective of Japanese occupational hereditary succession, an investigation into the theme of local politics in Japan must consider its historical background and analyze its social contributions and support of the population.

In light of demographic shifts, the extant frameworks of local politics are proving inadequate. However, there is a dearth of autonomous and institutional forces capable of effecting radical reforms to local politics in a manner that aligns with the realities and future needs of the population. Prior studies have identified shortcomings in the local politics situation with regard to the democratic function (Matsuoka 2021; Miyazaki 2022;

Sasaki 2024; Taniguchi 2024). However, few papers offered insights into potential solutions to these challenges. One paper addresses the case of the Kyoto town assembly, in which the enactment of a basic ordinance and the review of the functions of the town assembly itself were considered (Matsuoka 2021). The other paper analyzes the anticipated consequences of the proposed increase in remuneration for town assembly members (Miyazaki 2022). These studies present novel insights on the subject matter, and no other research is currently available. Consequently, this chapter will contribute to the policy discourse by offering ideas and recommendations for addressing these challenges.

This chapter is based on a comprehensive literature analysis of overviews on local politics in the contemporary setting. It should be noted that this chapter does not include a detailed survey investigating the specific area or field of local politics; neither does it include interview research. Consequently, this chapter does not offer a comprehensive review of local politics in Japan from a political science studies perspective. Nevertheless, this limitation does not negate the importance of academic analysis of research. While the scope of discussion is basically in Japan, some implications might have a global or regional application given demographic change similar to that observed in Japan.

3 Historical Review of Local Politics

3.1 Local Politics in Economic Growth (1950–1990)

In the aftermath of the war, Japan was afflicted with numerous scars, and the social fabric was rended by poverty and insecurity. It was only following the economic boom that was initiated by the Korean War (June 25, 1950–July 27, 1953) that Japan's economic recovery commenced in earnest. Concurrently, with the advent of the Cold War, the Allied Powers' policy of occupying Japan underwent a transformation, evolving from sanctions against Japan to the incorporation of Japan into the Western bloc. At that time, the Communist Party and the Socialist Party held considerable political influence in Japan, supported by trade unions. To counter the perceived threat of communism and socialism, the Liberal Democratic Party (LDP) was formed by merging the conservative Liberal Party and the Democratic Party of Japan. This was known as the 1955 Regime (Fukui 2023).

Following the merger of the two conservative parties, the LDP assumed the role of the leading party, while the Socialist Party functioned as the leading opposition party until the conclusion of the Cold War. During this period, the LDP placed the responsibility for national security in the hands of the Japan–U.S. Security Treaty, promoted economic growth, and worked assiduously to enhance the living standards of the population (Fukui 2023).

Local politics served as a conduit for the redistribution of centrally accumulated wealth to local areas in a manner that was deemed optimal. This approach, which was characterized by a uniformity of policy across Japan, had the effect of curbing regional economic disparities, contributing to national equality and the formation of an egalitarian society, which was referred to as a 100-million-population middle-class society. Consequently, a significant number of public policies were aligned with the requests put forth by the Socialist Party (Fukui 2023).

Conversely, the distribution of wealth gave rise to the emergence of interest politics, which in turn led to the proliferation of corruption within the local political landscape. A case in point is the collusion with the construction industry through public works budgets by the national and local governments, which led to Japan being derisively labeled a construction nation (Kitayama 2021). The 1970s saw the emergence of scandals involving financial impropriety such as the granting of illegal convenience and the abuse of power within the LDP. This occurred concurrently with Japan's rapid economic growth. This resulted in a notable reduction in public confidence in the political system (Fukui 2023).

The 1970s was a period during which the Japanese population was compelled to reconsider the trajectory of economic growth. This included addressing environmental pollution in industrialized areas, addressing student movements' dissatisfaction with social contradictions, responding to the sudden rise in energy resource prices due to the oil supply crisis in 1973 and after and 1979 and after, and grappling with the limitations of economic growth. The era in which the primary function of local politics was to guide and redistribute wealth has nearly come to an end, and the depopulation of rural areas has become a significant challenge.

The 1980s was a period of accelerated economic expansion in Japan, characterized by resilience in the face of environmental degradation, fluctuations in energy resources, and currency crises. The flourishing economy gave rise to real estate investment and prompted a period of speculation, which came to be known as the bubble economy. In 1990 to 1991, the Bank of Japan introduced a total volume regulation on real estate investment finance, which resulted in the bursting of the bubble and the onset of a prolonged period of economic stagnation that persists to the present day. During this period, Japan's national population reached its highest point at 128 million, and since 2008, there has been a decline in the national population.

In terms of population composition, the aging of the population has progressed rapidly, and the declining birthrate has become a notable phenomenon due to the increasing tendency for individuals to marry at later ages or to remain unmarried (Cabinet Office of Japan 2024). The aging of the population has resulted in a significant increase in the cost of medical care and long-term care, placing a considerable burden on the social security system and, subsequently, on the public (Cabinet Office of Japan 2024). The sustainability of the social security system is currently perceived as an issue due to shifts in the demographic equilibrium. These alterations in the demographic configuration and the augmented burden on the population about the social security system have an impact on people's lives, which in turn affects local politics. This has led to an increase in opportunities for liberal governors to promote innovative public policies in their prefectures (Er 2005).

3.2 Local Politics in Economic Stagnation (1991–2024)

This section will examine the role of local politics in contemporary Japan. It will consider the shift in focus from the redistribution of wealth from the center to the periphery to the fostering of lifestyles and industries that align with the needs and distinctiveness of the regional welfare and security measures. However, despite this shift, progress has been limited. This is due to multiple factors. First, they include the lack of human resources of local politicians partly due to the hereditary succession of local politicians, which is a significant contributor (Sakurai 2024). This issue will be discussed in the subsequent section.

Second, there has been a notable decline in the number of individuals engaged in local political processes, which has contributed to a significant deterioration in the state of local politics. The decline in participation in local politics has manifested itself in a reduction in voter turnout in local elections and a decrease in the number of candidates. Voter turnout, which was between 70% and 80% in the 1960s, has decreased to 40s%

(Taniguchi 2024). The number of local assembly members elected without voting is on the rise. In the 2023 spring unified local elections, approximately 25% of the elected officials were chosen in this manner due to the lack of alternative candidates (The Japan News 2023). In response to this development, the Ministry of Internal Affairs and Communications of Japan convened an advisory council on the revitalization of local politics and is striving to enhance it, yet the impact is not yet discernible.

There is a notable lack of female candidates, which contributes to the gender gap in local politics. Furthermore, the low level of political participation among young people represents a significant challenge. Young people are influenced by politicians who demonstrate concern for the elderly, which may lead them to perceive a lack of relevance between politics and their lives and futures (Bergman Engman 2022). This misperception may result in a lack of motivation among young people, who are eligible to vote at the age of 18 since 2019 by law, to engage in local politics. This contributes to low voter turnout and the exclusion of young people from the interests of local politicians. Consequently, the gap between Japanese generations may widen, potentially leading to a loss of societal solidarity.

Third, the constituency of local politics is undergoing a transformation. In the past, interest groups such as those representing local agriculture, forestry and fisheries industries, civil engineering and construction companies, trade unions, and medical associations constituted the support base for local politics, seeking economic benefits. Currently, the influence of such interest groups has relatively diminished, while that of emerging religious groups has grown covering the country.

Various religious groups emerged around this time, such as the Soka Gakkai, a Japanese religious organization, and the Family Federation for World Peace and Unification, commonly referred to as the former Unification Church, which was established in South Korea on May 1, 1954 by the late Sun Myung Moon. The Soka Gakkai provides support to its political party—the Komeito—and even plays a role in supporting the coalition partner—the LDP—in elections using its organizational votes. The former Unification Church adopt policies that support local politicians to secure their identity in society and cultivate followers (Imasaki 2022). The former Unification Church has a significant presence in the political sphere, with members serving as secretaries to politicians without compensation and campaigning for elections without financial remuneration (Imasaki 2022).

The former Unification Church has established a social environment that permits the implementation of its fundraising activities in accordance with the relevant legislation. Furthermore, it is developing its membership based on its relationships with politicians. The political activities of such religious groups are likely to contravene the constitutional principle of the separation of religion and government (Article 20, the Constitution of Japan). Nevertheless, such groups offer support to politicians, and their influence over local politicians has reached a point where public agencies, including the police, are unable to intervene due to concerns of illegality. This situation represents a significant social issue.

4 Issues and Challenges of Local Politics

4.1 Hereditary Succession Politicians

A distinctive feature of Japanese politics is the practice of hereditary succession among politicians (Sakurai 2024). Hereditary succession denotes the transmission of a designated position, such as an official rank, peerage, or occupation, from one generation to the next. Hereditary succession constitutes a traditional form of authority, as defined by Max Weber as one of the legitimate rules (Weber [1922] 1978).

In the context of the previous Civil Code of Japan (1898–1947), which was based on the household legal structure system (family system), succession in households was of paramount importance to the Japanese people. The primogeniture heritage system may be regarded as a constituent element of the broader concept of hereditary succession. Consequently, the Japanese have long practiced a hereditary succession system. Despite the abolition of the family system in the Civil Code in 1947, the hereditary nature of certain traditions and businesses has remained unchanged. This suggests that these hereditary traditions and businesses possess a distinctive culture that has remained unaltered over time in Japan.

The value of inheriting traditional skills or businesses through hereditary succession is widely recognized. However, there is a paucity of support for hereditary succession in public office, with the exception of the political sphere. Indeed, the practice of hereditary political succession is not confined to the Diet members but is also evident in local assembly members across Japan. This section focuses on the characteristics and impacts of hereditary politicians.

Hereditary succession is a system that is unique to Japanese politics. It places the highest priority on blood and family ties and does not necessarily emphasize the capability and efforts of politicians. The system is based on the concept of pedigree legitimacy, which was seen in samurai society before the nineteenth century (Sakurai 2024). This is typically represented by the Tokugawa shogunate succession. This system is closely related to the traditional culture of Japanese rule and governance.

In hereditary succession, politicians may inherit the support groups and individual supporters of the single-seat constituency system. In general, this method upholds the vested interests of both politicians and their supporters. The ties between politicians and their supporters lead to distribution of wealth from the center to the periphery. Such a mechanism has been at the heart of LDP politics since 1955 when the LDP was founded.

The number of politicians who have inherited their position is not included in official statistics; however, it is documented in private research at the national level. The number of politicians who can be considered hereditary is contingent upon the precise definition of the term hereditary (Tamura 2007). In a narrow sense, a hereditary politician is defined as "a person whose parent, stepparent, or grandparent is a member of the National Diet, or who has a member of the National Diet among relatives within the third degree of kinship and who runs for political office from the same constituency" (Tamura 2007, 88–91). A recent research blog has indicated that, as of September 2021, the proportion of hereditary politicians in the House of Representatives has undergone a slight decline from 25% during the period 1970 to 2020 to 20% at the present time (Research blog 2021).

In a broad sense, the term of hereditary politicians encompasses "individuals who have inherited the influence of politicians in elections, as well as those whose relatives are politicians and have been motivated to pursue a career in politics" (Ando 2022, 102–3). This definition excludes those who have inherited wealth or other resources that have enabled them to enter politics without necessarily having a familial connection to the field (Ando 2022).

In accordance with this definition, approximately 40% of the elected members of the House of Representatives in 2012 and 2014 were hereditary members (Ando 2022) in the central political context. Although no survey exists that considers hereditary members in the local political context, the prevalence of hereditary politicians is further accentuated by instances in which governors, mayors or local assembly members are relatives of politicians. Hereditary succession can be found both in the national and local assemblies, a phenomenon that is rare in other countries than Japan (Thompson 2012).

Hereditary succession politics may contribute to a distribution mechanism during economic growth. There is however an analysis that the attraction of subsidies to local industries by hereditary succession politicians has weakened the industrial competitiveness of the region overall (Asako et al. 2015). The recent research finds that most Japanese dislike hereditary succession candidates while they value specific attributes of hereditary succession politicians such as their political networks (Miwa et al. 2023). Japan is undergoing a demographic transition, which presents challenges for the social system, industrial structure, and working environment. In this context, the ability of politicians to provide wisdom and leadership is of paramount importance, regardless of their hereditary background. This is also relevant at the local level in Japan.

4.2 Ethics of Local Politicians

A further distinctive feature of Japanese local politics is the issue of ethical standards concerning political funding and electoral malpractice. These issues have their roots in the fundamental structure of Japanese politics and continue to be a source of concern in the present day (Fukui 2023). The political structure of the LDP, formed in 1955, intertwines central and local politics, organizing party members on a national scale. In Japan's forty-seven prefectures, there are local organizations known as LDP prefectural federations. To run for office with the LDP's endorsement in local politics, it is necessary to receive the recommendation of the LDP prefectural federation in advance (Fukui 2023).

While this party-driven politics contributes to the promotion of professional politicians, it also functions as an election apparatus that employs a range of strategies to guarantee the success of individuals affiliated with the LDP organization. The necessity for election funds inherent to election campaigns gives rise to the occurrence of scandals related to such funds. These have manifested repeatedly in both local and central politics, resulting in instances where politicians have faced legal prosecution.

Local politics, supported by central politics, facilitates the transfer of election funds from national lawmakers to prefectural assembly members and, subsequently, from prefectural assembly members to town assembly members. While the procedures set forth in the Political Funds Control Act of 1948 are generally regarded as appropriate, there are instances where this is not the case. Issues pertaining to the intersection of politics and money are unique to the LDP (The Mainichi 2024). National organizations such as the Japan Communist Party and the Komeito, which has a presence in major cities, do not face issues related to politics and money in public. Similarly, opposition parties and smaller parties targeting trade unions and swing votes also tend to avoid such problems.

The Political Funds Control Act states, "Political organizations must be conscious of their responsibilities and, in the receipt of their political funds, must conduct themselves openly and fairly in accordance with this law so as not to arouse suspicions among the people" (Article 2, Paragraph 2 [philosophy]). However, this law is commonly referred to as a toothless law, and there are many loopholes and excuses within the regulations set by the law (The Mainichi 2024). After all, while this law establishes a framework that seeks political ethics from politicians themselves, it is inherently considered impractical to achieve. In this sense, the political arena in Japan might be, much like the realms of TV entertainment and show business, a unique world where societal ethics do not apply.

Currently, political parties that have submitted declarations to central politics receive political subsidies from the government under certain conditions by law. However, the LDP, deeming this insufficient, hosts parties for corporate donations and political fundraising (The Mainichi 2024). These funds flow back into local politics, providing financial support for candidates endorsed by the LDP in local politics. The ongoing LDP financial impropriety controversy, which has unfolded under the Kishida administration and the leadership of the LDP President, has given rise to a significant degree of discourse and has had a discernible impact on the local political landscape.

Professional politicians, when defeated in elections, lose their parliamentary badges and are unable to receive parliamentary remuneration. Being a professional politician is an extremely unstable occupation that can be sustained by winning elections. Therefore, there are not many common people who aspire to such an unstable profession. In this sense, the reality is that individuals seeking to enter local politics, regardless of age, are extremely limited.

The purpose of local politics is not to provide a source of livelihood for professional politicians. Rather, it is to devise policies for the population of a particular locality and to ensure that these policies are implemented by the relevant administrative authorities. In contemporary Japan, at a pivotal moment in its political history, it is crucial to ensure that local politics is not constrained by the agendas of the central government. Instead, there is a need for a dynamic shift in approach, whereby local politics exert a tangible influence on the decisions made at the national level.

The Meiji Restoration of 1868 laid the groundwork for modernizing Japan based on the initiative of peripheral areas in western Japan, such as Choshu, Satsuma, and Tosa. As a result, the 15th shogun and central political figure at the time, Tokugawa Yoshinobu, stepped down from the shogunate, leading to the peaceful transfer of Edo Castle, the residence of the Tokugawa shogunate and the center of central politics at the time. The Emperor in Kyoto moved from the Kyoto Imperial Palace to Edo Castle, establishing it as the Imperial Palace in Tokyo.

The historical events mentioned above were achieved through the initiative of peripheral areas, driven by a shared sense of crisis in the central politics of the Tokugawa shogunate that it could not cope with international politics involving Western major powers. Even today, a similar sense of crisis is voiced against the coalition government of the LDP and the Komeito. However, the fundamental problem is that there is no opposition party in Japan that is deemed a reliable alternative to the LDP. The period between August 2009 and December 2012, during which the Democratic Party of Japan assumed office, was characterized by significant political challenges. The memories of these times, which coincided with the crisis caused by the East Japan Great Earthquake and the damage caused by the Fukushima Nuclear Power Plant, continue to have a profound impact on the Japanese population.

It is thus hoped that scholars, businesspeople and citizens, untainted by the influence of money and scandals, will play active roles in both local and central politics. Particularly, there is an expectation that women will provide leadership in politics. Nevertheless, it is conceivable that confronting the established political parties may present a significant and formidable challenge. To justify this, there needs to be a shared perception of crisis among the citizens. It is reasonable to hope that the untapped power of local politics will be effectively demonstrated within the values and procedures of contemporary democracy.

5 Politics for the Future Democracy

5.1 An Era of Diversity

In a social environment where economic growth is not anticipated, the realization of a diverse society in the community has become a goal as Japan paves the way forward to a mature democratic nation (MHLW, n.d.). In essence, the objective is to acknowledge the multiplicity of individuals within the population and to facilitate the coexistence of those occupying disparate positions within the community. It is incumbent upon local governments to provide support for this realization, respond to the requests of local citizens, and thereby strive to improve their well-being. Considering these policy considerations, we will examine measures pertaining to the three primary factors of human resources, goods, and money, with a view to revitalizing local politics in Japan.

First, regarding the matter of human resources, it would be prudent to implement legal restrictions pertaining to the hereditary succession of politicians for the purpose of occupying local assembly members and chief roles. It is recommended that the quotas for local assembly members and chiefs be created through the prohibition of hereditary succession of politicians be transferred to the public domain. It is imperative to enhance the working conditions to facilitate the participation of educated professionals and women in the local assembly.

Second, regarding the matter of goods, it is becoming increasingly apparent that digital society is set to evolve further in the future. Consequently, it is imperative that the introduction of digital devices and technologies within local governments is initiated at an earlier stage than has hitherto been the case with central governments (JCIE 2021). In addition to elections, multiple other possibilities exist, including the digital broadcasting of local assembly deliberations, virtual dialogue with local assembly members and chiefs, and the installation of digital suggestion boxes.

Third, regarding the matter of money, it would be prudent to abolish the money deposit system currently in place for candidates seeking election, thereby ensuring that any individual is able to run for office. The delivery of election speeches and the conduct of election campaigns will be conducted via digital devices, thereby eliminating the necessity for the expenditure of funds on the production and dissemination of printed materials such as posters and election campaign vehicles. Should such radical reforms be implemented, it is possible that young people may become more engaged in the electoral process, with some even pursuing careers in local politics.

5.2 It Is Time to Change

In April 2024, the Population Strategy Council, a group of private sector experts, published an analysis indicating that by 2050, 40% of all municipalities in Japan, or 744 in total, will have experienced a reduction of 50% in the number of women in their 20s and 30s (Nikkei Newspaper 2024). This demographic shift could potentially lead to the dissolution of these communities, given their lack of self-sustainability. The municipalities identified by the Population Strategy Council as being at risk of disappearing are distributed in a significantly uneven manner across the eastern region of the country.

This forecast of future events had a profound impact on the public. It is not yet clear whether this prediction will prove accurate. However, it is evident that a significant number of local authorities are uncertain as to their ability to manage local government in the same manner as before, given the rapid changes occurring in the demographic structure. In the event of a future decline in the financial resilience of local authorities due to an aging and shrinking population, they will be compelled to rely on the central government to a greater extent (Kato 1988). It is inevitable that most local governments will be required to undergo a significant shift in their strategic direction in the future.

To develop and implement policies that are tailored to the specific needs of each region, it is essential to consider the unique characteristics of each region, including its demographic composition, industry, healthcare system, and financial situation. In other words, the role of local politics should be to develop and implement regional welfare and social security systems that are responsive to the challenges of downsizing, with a focus on reducing administration costs and personnel. These systems are based on the provision of public pensions, healthcare and long-term care for the elderly, as well as support for fostering children with younger generations. Municipalities with smaller civil jurisdictions have primary responsibility for implementing social welfare measures.

It is of the utmost importance that local politics plays a central role in fostering more conducive social environments and problem-solving mechanisms in collaboration with local administrative bodies and stakeholders in diverse society. This will necessitate a considerable degree of political fortitude and expertise. The inherent challenges associated with this demanding work make it particularly challenging for politicians who have been appointed to their roles through hereditary succession. Instead, it will be necessary to employ individuals who possess the requisite multifaceted knowledge and experience in each field. This serves to illustrate that the discrepancy between the prevailing state of local politics and the desired ideal is considerable.

It is therefore necessary to implement policies that facilitate the introduction of new talent into professional local politics, rather than hereditary succession. It would be beneficial to consider candidates from diverse backgrounds, including young people, women, retired seniors, and individuals with disabilities who have had few opportunities to engage in local politics. Implementing such an initiative in a relatively small civil jurisdiction could serve as a pilot project, with subsequent expansion to larger cities.

In this context, it is of the utmost importance to cultivate a supportive social environment. This may be achieved by fostering collaboration with existing local political parties, establishing preliminary study groups for new entrants, and developing a support system for their candidacies. Furthermore, individuals may engage in grassroots, bottom-up support activities within local communities and professional associations. These actions are undertaken with the collective goal of influencing the future trajectory of society.

The implementation of these actions in an effective manner will be contingent upon the establishment of national forums comprising citizens. These forums will facilitate the achievement of a consensus on the fundamental concepts that citizens desire and are prepared to forego in each region. The objective of the regional forums is to facilitate multilayered and multidimensional consensus-building dialogues with the aim of strengthening consensus-building channels based on a bottom-up approach (Tanaka 2004).

It is recommended that public policy be established and implemented at the local level under the leadership of local governors or mayors to facilitate the fostering of local political human resources projects from a neutral standpoint. In consideration of their eligibility in financial power and their influential effects for the public, it is proposed that the governors of Tokyo and Osaka should assume a leadership role in this endeavor; however, this is not intended to be an exclusive designation, and any local governor or mayor is encouraged to participate.

6 Conclusion

This chapter presents an overview of the evolution of the roles of local politics in Japan from the postwar period until the present day. Subsequently, the chapter considers the issues and challenges currently facing local politics in Japan. The declining birthrate and aging population in Japan represent significant factors, and the projections of demographic shift until 2070 are clear. In light of these circumstances, it is evident that radical reform of local politics represents a crucial step for the Japanese society to maintain and enhance its quality of life in the longer term. The advent of capable and seasoned newcomers in local politics, actively engaged in local assemblies and pertinent political activities, can facilitate this transformation. This chapter puts forward potential strategies for encouraging newcomers to engage with local politics. It is recommended that public policy be established to facilitate this endeavor from a neutral standpoint. This is an essential measure for fostering a local society where individuals can repose their hopes for the future, overcoming the hereditary succession of local politicians and ethical issues. This chapter provides an initial idea of policy on local political management; however, it does not present an empirical analysis or investigation of the specific field of local politics in Japan to support its implementation. Such issues will be addressed in future studies.

AI Acknowledgment

The author acknowledges the use of the AI systems DeepL and ChatGPT for translation from Japanese into English and English editing work, but no use of generative AI or AI-assisted technologies in the preparation or completion of the essential authoring tasks in this manuscript. The prompts used include "Please translate this sentence into English" and "Please correct this sentence for academic writing." The output from these prompts was used for English writing and English editing.

Informed Consent

The authors declare that informed consent was not required as there were no human participants involved.

Conflict of Interest

The author declares that there is no conflict of interest.

Bibliography

Ando, Yuko. 2022. *The Liberal Democratic Party's Perception of Women: The Political Orientation of "Family-Centrism"* [in Japanese]. Akashishoten.

Asako, Yasushi, Takeshi Iida, Tetsuya Matsubayashi, and Michiko Ueda. 2015. "Dynastic Politicians: Theory and Evidence from Japan." *Japanese Journal of Political Science* 16 (1): 5–32. https://doi.org/10.1017/S146810991400036X.

Bergman Engman, Axel. 2022. "Political Apathy in Japan: A Study on How Japanese Political Parties Address Youth." Master's thesis, Lund University, August 18. https://lup.lub.lu.se/student-papers/search/publication/9097799.

Cabinet Office of Japan. 2024. "Section 1: Current Population Situation and Issues." [in Japanese]. https://www5.cao.go.jp/keizai-shimon/kaigi/special/future/sentaku/s3_1_2.html.

Er, Lam Peng. 2005. "Local Governance: The Role of Referenda and the Rise of Independent Governors." In *Contested Governance in Japan: Sites and Issues*, edited by Glenn D. Hook. Routledge.

Etoh, Toshiaki. 2020. "Development of Local Government Governance in Japan: Development of Intergovernmental Relations and One More Step." *Annual Journal of Social Sciences* 40: 47–73. [in Japanese]. http://id.nii.ac.jp/1188/00003700/.

Fukui, Haruhiro. 2023. *Party in Power: The Japanese Liberal-Democrats and Policymaking.* University of California Press.

Imasaki, Tsunehide. 2022. "Unification Church's Ex-Member Explains How It Gains Political Influence." *NHK World Japan*, September 16. https://www3.nhk.or.jp/nhkworld/en/news/backstories/2094/.

Japan Center for International Exchange. 2021. "Japan's Democracy: Lessons and Reflections. 1st Panel Discussion—The Current State of Japan's Democracy." https://www.jcie.org/programs/expanding-support-for-democratic-governance/japans-democracy-lessons-reflections/.

Kato, Tomiko. 1988. "Changes in the Powers and Functions of the Nation, Prefectures, Municipalities, and Residents." *Organization Science* 22 (2): 2–11. [in Japanese]. https://www.jstage.jst.go.jp/article/soshikikagaku/22/2/22_20210831-89/_pdf/-char/en#:~:text=*%20%E9%83%BD%E9%81%93%E5%BA%9C%E7%9C%8C%20*%20%E7%94%BA%E6%9D%91%20*%203%205.

Kitayama, Toshiya. 2021. "MOF and Construction State in Historical Time." *Policy Science* 28 (3): 73–93. [in Japanese]. https://doi.org/10.34382/00014306.

Matsuda, Naoki. 2003. "The Historical Background, Significance, and International Positioning of Decentralization and the Current Problems of the Japanese Centralized Financial System." *Journal of National Tax College* 43: 92–209. [in Japanese]. https://www.nta.go.jp/about/organization/ntc/kenkyu/ronsou/43/matsuda/hajimeni.htm.

Matsuoka, Kyomi. 2021. "Local Assembly Reform and Transformation of the Citizen Consciousness: Time Series Analysis of the Political Awareness Survey by Kyoto Citizens." *Scientific Reports of Kyoto Prefectural University, Public Policy* 13: 1–18. [in Japanese]. https://kpu.repo.nii.ac.jp/records/6277.

MHLW (Ministry of Health, Labour, and Welfare of Japan). n.d. "Toward the Realization of a Diverse Society in Community." Accessed January 18, 2025. [in Japanese]. https://www.mhlw.go.jp/stf/seisakunitsuite/bunya/0000184346.html.

Ministry of Internal Affairs and Communications of Japan. 2024a. "History of the Local Self-Government System." [in Japanese]. https://www.soumu.go.jp/main_sosiki/jichi_gyousei/bunken/history.html.

Ministry of Internal Affairs and Communications of Japan. 2024b. "Overview of the Local Government System." [in Japanese]. https://www.soumu.go.jp/main_sosiki/jichi_gyousei/bunken/history.html.

Ministry of Internal Affairs and Communications of Japan. 2024c. "Regional Administration and Municipal Mergers." [in Japanese]. https://www.soumu.go.jp/kouiki/kouiki.html.

Miwa, Hirofumi, Yuko Kasuya, and Yoshikuni Ono. 2023. "Voters' Perceptions and Evaluations of Dynastic Politics in Japan." *Asian Journal of Comparative Politics* 8 (3): 671–88. https://doi.org/10.1177/20578911221144101.

Miyazaki, Kenta. 2022. "The Salary of Members and Elections and Activity in Japanese Local Assemblies: The Effect of Amount of Salary and Its Voluntary Increase." *Waseda Commercial Review* 463: 1–36. [in Japanese]. https://waseda.repo.nii.ac.jp/records/76937.

Nikkei Newspaper. 2024. "40% of Local Governments at Risk of Disappearing, Female Population Halved in 30 Years—Population Strategy Council." April 24. [in Japanese]. https://www.nikkei.com/article/DGXZQOUA230SG0T20C24A4000000/.

Research Blog. 2021. "Visualize the Hereditary Status of Parliament Members." September 22. [in Japanese]. https://1manken.hatenablog.com/entry/Hereditary-politicians.

Sakurai, Yukio. 2024. "It Is Time to Reconsider the Hereditary Succession of Politicians and Medical Practitioners in Japan: Reform Ideas to Overcome the Adverse Effects." *Rest: Journal of Politics and Development* 14 (2): 181–93. https://therestjournal.com/2024/07/31/it-is-time-to-reconsider-the-hereditary-succession-of-politicians-and-medical-practitioners-in-japan-reform-ideas-to-overcome-the-adverse-effects/.

Sasaki, Nobuo. 2020. "The Japanese Democracy Is Now Facing a Serious Crisis—Local Municipal." *Economic Review, Chuo University* 60 (5–6): 235–53. [in Japanese]. https://chuo-u.repo.nii.ac.jp/records/12502.

Statistics Bureau, Ministry of Internal Affairs and Communications of Japan. 2024. "Election-Related Materials (as of the End of December 2023)." [in Japanese]. https://www.soumu.go.jp/senkyo/senkyo_s/data/ninki/touhabetsu.html.

Tamura, Shigeru. 2007. "A Study of Hereditary Politics." *Journal of Law and Politics (Hosei riron)* 39 (2): 86–113. [in Japanese]. https://niigata-u.repo.nii.ac.jp/records/29818.

Tanaka, Shigeaki, ed. 2004. "On the Legal Involvement in Bioethics." In *Perspectives on Modern Law: Aspects of Self-Determination* [in Japanese]. Yuhikaku Publishing.

Taniguchi, Naoko. 2024. "An Analysis of Public Attitudes Toward Local Politics in Japan." *Journal of Law, Politics, and Sociology* 97 (2): 129–47. [in Japanese]. https://aslp.law.keio.ac.jp/pdf/AN00224504-20240228-0129.pdf.

The Japan News. 2023. "Editorial: Lack of Candidates for Office Accelerates Decline in Regional Areas." *The Yomiuri Shimbun*, April 25. https://japannews.yomiuri.co.jp/editorial/yomiuri-editorial/20230425-105659/.

The Mainichi. 2024. "Editorial: Japan's Revised Political Funds Law, A Stopgap that Mocks Public Trust." June 20. https://mainichi.jp/english/articles/20240620/p2a/00m/0op/013000c.

Thompson, Mark Richard. 2012. "Asia's Hybrid Dynasties." *Asian Affairs* 43 (2): 204–20.

Weber, Max. (1922) 1978. *Economy and Society: An Outline of Interpretive Sociology*. University of California Press. Originally published as *Wirtschaft und Gesellschaft* in 1922.

CHAPTER 8

Japan's Immigration Governance: Legal Reform, Social Integration, and Democratic Accountability

Abstract

This study examines Japan's immigration governance through a comprehensive analysis of legal terminology, institutional structures, and policy discourse. Despite the growing economic reliance on foreign workers, the government continues to employ the term "policy on foreign nationals" rather than "immigration policy," reflecting a deliberate rhetorical strategy that obscures the broader social and legal implications of migration. This terminological ambiguity, reinforced by political statements, has contributed to public misunderstanding and hindered the development of a coherent legal framework. Policy decisions remain dominated by the executive, with minimal legislative oversight or public participation, resulting in a fragmented system narrowly focused on labor supply. Drawing on legal and administrative analyses and a comprehensive literature review, the study identifies critical deficiencies in transparency, integration policy, and the protection of migrants' rights. In response, it proposes three interrelated reforms: foundational legislation to clarify legal definitions and responsibilities; a comprehensive integration strategy securing labor, social, and educational rights; and institutional reforms—including the creation of a National Forum on Immigration Policy—to strengthen democratic oversight and participatory policymaking. These measures are essential to align Japan's immigration governance with constitutional principles and international human rights standards. Future research should incorporate field-based perspectives and cross-national comparisons to better understand migrant experiences and policy implementation challenges.

Keywords: Immigration Policy, Foreign Workers, Law Reform, Social Integration, Democratic Accountability

1 Introduction

It is widely argued that Japan has effectively functioned as an immigrant-receiving country for more than a decade (Miyajima 2022; Liu-Farrer 2024). However, the validity of this characterization depends on how the term "immigrant" is defined. This term remains undefined in Japanese law, and the absence of a legal definition for "immigrant" is a critical issue in itself. For statistical purposes, the United Nations defines an international migrant as any individual who has changed their country of usual residence, regardless of legal status, type of movement, or underlying motive (United Nations, n.d.). Despite the absence of a legal definition of the term "immigrant," Japan is undeniably moving toward becoming what may be described as a "de facto" immigrant society (Saito 2024). The country's distinctive demographic trajectory, marked by rapid population aging and persistently low birth rates, has led to severe labor shortages across a wide range of sectors. These demographic and economic pressures have prompted a critical reassessment of Japan's immigration policies.

Recent data illustrates this trend. As of the end of 2024, Japan's foreign resident population reached 3,768,977, consisting of 3,494,954 mid- to long-term residents and 274,023 special permanent residents (ISA of Japan 2025a). The foreign resident population accounts for 2.7% of Japan's total population (Suzuki 2025). This represents a significant year-on-year increase of 10.5%, or 357,985 individuals, compared to the previous total of 3,410,992 in 2023 (ISA of Japan 2025a). Although the proportion of foreign resident population remains relatively low in comparison to other developed countries, this figure has nevertheless reached a record high in Japan. The most common visa categories among foreign residents as of the end of 2024 were, in descending order, as follows: permanent residents (918,116), technical intern training (456,595), engineers/specialists in humanities/international services (418,706), students (402,134), and family stay (305,598). All of these categories saw an increase compared to the previous year (ISA of Japan 2025a).

A more detailed breakdown by nationality reveals important trends in immigration patterns and demographic shifts. As shown in Table 1, there

Table 1: The Number of Immigrants to Japan by Nationality

Nationality	End 2022	End 2023	End 2024	Two-Year Change (%)
Total Number	3,075,213	3,410,992	3,768,977	+18.4
Chinese	761,563	821,838	873,286	+12.8
Vietnamese	489,312	565,026	634,361	+22.9
South Korean	411,312	410,156	409,238	-0.5
Filipino	298,740	322,046	341,518	+12.5
Nepalese	139,393	176,336	233,043	+40.2
Brazilian	209,430	211,840	211,907	+1.2
Indonesian	98,865	149,101	199,824	+50.5
Burmese	56,239	86,546	134,574	+49.0

Source: ISA of Japan (2025a).

has been notable growth among specific immigrant populations, particularly from Vietnam, Nepal, Indonesia, and Myanmar. Among these groups, Vietnamese nationals experienced the most significant increase, with a 22.9% rise over a two-year period. Similar upward trends are evident among Nepalese, Indonesian, and Burmese residents, while the numbers of South Korean and Brazilian nationals have remained relatively stable. The comparatively modest increases in the Chinese and Filipino populations, relative to the more rapid growth from other Asian countries, suggest a diversification in the sources of immigration to Japan. This growth reflects Japan's increasing reliance on labor from South and Southeast Asia, particularly in sectors such as manufacturing, wholesale and retail trade, accommodation and food services, construction, and other service industries.

At the community level, the increasing visibility of foreign workers highlights both their contributions and the challenges associated with immigration. Local debates are particularly pronounced in municipalities with concentrated immigrant populations, such as the Kurdish community in Kawaguchi City, where foreign residents constitute 8.4% of the local population (Suzuki 2025). This population includes individuals with irregular legal status (Kato 2019; Kato and Liu-Farrer 2022). In such contexts, sustained dialogue among central and local governments, residents, and community leaders is crucial. Integrating bottom-up community engagement with top-down policy initiatives can address localized concerns, foster mutual understanding, and yield more effective integration strategies (Nagayoshi 2021; Watado 2019). A governance framework that emphasizes transparency, public participation, and context-sensitive dialogue is essential for building a sustainable and socially cohesive immigration policy.

Social media has emerged as an influential medium for the rapid dissemination of local information, including reports of labor rights violations, administrative limitations, and community-level tensions. The immediacy and broad reach of such platforms constrain the state's ability to shape public narratives through selective disclosure or centralized messaging. This evolving information environment underscores the need for more transparent, responsive, and participatory governance. However, social media discourse often includes negative portrayals of foreign residents, including accusations of welfare misuse, administrative shortcomings in enforcement, and perceived leniency by law enforcement or judiciary. Some sources and news reports have indicated a growing trend of such narratives online (Annio 2025; The Mainichi 2025), and while some of these concerns may stem from genuine experiences, many are based on misinformation or unfounded generalizations that exacerbate social tensions. The viral spread of such content has been noted to pose additional challenges for fostering informed public debate and constructive policy discourse.

Recent data challenges the common perception that immigration has caused a rise in crime or a decline in public safety. In 2023, Japan recorded 703,351 reported crimes. Of the cleared cases, 5.8% involved foreign residents (Ministry of Justice of Japan 2024). The crime rate among foreigners was about 0.3%, slightly higher than the 0.15% to 0.2% rate among Japanese citizens. This difference is not statistically significant from a macro perspective and does not always support claims of a foreign-driven crime surge to date. Moreover, the nature of crimes committed by foreigners may mirror those committed by Japanese nationals. Theft remains the most common offense, followed by bodily injury and fraud.

The study aims to contribute to a more informed and inclusive public discourse on immigration policy by examining these tensions. The analysis examines Japan's immigration regime, which is constrained by inherent structural contradictions while pragmatically addressing labor shortages and demographic decline. Japan's approach to immigration governance is often characterized by deliberate ambiguity and a perceived lack of democratic legitimacy (Komine 2014; Chiavacci 2025; Wakisaka 2024; Takaya 2025). This phenomenon is often characterized as a "de facto immigration policy" or a "policy on foreign nationals." In practice, this regime comprises both formal policies targeting foreign nationals and informal, ad hoc measures. These factors reflect competing pressures, including economic imperatives, entrenched nationalist ideologies, and the growing influence of international human rights norms.

The lack of transparency and limited civic participation in Japan's immigration policymaking process has contributed to a growing disconnect between governmental decision-making and public understanding. This disconnect has facilitated the spread of misinformation, heightened public anxiety, and intensified backlash against immigration. Japan's reactive and fragmented approach to immigration stands in stark contrast to the proactive, coordinated strategies adopted by other advanced democracies confronting comparable demographic challenges.

This chapter posits that Japan has experienced a gradual, implicit shift toward a more open immigration regime. Nevertheless, this transformation has occurred in the absence of substantive public deliberation or democratic consensus. Accordingly, it is argued that immigration policy should not be determined solely by the executive branch or ruling political parties. Instead, it is imperative that such initiatives are grounded in democratic legitimacy, reflect national identity, and involve broad-based public engagement. A forward-looking immigration strategy must carefully balance economic necessity with the principles of social inclusion and human rights protection.

2 Methodology

The central argument advanced in this study is that although Japan's current approach may offer a pragmatic short-term response to labor market demands, it remains fragmented, opaque, and insufficiently grounded in a coherent legal framework. This absence of institutional clarity poses significant long-term risks, including threats to the sustainability of Japan's socio-economic model, weakened social cohesion, and inadequate protection of foreign workers. The overarching question guiding this inquiry is as follows: How do economic imperatives, nationalist ideologies, and international human rights norms shape Japan's policy on foreign nationals, its de facto immigration practices, and the legal framework established under the Immigration Control and Refugee Recognition Act (ICRRA)?

This study adopts a multidisciplinary, mixed-methods approach grounded in law studies, political science, and policy studies to analyze the legal, institutional, and socio-economic dimensions of Japan's immigration policy. By integrating quantitative data analysis with qualitative content analysis and legal interpretation, the research offers a comprehensive framework for understanding how immigration policy is formulated, implemented, and experienced. The legal analysis focuses on the ICRRA and related statutory instruments. Through close reading and interpretive analysis, the study evaluates the coherence of Japan's legal framework with international standards and normative benchmarks. Attention is given to the structure, scope, and practical operation of immigration laws, with particular emphasis on labor rights, residency status, and access to public services. This legal inquiry helps assess whether Japan's immigration regime reflects a rights-based, utilitarian, or control-oriented approach and how such legal positioning affects the lived realities of foreign residents.

The quantitative component utilizes time-series data obtained from the Ministry of Health, Labour, and Welfare (hereinafter MHLW) and the Immigration Services Agency (ISA) of Japan. These data sets are used to identify long-term trends in immigration flows and labor market participation among foreign workers. Disaggregated by nationality, visa category, and employment status, the data enables an examination of how the composition of the foreign resident population has evolved over time. In addition, regression models are employed to explore the relationship between the inflow of foreign workers and key economic indicators, such as labor shortages, wage levels, and employment rates. This empirical analysis provides a data-driven foundation for evaluating the extent to which immigration policy aligns with Japan's economic conditions and workforce needs.

The qualitative component involves systematic content analysis of key policy documents, including government websites (i.e., Ministry of Justice, n.d.), ministerial reports (i.e., ISA 2024), and parliamentary debates (i.e., House of Representatives 2018). This analysis aims to uncover the dominant narratives, institutional logic, and rhetorical framings that inform immigration policymaking. Furthermore, a thematic review of academic literature in both English and Japanese situates the discourse within its broader socio-political context, particularly the interplay between economic imperatives, nationalist ideologies, and evolving international human rights norms.

While prior scholarship by Liu-Farrer, Douglass, Tsuda, and others listed in the References has provided valuable insights into Japan's labor-centered immigration model, return migration, and regional integration, these studies often focus on either macroeconomic trends or localized migrant experiences. By contrast, this study contributes to the literature by directing attention to the legal-structural dimensions of immigration policy, a dimension that has received comparatively little scholarly focus in Japan. It further considers how these structural aspects shape, constrain, or reinforce the practices and norms of democratic governance.

3 Legal and Policy Frameworks of Japan's Immigration Policy

3.1 Legal and Policy Frameworks of Immigration Policy

(1) Legal and Policy Frameworks

Japan's immigration legal framework, primarily governed by the ICRRA, mandates that all foreign nationals obtain a specific residence status, which meticulously delineates the permissible scope of their activities within the nation's borders. The ICRRA serves as the foundational legal instrument regulating entry, residence, employment, and deportation of foreign nationals in Japan, functioning as the central pillar of immigration control. Since its initial enactment in 1951, the ICRRA has undergone numerous revisions, reflecting the dynamic interplay of evolving socio-economic pressures, shifting demographics, and perceived societal needs. These amendments reveal a reactive approach to immigration management.

A key distinction between Japan's approach and the established practices of many Western nations lies in its reluctance to embrace permanent residency as a primary pathway for immigrants upon initial entry. Instead, Japan's immigration policy is more accurately characterized as a preference for temporary, purpose-specific, or limited-term migration, strategically designed to address specific, often acute, labor shortages within targeted sectors of the economy (Wakisaka 2024; Liu-Farrer 2024). In practice, this means that the Japanese government tends to issue short- or medium-term residence permits tied to employment categories, rather than long-term settlement rights. This structural reliance on sector-specific migration schemes underscores the instrumental nature of Japan's immigration policy, which prioritizes economic necessity over demographic renewal or multicultural integration.

The ambiguity inherent in Japan's immigration policy is rooted in its historical trajectory. Prior to the 1990s, Japan operated under a "no immigration" policy, the origins of which can be traced to a complex interplay of postwar historical context and socio-cultural values (Watado 2019). During the period of rapid postwar economic growth, the Japanese government prioritized a policy of full employment, achieving an unemployment rate consistently below 3.0% for Japanese citizens of working age. This context obviated the perceived necessity for large-scale foreign workers' migration for industrial purposes. The absence of a perceived need, coupled with cultural homogeneity and concerns about social cohesion, solidified the "no immigration" stance.

The economic landscape of Japan underwent a significant transformation in the 1990s, driven by a confluence of interconnected factors. A sustained decline in the birth rate, coupled with an aging population, resulted in severe labor shortages across a spectrum of sectors, including manufacturing, construction, agriculture, and the burgeoning care services industry (Watado 2019). Simultaneously, the forces of globalization and intensified international economic competition compelled Japanese companies to reduce variable expenditures and enhance operational efficiency, thereby generating an increased demand for low-cost foreign workers.

To address these challenges, the Japanese government introduced a number of piecemeal policy measures rather than a unified immigration reform. For example, the government introduced a system permitting foreign students and legally designated dependent foreigners to engage in part-time employment, limited to 28 hours per week, with extended allowances during holiday periods. This framework, established under Article 19 of the Enforcement Regulations of the Immigration Control Act (amended in 1992), was intended to ensure that students' primary purpose remained study, while allowing limited labor participation. This measure effectively positioned the student visa category as a supplementary channel for addressing labor shortages. It has been observed that this legal exception has effectively served as the regulatory basis that enables young people from Southeast and South Asia to obtain student visas by enrolling in Japanese-language schools or vocational colleges, while in practice facilitating their engagement in demanding manual labor (Idei 2019). Similarly, dependents of foreign professionals—spouses or children—were allowed to engage in part-time work within the same hourly limits, thereby expanding the labor pool without formally recognizing them as migrant workers. This development illustrates the de facto character of Japan's immigration policy, which has relied on the instrumental use of existing visa categories to accommodate labor migration in the absence of a comprehensive, overarching policy framework (Rehm 2023, 2024).

In order to address labor shortages, the Japanese government expanded the scope and reach of the Technical Intern Training Program (TITP) step by step (JITCO, n.d.). Initially conceived in 1993 as a skills transfer program aimed at fostering human resource development in developing countries, Japan's TITP functioned in practice as a proxy for importing low-skilled foreign workers to address domestic labor shortages. This unofficial role resulted in documented cases of exploitation, as "trainees" were denied legal labor protections. Despite the implementation of amendments in 2009/2010, which sought to extend certain rights to workers, instances of abuses continued to occur, largely attributable to inadequate oversight and dependence on intermediary organizations. Consequently, the government enacted the Act on Proper Technical Intern Training and Protection of Technical Intern Trainees (2016). The 2016 Act outlines the fundamental principles that must be observed when implementing proper training programs and protecting trainees. It emphasizes the responsibilities of organizations in implementing and supervising the program and established the Organization for Technical Intern Training (OTIT) to monitor compliance and investigate abuses.

This legislation identified a pivotal shift, formally clarifying that the program's purpose was to facilitate skills transfer, rather than to provide inexpensive labor, and prioritizing the rights and welfare of foreign trainees. However, it is important to note that this program was not accompanied by a formal adoption of an explicit "immigration policy." Rather than articulating a coherent policy vision, the government opted for incremental, case-by-case adjustments, introducing new visa categories while maintaining the official rhetoric of "no immigration." This ad hoc approach highlights the reactive and often inconsistent nature of Japan's immigration policy.

In 2019, Japan further diversified its labor migration framework through the introduction of the "Specified Skilled Worker" (SSW) visa. This new status was created under the revised Immigration Control Act to attract foreign nationals with certain skill levels in industries facing chronic labor shortages, such as construction, agriculture, food service, and eldercare. The SSW system comprises two categories: (i) Specified Skilled Worker, allowing up to five years of residence for workers with basic skills and (ii) Specified Skilled Worker, granting renewable residence status and family accompaniment for more experienced workers. Although it does not mark a fundamental paradigm shift toward an immigration state, the SSW visa reflects a growing institutionalization of labor migration under Japan's selective and pragmatic framework.

The spectrum of immigrant statuses in Japan is diverse and encompasses a range of categories, each designed to serve specific purposes. These include employment-based visas (e.g., "Engineer/Specialist in Humanities/International Services," "Highly Skilled Professional"), which are targeted toward skilled professionals expected to make significant contributions to the Japanese economy; non-employment visas (e.g., "Student," "Dependent"), facilitating educational pursuits or family reunification; and the "Specified Skilled Worker" visa, a more recent category established to address specific, identified labor market demands in sectors facing critical shortages. Japan also utilizes a variety of foreign worker programs, most notably, the TITP.

While the programs were originally designed for the purpose of human resource development in emerging nations, they have been the subject of persistent criticism for their role in channeling low-cost labor, with reports indicating that many of these workers face substandard or rights-violating working conditions (United Nations 2022, 8–9; Matsumoto 2023). Consequently, the government's use of fragmented visa mechanisms has led to conceptual ambiguity between "immigration policy" and "foreign national policy." Within the context of Japan, the government employs the term "policy on foreign nationals" in lieu of "immigration policy." Nevertheless, the general public tends to interpret "immigration policy" as the appropriate term, and this interpretation is consistent with common usage in English-language discourse. The use of inconsistent terminology has been identified as a contributing factor to conceptual confusion, which, in turn, complicates public debate and academic analysis.

(2) Judicial Stance

The legal status of immigrants in Japan has been significantly shaped by case law, with key court decisions defining its contours. The McLean Case (Supreme Court Grand Bench Decision, October 4, 1978) established a pivotal precedent by affirming the government's broad discretionary authority in immigration matters (Courts of Japan 1978). The ruling at issue addressed a constitutional and legal challenge to the Minister of Justice's decision to deny renewal of a foreign national's period of stay on the grounds of political activity within Japan. In its judgment, the court reaffirmed the principle of state sovereignty in the realm of immigration control and expressly held that foreign nationals do not enjoy a constitutionally protected right of residence in Japan.

The academic debate has unfolded on multiple fronts, including the tension between broad administrative discretion and the protection of individual rights, the consistent application of international standards and constitutional principles, and concerns regarding substantive fairness, the principle of minimum necessary restriction, and the hierarchy and coordination of legal norms (Tokugawa 2011). Yet despite these persistent critiques, the McLean decision has remained a cornerstone of Japanese immigration jurisprudence for nearly half a century. Its endurance lies in the court's clear affirmation of state sovereignty in immigration control, which has provided a stable doctrinal foundation for administrative practice. Consequently, immigration authorities continue to rely on McLean as a guiding principle in their decision-making, even as broader legal and normative debates about human rights and constitutional interpretation have evolved.

The Calderon Family Case (administrative decision, March 2009) exemplified the tension between the rigid application of immigration control and the protection of fundamental rights, most notably, the right to family unity. Central to the dispute were questions concerning the interpretation of the ICRRA in relation to a Filipino family's residence status. The Tokyo Immigration Bureau's decision to order the deportation of the parents, while simultaneously granting special residency to their daughter who was born and raised in Japan and had achieved full social and linguistic integration. This decision demonstrated the discretionary yet fragmented application of immigration law. This outcome highlighted the legal and normative challenges of reconciling statutory enforcement with constitutional principles and international human rights norms.

A further incident underscored these doctrinal tensions. In March 2021, the death of a 33-year-old Sri Lankan woman in custody at the Nagoya Regional Immigration Services Bureau, following a rapid deterioration in her health, raised critical questions concerning the state's duty of care under both domestic law and international human rights obligations. The case prompted renewed scrutiny of Japan's immigration detention regime, including the adequacy of statutory safeguards for detainee health, the legal framework governing accountability and independent review, and the extent to which existing practice aligns with constitutional protections and international standards.

Although Japan is a signatory to the 1951 Convention Relating to the Status of Refugees (hereinafter "1951 Convention"), its refugee recognition rate remains strikingly low in comparison with international standards, with the vast majority of asylum applications being rejected. In 2020, litigation was initiated challenging the prolonged detention of asylum seekers in immigration facilities. The Tokyo District Court subsequently held that certain instances of detention were unjustifiably lengthy and awarded damages to the plaintiffs (Tokyo District Court, June 20, 2025). This judgment represented an important development in acknowledging and safeguarding the human rights of individuals confined within Japan's immigration detention system, thereby establishing a meaningful precedent for future adjudication. While residency permits are occasionally granted on humanitarian grounds, such outcomes remain exceptional, underscoring the restrictive character of Japan's asylum policy.

3.2 Developments in Immigration Policy After 2018

This section examines recent developments in Japan's immigration policy since 2018, focusing on administrative and legislative perspectives.

(1) Administrative Stance

An analysis of the immigration policy statements made by recent Japanese prime ministers from the Liberal Democratic Party (LDP) shows a nuanced and evolving administrative stance on foreign workers. This stance demonstrates Japan's cautious and incremental approach to balancing economic necessity with political and social resistance to large-scale immigration.

Shinzo Abe's administration (2012–2020, second term) employed a top-down decision-making process within existing institutional frameworks, facilitated by his strong political authority at the time. In the government's written response to a question submitted by a member of the House of Representatives on March 9, 2018, regarding foreign workers and immigrants (House of Representatives 2018), the government stated that it was "actively accepting foreigners with specialized and technical skills" due to labor shortages but only within the framework of existing legislation. The response emphasized the necessity of reviewing the system for admitting such foreign nationals, while carefully avoiding the use of the term "immigration."

On December 25, 2018, the government adopted the Comprehensive Measures for Accepting and Coexisting with Foreign Workers (ISA of Japan 2025b). These measures aim to build a society in which Japanese and foreign residents can live together in safety and security by supporting the proper acceptance of foreign workers and promoting social integration. They cover key areas of daily life—such as employment, education, healthcare, and housing—and are updated annually to reflect evolving demographic and labor conditions.

In 2019, the Abe administration introduced a major policy reform under the revised ICRRA, establishing two new residency statuses: Specified Skilled Worker (SSW) Type 1 and Type 2 (Prime Minister's Office of Japan 2019). SSW Type 1 permits foreign workers with designated skill sets to work in fourteen specific sectors, such as nursing care, construction, and agriculture, for up to five years, without family accompaniment. SSW Type 2 is intended for workers with more advanced skills, allowing longer stays and the option to bring family members. The policy requires Japanese language proficiency, guarantees equal pay with Japanese nationals, and mandates the provision of support systems for daily life and employment integration.

While this reform represented a significant expansion of labor migration, the government consistently maintained that it did not constitute an immigration policy. To legitimize the reform, it employed discursive strategies such as referring to it as the "utilization of foreign human resources" (Chiavacci 2025; Takaya 2025). This rhetorical framing aligned the reform with existing legal and policy frameworks, allowing the government to expand foreign labor without triggering political backlash. The administration thus relied on linguistic and procedural ambiguity to manage public perception and maintain social consensus.

This perception was reinforced by repeated statements from Prime Minister Abe, disseminated through mass media, particularly NHK, stressing that "the government has no intention to promote a so-called immigration policy." This stance was largely intended to reassure nationalist supporters opposed to immigration (Yamada 2018; Higuchi et al. 2024).

Such communication strategies illustrate how the government prioritized narrative control over transparent policy articulation, relying on public misunderstanding to sustain legitimacy.

Fumio Kishida's administration (2021–2024) largely maintained the Abe administration's approach, avoiding explicit reference to an "immigration policy." In June 2022, Kishida endorsed a unified government strategy titled the "Roadmap for the Realization of a Society Living in Harmony with Foreign Nationals" (ISA of Japan 2022a). This five-year plan (FY 2022–2026) aims to enhance the social and administrative environment for foreign residents through improved oversight, regional cooperation, and multilingual information provision. Kishida also approved the Foreign Human Resources Training and Employment Program in February 2024, scheduled for implementation in 2027 (Prime Minister's Office of Japan 2023). This new program, intended to replace the TITP, seeks to enhance skills development and improve working conditions, representing an incremental move toward systematized labor migration management. In June 2024, the ICRRA was partially amended to facilitate these reforms by streamlining admission procedures and strengthening oversight of working conditions.

Japan International Cooperation Agency (JICA), a government-related implementing body responsible for Japan's official development assistance, published a report titled *Living with Foreigners in 2030/40: A Study of Initiatives for a Coexistence Society* in March 2022 (JICA 2022). The report's projections regarding future demand for foreign residents provide an important empirical reference point for the present analysis. The concept of a "coexistence society," which features prominently in the report, is closely linked to the broader notion of a "multicultural coexistence society." This terminology reflects liberal normative assumptions and implicitly advances a policy orientation that presumes acceptance of, and alignment with, multicultural coexistence as a desirable societal model, despite the fact that no clear consensus on such a model has been established among the national population.

Shigeru Ishiba's administration (2024–2025) has gradually expanded pathways for foreign workers and, in select cases, begun to consider humanitarian admissions (Prime Minister's Office of Japan 2025). Compared with his predecessors, Ishiba has demonstrated a slightly more open stance toward long-term integration, emphasizing demographic sustainability and regional revitalization. Notably, immigration issues gained unprecedented visibility during the 2025 House of Councillors election campaign, reflecting growing public engagement. Following the election, Minister of Justice Keisuke Suzuki held a press conference on July 30, 2025 at the Japan National Press Club (JNPC 2025), stating that if current trends continue, foreign residents could exceed 10% of Japan's population—approximately ten million—by 2040. This marked a notable shift toward greater policy transparency and acknowledgment of Japan's structural dependence on foreign labor.

However, it is unlikely that this announcement alone significantly enhanced public understanding. The unilateral nature of the disclosure underscores the continuing absence of participatory mechanisms or public deliberation in shaping immigration policy. While Japan's administrative stance has become more explicit, it remains characterized by incrementalism, rhetorical caution, and limited engagement with broader civil society.

Sanae Takaichi, who was inaugurated as Japan's 104th Prime Minister on October 21, 2025, outlined her policy toward foreign nationals during her inaugural press conference that evening. She emphasized the rejection of unrestricted immigration in order to prioritize the livelihoods and security of Japanese citizens, while pursuing a model of orderly coexistence. The core components of her policy include stricter immigration controls; a review of restrictions on land acquisition by foreign nationals; reforms to the Technical Intern Training Program and the Specified Skilled Worker scheme to facilitate selective labor intake; measures to address unpaid taxes and medical fees; and tighter requirements for the acquisition of Japanese nationality. The policy framework also establishes a dedicated ministerial portfolio and an inter-ministerial council designed to balance national protection with regulated integration. Takaichi also framed these reforms as a necessary shift in Japan's policy toward foreign nationals— an agenda that has received broad public support. Close attention will be required to assess how, and to what extent, her policy agenda will be implemented through subsequent legal and policy reforms.

(2) Legislative Stance

The National Diet of Japan has seen increased activity on immigration issues, marked by the formation of cross-party coalitions and efforts from individual lawmakers. Notably, the LDP is leading a parliamentary group to expand foreign worker acceptance and promote integration, reflecting economic pressures and the need for labor diversification. This is because the LDP has historically enjoyed the support of agricultural and industrial societies that rely on foreign workers. Simultaneously, a cross-party coalition is advocating for the protection of foreign workers' rights and a multicultural society, engaging in vigorous debates on revising the TITP and the ICRRA.

Recent deliberations in the National Diet have centered on legislative and administrative reforms to TITP, with the aim of enhancing statutory protections for workers and preventing exploitation, as reflected in the administrative stance. Parallel discussions have addressed the reform of immigration detention facilities, particularly in relation to the legality and proportionality of prolonged detention. Consideration was also given to measures for facilitating social integration, including language education programs and community engagement initiatives. Collectively, these debates reflect the complex and evolving legal and policy framework governing immigration in Japan, highlighting the interplay between statutory regulation, administrative practice, and broader human rights considerations.

The 2024 revision to the ICRRA introduces significant changes to the country's asylum and immigration system. A key provision is a new deportation rule for asylum seekers with three rejected applications. This measure was intended to streamline the system and deter abusive claims (ISA of Japan 2025c). Article 22-4 also introduces provisions to regulate the revocation of permanent resident status for individuals who continuously fail to pay tax or social insurance premiums or who are sentenced to imprisonment for certain crimes. Human rights organizations fear the new three-rejection rule will infringe on the rights of asylum seekers and reinforce Japan's historically restrictive refugee policy. Notably, the Japan Federation Bar Association, a lawyers' group, submitted a statement opposing the 2023 Bill for Amendments to the ICRRA. The organization expressed concerns that specific provisions of the bill risked violating foreign immigrants' human rights, particularly regarding legal representation and the potential for increased detention periods (Japan Federation of Bar Associations 2023).

On the other hand, the 2024 revision to the ICRRA establishes a new category of "complementary protection" for individuals who do not meet the strict criteria of the 1951 Refugee Convention but face serious harm if repatriated, such as those fleeing armed conflict or natural disasters (The Mainichi 2024). This provision brings Japan's policy more in line with international protection standards by acknowledging a broader range of humanitarian needs. The amendment also revises immigration detention policy, introducing more flexible provisions for supervised release (ISA of Japan 2025c). These changes are designed to reduce the length of detention by allowing temporary release under conditions like regular check-ins with immigration authorities.

In summary, Japan's immigration policy remains primarily economically driven, prioritizing selective labor-based admissions over a rights-based approach to integration. Judicial decisions, such as the McLean Case, underscore the broad discretion afforded to the state, with only limited exceptions grounded in humanitarian considerations. A partial shift occurred under the Abe administration in 2019 with the introduction of the SSW visa, which sought to address labor shortages without reframing immigration as a long-term settlement issue. The 2024 amendments to the ICRRA introduced measures for complementary protection; however, they largely tightened asylum regulations, reflecting a cautious and restrictive approach to reform. Collectively, these developments illustrate the persistent tension between national security, immigration control, and the protection of fundamental human rights (Higuchi et al. 2024).

4 Issues of Japan's Immigration Policy

Japan's immigration policy has undergone considerable evolution in recent years, yielding both advantages and adverse consequences. This section offers a detailed examination of the multifaceted impacts of these policy shifts on the Japanese economy, society, and labor market.

4.1 Pros and Cons Analysis on Japan's Immigration Policy

One of the foremost advantages of accepting immigrants is the supplementation of the labor force. As of October 2024, the number of foreign workers in Japan reached 2,302,587, a 12.4% increase from the previous year, according to the MHLW of Japan (2025). This influx has proven critical in mitigating labor shortages across numerous sectors of the Japanese economy. Moreover, empirical estimations indicate that the influx of approximately 775,000 foreign workers into Japan between 2014 and 2021 contributed to a 0.87% increase in real GDP, exerted downward pressure on the consumer price index and GDP deflator, and produced mixed effects on labor and asset markets, including a slight reduction in skilled labor real wages and a rise in real land prices (Economic and Social Research Institute 2023).

Certain industries have become particularly reliant on foreign workers. The construction sector has witnessed a doubling of foreign workers, from approximately 70,000 to 140,000, in just five years (MHLW 2025). The healthcare and welfare sector has experienced a more than threefold increase in foreign workers' participation, with numbers rising from approximately 260,000 to 900,000. The agricultural and manufacturing sectors have also seen notable increases in foreign workers' participation. These trends highlight the increasing embeddedness of foreign workers in key sectors of the Japanese economy.

Japan has seen a growing influx of highly skilled professionals, facilitated by initiatives such as the Highly Skilled Professional ("J-Skip") visa (Ministry of Foreign Affairs of Japan 2023). By 2024, approximately 40,000 foreign nationals held this status, reflecting a 20.5% increase from the previous year. The policy is intended to boost innovation and productivity in key economic sectors (Cao 2024). Concurrently, affluent Chinese immigrants have increasingly entered through the business manager visa program, which grants residency in exchange for economic contribution. Together, these trends indicate a shift in the composition of Japan's immigrant population, emphasizing skilled labor and investment-based migration, with potential implications for the country's long-term economic trajectory and integration policies.

Despite certain advantages, Japan's immigration policy continues to generate a range of negative consequences, as is also the case in other countries. Although the employment of low-cost foreign workers may enhance corporate performance, the associated drawbacks such as fiscal strain, social tensions, and concerns about public safety are often borne by the public sector. This transfer of responsibility may result in a greater tax burden for citizens (Borjas 2019). As a result, there is only limited evidence that labor immigration yields net benefits for Japanese society (Fukui 2023). Some scholars of economics argue that these policies may suppress wages and increase economic inequality (Fukui 2023). From this perspective, economic gains tend to be concentrated in the business sector, while the resulting social costs are shifted to the public sector and ultimately conducted by the general public. This raises important concerns about fairness and distributive justice (Fukui 2023, 2024).

The relative lack of comprehensive integration policies has led to difficulties for immigrants, especially concerning language acquisition and cultural adaptation (Nagayoshi 2021; Liu-Farrer 2024). Further, there have been persistent reports of labor exploitation, particularly within the TITP, including issues of low wages and harsh working conditions. Many immigrants, especially those in low-skilled jobs, encounter barriers to career advancement. For example, the majority of South American *Nikkeijin* (persons of Japanese descendant) workers remain in temporary positions even after as many as thirty years of employment in Japan.

Furthermore, the children of immigrants often face significant educational hurdles, even to the extent of failing to enroll in school at all in some cases and dropping out before completing their education in others. The increasing number of foreign workers has also raised questions about the long-term sustainability of Japan's social security system, notably, concerning pension and healthcare provisions. Finally, there are rising concerns about public security related to immigration, although these are often not fully substantiated by empirical evidence as evidenced before. These challenges underscore the need for a more integrated approach to immigration policy that addresses both economic needs and social integration.

In response to these challenges, Japan has implemented several specific policy adjustments. Starting in January 2025, the country will expand its Startup Visa program nationwide, offering greater flexibility for foreign entrepreneurs. Moreover, there is a growing recognition of the necessity for improved support systems for immigrants, including enhanced language programs and targeted measures to address and combat discrimination. From a labor law perspective, Japan has also begun to strengthen the legal protections afforded to foreign workers, reflecting an evolving understanding that fair labor conditions are integral to sustainable immigration policy. The government has introduced stricter review procedures for, and is actively considering applying fundamental labor law principles—such as minimum wage guarantees, occupational safety standards, and the right to collective representation—to trainees in the TITP, in an effort to address reported abuses within the program. Such efforts indicate a gradual shift toward aligning immigration-related employment schemes with the broader framework of Japan's Labor Standards Act and international labor norms. Finally, Japan has adopted a formal policy to accept foreign workers more openly in professional or technical fields.

Despite notable efforts, critics argue that Japan's immigration policy remains a fragmented and incremental approach and may be inadequate to meet long-term demographic challenges (Hashimoto 2019; Higuchi

2023). The government continues to avoid formally recognizing its shift toward a more open immigration stance, largely due to concerns over political backlash. This reluctance has impeded the development of comprehensive and effective integration strategies. It also reflects a deeper tension between economic necessity and enduring socio-cultural resistance.

To sum up this section, while Japan's evolving immigration policy has yielded substantial economic benefits and helped to alleviate critical labor shortages, it has also introduced a range of complex social and policy-related challenges. Scholars have expressed concerns that the public sector may bear disproportionate costs, such as increased tax burdens and social tensions, while the benefits accrue mainly to private industry. Some also argue that immigration may suppress wages and widen economic disparities (Fukui 2023, 2024; Borjas 2019). The ability to effectively manage these issues will ultimately be decisive for the success of the country's evolving immigration strategy. This, in turn, will shape the broader impacts on the future of Japan's economic and social landscape.

4.2 Comparison with Other Countries

A comparison of Japan's immigration law and policies with those of South Korea reveals several notable distinctions. While Japan's legal framework is primarily anchored in the ICRRA, South Korea operates under a more comprehensive set of legislation, including the Nationality Act, the Immigration Control Act, the Multicultural Families Support Act, and the Framework Act on Treatment of Foreigners (Korea Immigration Service, n.d.). South Korea has also developed a clearly defined national strategy, as articulated in its 4th Master Plan for Immigration Policy (2023–2027), outlining a long-term vision for a global nation in which citizens and immigrants progress together. Japan, by contrast, lacks a comparable comprehensive, long-term immigration strategy, reflecting a more incremental and reactive approach.

South Korea provides clearer pathways to citizenship and permanent residency, particularly for spouses of Korean nationals or significant investors, whereas Japan's pathways are less transparent, more restrictive, and subject to greater administrative discretion—reflecting a policy approach characterized by intentional ambiguity. Additionally, South Korean policies place greater emphasis on social integration and multiculturalism, implementing measures to support multicultural families and promote societal inclusivity, whereas these elements are less prominent in Japanese policy. While both countries face criticism regarding their treatment of refugees and asylum seekers, South Korea's plan explicitly prioritizes human rights protection, whereas Japan has been scrutinized by United Nations experts over detention practices for refugee applicants (United Nations 2022).

Although both nations maintain relatively restrictive immigration policies compared to many Western countries, South Korea's approach is more integrated, strategic, and forward-looking. Japan's policy remains focused on temporary labor migration and strict control, with reforms targeting immediate issues rather than a fundamental reorientation of the overall immigration framework. While such an incremental approach may address short-term labor needs, it risks falling short of establishing a sustainable and equitable system that integrates foreign residents and responds to long-term demographic and social challenges. Nevertheless, South Korea faces parallel challenges, and experts have emphasized the need for structural reforms to facilitate social integration (Lee 2024).

In this context, the ISA of Japan has explored potential mechanisms for the acceptance of foreign workers (ISA of Japan 2022b). Proposed measures include the introduction of a labor market test to assess domestic labor conditions before admitting foreign workers, the establishment of an acceptance cap aligned with industrial needs, and systems involving financial obligations, such as employment taxes or quotas, to balance the costs and benefits of foreign worker intake. The ISA report also considers agreements with sending countries to standardize skill levels and facilitate orderly admission in specific sectors. These findings have been filed as reference data for policy deliberation.

A comparative analysis of immigration policies in Europe provides critical insights and highlights potential best practices that can inform both national and regional policy design (Assari and Najand 2023; Kokkonen and Linde 2025). Immigration has become one of the most salient and polarizing issues in contemporary European politics, exerting noteworthy influence on electoral outcomes, party system realignments, and the framing of public discourse. Beyond questions of border control and asylum management, immigration debates encompass a wide spectrum of issues, including labor market integration, social welfare provision, cultural identity, and security concerns. These dynamics reveal the necessity of developing a comprehensive, context-sensitive, and interdisciplinary framework for analyzing immigration, one that accounts for the interplay between law, economics, sociology, and political science.

The comparative experience of European welfare states, particularly Germany and Sweden, is highly instructive for understanding the complex interaction between immigration policy, social integration, and political legitimacy. The cases of Germany and Sweden illustrate these dynamics with particular clarity. In Germany, immigration has been managed through a dual framework that distinguishes between humanitarian admission (asylum and refugee protection) and labor migration, the latter institutionalized through the 2005 Immigration Act and subsequent Skilled Workers Immigration Act of 2020. The arrival of large numbers of asylum seekers in 2015 reshaped political alignments, contributing to the rise of the Alternative für Deutschland (AfD) and sparking intense debates over national identity, integration, and social cohesion. Despite Germany's efforts to promote integration through structured language programs, vocational training, and pathways to permanent residency, challenges such as labor market segmentation, uneven municipal capacity, and right-wing mobilization persist, revealing the limits of administrative coordination in managing large-scale immigration.

In Sweden, long considered a paradigmatic example of humanitarian openness, immigration policy has evolved from a rights-based and inclusive model toward a more restrictive and security-oriented framework, particularly following the 2015 to 2016 refugee crisis. Immigration policy has not only influenced party competition but has also unsettled long-standing narratives of social solidarity and welfare universalism. Sweden's experience demonstrates the tension between maintaining generous welfare provisions and ensuring equitable access amid growing diversity, as well as the political consequences of welfare strain and perceived cultural fragmentation. The rise of the Sweden Democrats (SD) underscores how immigration can become a decisive factor in transforming consensus-oriented political systems into more polarized arenas.

These examples demonstrate the inherent difficulties in regulating immigration exclusively through government legislation, as policy implementation often encounters human error, administrative limitations, and unanticipated social consequences. They also highlight that even in advanced welfare democracies, the sustainability of immigration policy depends on effective coordination between legal design, administrative capacity, and societal acceptance. Such developments underscore how immigration functions as a critical axis of social and political contestation across Europe, while simultaneously highlighting the importance of developing policy approaches that balance humanitarian commitments with the demands of social integration and political stability.

Japan, in formulating and implementing its own immigration framework, should closely examine these European experiences, which offer instructive lessons regarding the risks of inadequate policy design, poor public communication, and the unintended amplification of social tensions. Neglecting such lessons may exacerbate public dissatisfaction, intensify anti-government and anti-establishment sentiment, and impose considerable social and political costs. By drawing on comparative insights, policymakers can anticipate potential pitfalls and craft more balanced, legitimate, and socially sustainable immigration strategies.

5 Discussion

5.1 Challenges

Japan's immigration policy is marked by a fundamental duality. Substantial numbers of immigrants have been admitted, yet the state has refrained from articulating a formal, comprehensive immigration policy. The government has consistently asserted that it is "not adopting a so-called immigration policy," while at the same time enacting measures under the ICRRA that allow the entry and employment of foreign workers. These measures are narrowly constructed and directed toward strategically selected sectors, thereby reinforcing the discretionary character of immigration governance under the existing legal framework. This duality underscores a deeper contradiction between cultural nationalism, which has shaped Japan's postwar constitutional and political order, and the economic imperatives articulated by industrial sectors. The persistence of this tension has been recognized as a critical factor shaping both the content of immigration law and the public perception of immigration-related policies (Liu-Farrer 2020).

Public sentiment regarding immigration in Japan presents a nuanced and often contradictory landscape, creating a complex interplay with government policy decisions. According to the 2020 Cabinet Office Public Opinion Survey on the Improvement of the Environment for Accepting Foreigners, a majority (51.2%) of respondents indicated support for expanding the acceptance of foreign workers, while a substantial minority (38.1%) expressed opposition (Cabinet Office of Japan 2020). Proponents of increased immigration primarily cited contributions to Japan's economic development and the alleviation of persistent labor shortages as key justifications. Conversely, opponents voiced concerns related to potential deterioration of public safety and the displacement of Japanese workers from employment opportunities. These survey results suggest a generally favorable, albeit cautious, public attitude toward accepting foreign workers. A significant undercurrent of anxiety persists regarding the potential social and cultural ramifications of large-scale immigration, highlighting the challenges inherent in fostering a truly inclusive and cohesive society.

Government policy, while ostensibly aimed at addressing labor shortages and promoting economic growth through the expansion of foreign worker acceptance, also seeks to mitigate these public concerns through an emphasis on social integration and the maintenance of public safety. The establishment of the Comprehensive Measures Council for Acceptance and Coexistence of Foreign Human Resources, for example, reflects a commitment to facilitating a more harmonious multicultural society. However, policy implementation in crucial areas, such as protecting foreign workers' rights, enhancing social security provisions, and strengthening Japanese language education, has not fully met public expectations. This divergence between stated policy objectives and perceived outcomes underscores the ongoing need for more effective and responsive policy interventions to address the concerns of both the Japanese public and the foreign worker population.

This complex interplay between public opinion and policy is further complicated by a cultural nationalism prevalent in postwar Japan (Liu-Farrer 2020). This ideology, which emphasizes cultural homogeneity and a distinct sense of Japanese identity, has functioned as a significant impediment to a full and transparent acknowledgment of the nation's evolving immigration reality. It has also hindered the development of institutional and cultural frameworks necessary to effectively accommodate the growing immigrant population. Furthermore, this ideology perpetuates a binary distinction between "Japanese" and "foreigner," fostering challenges related to belonging, identity, and social integration for immigrants and their children (Davison and Peng 2021; Laurence et al. 2022).

In contrast to this ideologically motivated reluctance, economic imperatives have steadily increased Japan's reliance on foreign workers, effectively positioning the country as a de facto immigration state. The recent abolition of the TITP and the proposed establishment of a "Nurturing and Working" system may be viewed as preliminary institutional adjustments, signaling a gradual acknowledgment of Japan's evolving immigration reality. Nonetheless, the continued absence of a comprehensive and clearly articulated immigration policy framework poses enduring challenges, particularly in safeguarding the rights of foreign workers and in fostering broader societal recognition and acceptance of immigrants within Japan.

A pressing issue must be addressed. In municipalities such as Kawaguchi City, the rapid increase of foreign residents, including many refugee applicants, exposes structural gaps in migration law. Applicants may reside lawfully or remain de facto without status, creating strains on local communities and recalling the precedent of the Iranian visa waiver, which was terminated after rising public order concerns. Although administrative discretion permits flexible responses, the delineation of responsibilities between national and municipal authorities remains unclear, often leaving local governments to manage social services, housing, and integration support with limited guidance or resources from the central government. Coordination between central and local authorities has been limited, resulting in uneven enforcement, inconsistent support for immigrants, and potential legal uncertainties at the local level.

Finally, a Visa exemption policy exemplifies the tension between diplomatic reciprocity and domestic security. The rule of law requires that discretionary powers be exercised with necessity and proportionality, yet current practice lacks institutional mechanisms to reconcile these imperatives. Developing clear frameworks that define the roles and obligations of national and municipal governments would help ensure that visa and immigration policies are implemented consistently while addressing local needs. A framework for the conditional and transparent revocation of visa exemptions is therefore needed to balance international commitments with the protection of local communities.

5.2 Opportunities

Despite the challenges, these circumstances also present significant opportunities. To effectively capitalize on them, several key areas warrant focused attention.

First, the development and implementation of comprehensive integration strategies are essential to promote social cohesion and intercultural understanding. This includes strengthening language education programs, expanding culturally responsive social services, and fostering cross-cultural dialogue. A practical policy framework should address the identification of responsible entities for implementing language and cultural education, the allocation of adequate financial resources, and the integration of such initiatives within the framework of compulsory education for citizens.

Second, there is a pressing need to reinforce labor protections for foreign workers and to establish clear pathways for career advancement, thereby enabling immigrants to contribute more fully to the Japanese economy and society. Third, policymakers must work to reduce disparities in healthcare access, ensuring that all residents, regardless of immigration status, can obtain timely and appropriate medical care. Finally, engagement with local communities is vital to addressing public perceptions and attitudes, fostering a more inclusive and welcoming environment for immigrants.

While no single comprehensive solution to the complex challenges of immigration exists, scholars and political leaders are pursuing multifaceted approaches. Scholarly contributions span several disciplines. Sociologists and cultural anthropologists focus on fostering social integration and multicultural coexistence by promoting understanding of immigrant cultures and lifestyles, aiming to reduce prejudice and discrimination. Legal and political science scholars advocate for policy changes, including revisions to discriminatory laws and systems, improved refugee recognition processes, and enhanced labor protections for foreign workers. Economists contribute by demonstrating the positive economic impacts of immigration while simultaneously addressing related challenges such as employment disparities.

While Japan's immigration policies often prioritize labor economics, a critical gap exists in addressing the human dimension of immigrant well-being. Although economic contributions are clearly valued, the integration challenges and overall welfare of foreign residents receive comparatively less attention, necessitating stronger institutional support (Keidanren 2022). Counterarguments to prioritizing immigrant well-being often rest on assumptions that economic efficiency should be the primary driver of immigration policy, that cultural homogeneity is crucial for social stability, and that immigrants bear sole responsibility for their successful integration.

However, many scholars challenge these assumptions, advocating for a more comprehensive approach that balances economic benefits with the well-being of all residents (OECD 2019). This necessitates a clear articulation of immigration policy objectives, accompanied by comprehensive plans to mitigate potential challenges associated with increased immigration. Meaningful public discourse, facilitated through various channels such as political parties, non-governmental organizations (NGOs), and community forums, is essential to ensure that policy decisions reflect the diverse perspectives and concerns of the Japanese population. An opaque and unilateral approach, characterized by a lack of transparency and public consultation, is antithetical to democratic principles and risks fueling social anxieties and undermining public trust.

Lastly, immigration policy remains a critical and complex political and social issue with far-reaching implications for a nation's long-term development, social cohesion, and collective identity. It also plays a significant role in shaping democratic legitimacy and national self-conception. Given its significance, immigration policy should not be formulated solely by governing parties, administrative bodies, or their closely affiliated stakeholders. Rather, it requires the broad consent of the public to ensure its legitimacy and sustainability. To that end, fostering informed and inclusive public discourse—with meaningful engagement across all generations—is essential. Without such democratic deliberation and transparency, government policy risks lacking public acceptance, potentially leading to social unrest and avoidable confusion.

5.3 Proposed Actions

The discussion in this chapter has highlighted three interrelated dimensions requiring particular attention in the reform of Japan's immigration policy.

First, structural and legal reform is essential. Japan's immigration governance remains fragmented, lacking a comprehensive statutory framework and relying heavily on administrative discretion. Reform should extend beyond immigration law to encompass related domains such as labor regulation, education, healthcare, and taxation. Only through such an integrated approach can legal certainty be enhanced, policy coherence ensured, and institutional accountability strengthened for both migrants and host communities.

Second, the protection of immigrants' social integration and human rights remains insufficient. Existing policies fail to provide adequate safeguards in critical areas, including labor protections, access to healthcare and education, and structured support for language acquisition and intercultural understanding. Moreover, local authorities often bear the operational responsibility for implementing these protections yet lack sufficient resources, guidance, or coordination with the central government, resulting in uneven access and inconsistent enforcement across municipalities. These deficiencies are particularly severe for low-skilled and undocumented migrants, who face structural barriers that undermine social cohesion and restrict upward mobility. Reform should therefore not be limited to utilitarian considerations but must also engage with communitarian dimensions—such as social identity, shared values, and historical narratives—while clarifying the complementary roles of national and municipal authorities in protecting human rights and facilitating integration so that responsibilities are clearly delineated and operationally feasible.

Third, the democratic legitimacy and sustainability of immigration policy depend on the establishment of transparent and participatory processes. To ensure credibility, inclusive public dialogue must be facilitated with active engagement from diverse stakeholders at both national and local levels. Particular attention should be given to region-specific concerns, whether they arise in densely populated metropolitan areas or in rural districts characterized by depopulation and aging populations. In the absence of broad consent and open deliberation, immigration policy risks exacerbating social division and eroding public trust.

To address these dimensions, this chapter proposes the establishment of a National Forum on Immigration Policy, composed of representatives from ministries, local governments, academia, and civil society and supported by a high-level policy task force under the authority of a cabinet minister. Such a public–private initiative would enable policymaking to proceed in a transparent, participatory, and strategically coordinated manner. The forum could be structured around a public forum, a high-level policy task force, and specialized working groups tasked with deliberating specific issues systematically. Although the process of consensus-building may be time-consuming, it represents a necessary cost of democratic governance and a prerequisite for constructing a sustainable and legitimate immigration policy in Japan.

6 Conclusion

Japan's immigration governance continues to be defined by ambiguity and policy incoherence. The persistent avoidance of the term "immigration policy," reinforced by political rhetoric, has obscured the government's objectives and contributed to public uncertainty. Despite growing dependence on foreign labor, there remains little clarity regarding the long-term direction of policy or the societal role of migrant communities.

Decision-making in this field is further constrained by limited transparency and concentration of authority within the executive. Parliamentary oversight and public deliberation remain minimal, while bureaucratic institutions tend to emphasize administrative control and labor market needs over social, legal, and human rights dimensions. This centralization of authority has also resulted in weak coordination with municipal governments, which often bear the practical burden of implementing integration, welfare, and community support measures without sufficient legal clarity or fiscal support. This narrow framing has left critical challenges of residence, integration, and inclusion insufficiently addressed, thereby weakening the legitimacy and coherence of governance.

At the societal level, the increasing visibility of migrant workers reveals both their essential contributions and the vulnerabilities they face. Social media and transnational communication have further eroded the state's ability to control narratives, exposing gaps between policy intent and lived realities. Municipal initiatives in education, housing, and intercultural programs have begun to fill some of these gaps, yet such efforts remain fragmented and highly dependent on local capacity. These developments highlight the urgency of building governance structures that are transparent, inclusive, and responsive to diverse stakeholders, including local governments, employers, civil society, and migrant communities themselves.

This study underscores that effective immigration governance must be grounded in three interrelated principles. First, foundational legislation should clarify the respective rights and responsibilities of national and municipal authorities to ensure coherent and accountable administration. Second, a comprehensive integration framework must secure labor protections, social inclusion, and equal access to basic public services, thereby enhancing migrants' ability to participate fully in society. Third, democratic legitimacy and sustainability depend on transparent decision-making, inclusive consultation, and independent oversight mechanisms that foster public trust and policy stability.

While this analysis focused on structural and discursive features, future research should incorporate empirical fieldwork and comparative perspectives to evaluate reform outcomes. In particular, examining how local and national actors negotiate their roles in implementing immigration and integration measures will be critical to understanding the evolving nature of Japan's migration governance. Such inquiry will be essential to advancing a more coherent, accountable, and sustainable immigration policy in Japan.

Bibliography

Annio, Francesca. 2025. "Why Is Kawaguchi's Kurdish Community Under Fire?" *Unseen Japan*, June 13. https://unseen-japan.com/kawaguchi-kurdish-community-under-fire/.

Assari, Shervin, and Babak Najand. 2023. "Anti-Immigrant Sentiments and Immigrants' Happiness." *International Journal of Travel Medicine and Global Health* 11 (3): 369–81. https://doi.org/10.30491/IJTMGH.2023.378697.1336.

Borjas, George J. 2019. "Immigration and Economic Growth." Working Paper 25836. National Bureau of Economic Research. Accessed September 16, 2025. http://www.nber.org/papers/w25836.

Cabinet Office of Japan. 2020. "Public Opinion Survey on the Improvement of the Environment for Accepting Foreigners." Survey Conducted in November 2019. Accessed September 16, 2025. [in Japanese]. https://survey.gov-online.go.jp/hutai/r01/r01-gaikokujin.html.

Cao, Thi Khanh Nguyet. 2024. "Materials: Introduction of Japan's Policy to Attract Highly Skilled Human Resources and the German Example." *The Faculty of Economics and Business Administration Journal, KUAS* 7: 39–46. Accessed September 16, 2025. [in Japanese]. https://www.jstage.jst.go.jp/article/kuasjournaleba/2024/7/2024_007_002/_pdf/-char/ja.

Chiavacci, David. 2025. "Dam Break in Japan's Immigration Policy: The 2018 Reform in a Long-Term Perspective." *Social Science Japan Journal* 28 (1). https://doi.org/10.1093/ssjj/jyae033.

Courts of Japan. 1978. "Supreme Court Grand Bench Decision." October 4. Accessed September 16, 2025. [in Japanese]. https://www.courts.go.jp/app/hanrei_jp/detail2?id=53255.

Davison, Jeremy, and Ito Peng. 2021. "Views on Immigration in Japan: Identities, Interests, and Pragmatic Divergence." *Journal of Ethnic and Migration Studies* 47 (11): 2578–95. https://doi.org/10.1080/1369183X.2020.1862645.

Economic and Social Research Institute, Cabinet Office of Japan. 2023. "Effects of Increasing Foreign Workers Using the GMig2 Model." ESRI Research Note no. 73. Accessed September 16, 2025. [in Japanese]. https://www.esri.cao.go.jp/jp/esri/archive/e_rnote/e_rnote080/e_rnote073.pdf.

Fukui, Yoshitaka. 2023. "The Labor Shortage Theory Is a Deceptive Emphasis on Markets." *Seiron* 623: 56–63. [in Japanese].

Fukui, Yoshitaka. 2024. "The Economic Impact of Immigrants Who Do Not Enrich the Nation." *Seiron* 635: 24–31. [in Japanese].

Hashimoto, Naoko. 2019. "Japan Runs the Risk of Repeating the Migration Mistakes Made by the 'West'." *Global Policy*, January 3. Accessed September 16, 2025. https://www.globalpolicyjournal.com/blog/03/01/2019/japan-runs-risk-repeating-migration-mistakes-made-west.

Higuchi, Naoto. 2023. "Japan's Incremental Immigration Reform: A Recipe for Failure." *nippon.com*, August 25. Accessed September 16, 2025. https://www.nippon.com/en/in-depth/d00920/.

Higuchi, Naoto, Nanako Inaba, and Sachi Takaya. 2024. "Japan's Paradoxical Migration Policy." *East Asia Forum*, August 16. https://doi.org/10.59425/eabc.1723802400.

House of Representatives, The Diet of Japan. 2018. "Response to Questions Regarding Foreign Workers and Immigrants Submitted by House of Representatives Member Soichiro Okuno." Accessed September 16, 2025. [in Japanese]. https://www.shugiin.go.jp/internet/itdb_shitsumon.nsf/html/shitsumon/b196104.htm.

Idei, Yasuhiro. *Immigration Crisis: Fake Foreign Students and the Frontline of Slave Labor*. [in Japanese].Kadokawa, 2019.

ISA (Immigration Services Agency) of Japan. 2022a. "Roadmap for the Realization of a Society Living in Harmony with Foreign Nationals."

Accessed September 16, 2025. [in Japanese]. https://www.moj.go.jp/isa/support/coexistence/04_00033.html.

ISA (Immigration Services Agency) of Japan. 2022b. "Research and Studies on the Systems and Environment for Accepting Foreigners in Various Countries." December. Accessed September 16, 2025. [in Japanese]. https://www.moj.go.jp/content/001391730.pdf.

ISA (Immigration Services Agency) of Japan. 2024. "Guidebook on Living and Working: For Foreign Nationals Who Start Living in Japan." Accessed September 16, 2025. https://www.moj.go.jp/content/001297615.pdf.

ISA (Immigration Services Agency) of Japan. 2025a. "Number of Foreign Residents as of the End of 2024." Accessed September 16, 2025. [in Japanese]. https://www.moj.go.jp/isa/publications/press/13_00052.html.

ISA (Immigration Services Agency) of Japan. 2025b. "Comprehensive Measures for Accepting and Coexisting with Foreign Workers." Accessed September 16, 2025. [in Japanese]. https://www.moj.go.jp/isa/support/coexistence/nyuukokukanri01_00140.html.

ISA (Immigration Services Agency) of Japan. 2025c. "Regarding the 2024 Amendment to the Immigration Control Act, etc." Accessed September 16, 2025. [in Japanese]. https://www.moj.go.jp/isa/01_00461.html.

Japan Federation of Bar Associations. 2023. "Statement Opposing the Bill for Amendments to the Immigration Control and Refugee Recognition Act." March 7. Accessed September 16, 2025. https://www.nichibenren.or.jp/en/document/statements/230309.html.

JICA (Japan International Cooperation Agency. 2022. *Foreigners in 2030/40: A Study of Initiatives for a Coexistence Society.* [in Japanese]. March. https://www.jica.go.jp/jica_ri/publication/booksandreports/20220331_01.html.

JITCO (Japan International Trainee & Skilled Worker Cooperation Organization). n.d. "What Is the Technical Intern Training Program?" Accessed September 16, 2025. https://www.jitco.or.jp/en/regulation/index.html.

JNPC (Japan National Press Conference). 2025. "Press Conference by Minister of Justice Keisuke Suzuki." July 30, 2025. Accessed September 16, 2025. [in Japanese]. https://www.youtube.com/watch?v=FMKMIADN1YQ.

Kato, Jotaro. 2019. "Living in 'Illegality': What Makes It Possible for Irregular Migrants to Live in Japan?" *Migration Policy Review* 11: 60–74. [in Japanese]. https://iminseisaku.org/top/pdf/journal/011/011_060.pdf.

Kato, Jotaro, and Gracia Liu-Farrer. 2022. "Becoming Illegal: The Institutional Mechanisms of Migrants' Illegalization in Japan." *Journal of Asia-Pacific Studies* 44: 183–97. https://doi.org/10.57278/wiapstokyu.44.0_183.

Keidanren. 2022. "Innovating Migration Policies." February 15. Accessed September 16, 2025. [in Japanese]. https://www.keidanren.or.jp/policy/2022/016.html.

Kokkonen, Andrej, and Jonas Linde. 2025. "Anti-Immigrant Attitudes and Political Participation in Europe." *Political Studies* 73 (1): 326–46. https://doi.org/10.1177/00323217241241438.

Komine, Ayako. 2014. "When Migrants Became Denizens: Understanding Japan as a Reactive Immigration Country." *Contemporary Japan* 26 (2): 197–222. https://doi.org/10.1515/cj-2014-0010.

Korea Immigration Service, Ministry of Justice of Korea. n.d. "Policy, Resources, and Vision & Mission." Accessed September 16, 2025. https://www.moj.go.kr/moj_eng/1780/subview.do.

Laurence, James, Akira Igarashi, and Kenji Ishida. 2022. "The Dynamics of Immigration and Anti-Immigrant Sentiment in Japan: How and Why Changes in Immigrant Share Affect Attitudes Toward Immigration in a Newly Diversifying Society." *Social Forces* 101 (1): 369–403. https://doi.org/10.1093/sf/soab115.

Lee, Jaeeun. 2024. "Immigration Policy Must Go Beyond Labor Supply: Experts." *The Korea Herald*, September 29. Accessed September 16, 2025. https://www.koreaherald.com/article/3484056.

Liu-Farrer, Gracia. 2020. *Immigrant Japan: Mobility and Belonging in an Ethno-Nationalist Society*. Cornell University Press.

Liu-Farrer, Gracia. 2024. "Immigrant Japan: The Reality of Immigration in a 'No-Immigration' Country." Translated by Yu Korekawa. *The Hitachi Global Foundation Global Society Review* 2: 11–16. Accessed September 16, 2025. https://www.hitachi-zaidan.org/global-society-review/vol2/assets/docs/pdf/vol2_article_gracia-liu-farrer_en.pdf.

Matsumoto, Akane. 2023. "Widespread Labour Standards Violations Among Japanese Businesses with So-Called Technical Interns." *Global Voices*, November 16. Accessed September 16, 2025. https://globalvoices.org/author/a-matsumoto/.

MHLW (Ministry of Health, Labour, and Welfare) of Japan. 2025. "Summary of Reporting Status of 'Employment Status of Foreign Nationals' (as of the End of October 2024)." [in Japanese]. Accessed September 16, 2025. https://www.mhlw.go.jp/stf/newpage_50256.html.

Ministry of Foreign Affairs of Japan. 2023. "Highly Skilled Professional Visa." March 15. Accessed September 16, 2025. https://www.mofa.go.jp/j_info/visit/visa/long/visa16.html.

Ministry of Justice of Japan. 2024. "White Paper on Crime." 2024 English Summary Version. Accessed September 16, 2025. https://www.moj.go.jp/content/001429738.pdf.

Ministry of Justice of Japan. n.d. "Immigration Control of Japanese and Foreign Nationals." Accessed September 16, 2025. https://www.moj.go.jp/ENGLISH/m_hisho06_00044.html.

Miyajima, Takashi. 2022. *Japan as an "Immigration Nation": Prospects for Coexistence* [in Japanese]. Iwanami Shoten.

Nagayoshi, Kikuko, ed. 2021. *Immigrant Integration in Japan: Current Status and Challenges* [in Japanese]. Akashi Shoten.

OECD. 2019. "Towards 2035 Strategic Foresight: Making Migration and Integration Policies Future Ready." Accessed September 16, 2025. https://www.oecd.org/migration/mig/migration-strategic-foresight.pdf.

Prime Minister's Office of Japan. 2019. "Ministerial Council on Acceptance and Inclusion of Foreign Human Resources." March 29. Accessed September 16, 2025. https://japan.kantei.go.jp/98_abe/actions/201903/_00046.html.

Prime Minister's Office of Japan. 2023. "Ministerial Council on Acceptance and Inclusion of Foreign Human Resources." June 9. Accessed September 16, 2025. https://japan.kantei.go.jp/101_kishida/actions/202306/09gaikoku.html.

Prime Minister's Office of Japan. 2025. "Ministerial Council on Acceptance and Inclusion of Foreign Human Resources." June 6. Accessed September 16, 2025. https://japan.kantei.go.jp/103/actions/202506/06gaikoku.html.

Rehm, Maximilien Xavier. 2023. "The Admission of Foreigners as 'Human Resources': The Contradictory Approach of Japan." *Global Resource Management Journal* 9: 74–91. https://doi.org/10.14988/00029524.

Rehm, Maximilien Xavier. 2024. "Re-examining the Roles of the Polity-Bureaucracy-Industry Triad in Japanese Immigration Policymaking: How Have the Major Actors' Levels of Influence Changed Since 1990?" *Electronic Journal of Contemporary Japanese Studies* 24 (1). Accessed September 16, 2025. https://www.japanesestudies.org.uk/ejcjs/vol24/iss1/rehm.html.

Saito, Jun. 2024. "Japan's Immigration Policy: De Jure and De Facto." Japan Center for Economic Research (JCER), December 17. https://www.jcer.or.jp/english/japans-immigration-policy-de-jure-and-de-facto.

Suzuki, Keisuke. 2025. "Immigrants and the Japanese." *The Sankei Shimbun*, August 6. Accessed September 16, 2025. [in Japanese]. https://www.sankei.com/article/20250806-RLPVDBGDRZAZXAA5PEASX6Y-CWA/.

Takaya, Sachi. 2025. "Policy Change and National Identification: The Discursive Institutionalism of Japan's Migrant Admission Policy." *Social Science Japan Journal* 28 (1). https://doi.org/10.1093/ssjj/jyaf002.

The Mainichi. 2024. "Editorial: Foreigners' rights must be protected as Japan's new refugee rules take effect." June 10. https://mainichi.jp/english/articles/20240610/p2a/00m/0op/012000c.

The Mainichi. 2025. "Japan to Review 'Africa Hometown' Program After False Claims About Immigrants Spread Online." September 18. https://mainichi.jp/english/articles/20250917/p2a/00m/0na/016000c.

Tokugawa, Shinji. 2011. "Immigration and Customary International Law: The McLean Case (Supreme Court, October 1978, Fourth Bench Decision)." In *100 Selected International Law Cases*, 2nd ed. [in Japanese], edited by Akira Kodera, Koichi Morikawa, and Yumi Nishimura. Yuhikaku.

United Nations. n.d. "International Migration." Accessed September 16, 2025. https://www.un.org/en/global-issues/migration.

United Nations, Human Rights Committee. 2022. "Concluding Observations on the Seventh Periodic Report of Japan." November 30. Accessed September 16, 2025. https://tbinternet.ohchr.org/_layouts/15/treaty-bodyexternal/Download.aspx?symbolno=CCPR%2FC%2FJPN%2F-CO%2F7&Lang=en.

Wakisaka, Daisuke. 2024. "Unraveling Migration Policy-Making in the Land of 'No Immigrants': Japanese Bureaucracy and the Discursive Gap." *International Migration Review* 58 (3): 1507–31. https://doi.org/10.1177/01979183231171557.

Watado, Ichiro. 2019. "Reconsidering 'Multicultural Symbiosis' in Japan: Between 'Multiculturalism' and 'Interculturalism'." *Migration Policy Review* 11: 187–207. [in Japanese]. https://iminseisaku.org/top/pdf/journal/011/011_188.pdf.

Yamada, Jun. 2018. "Why Are 'Foreign Workers' Not Called 'Immigrants'? Government and Media Framing in Japan." *Yahoo News Japan*, October 28. Accessed September 16, 2025. [in Japanese]. https://

news.yahoo.co.jp/expert/articles/7c5b33baf16e814c06313258cd3b-
34deb35ff5db.

PART III

Human Rights, Ethics, and Social Structures

CHAPTER 9

The Silent Influence: How Sub-Societal Structures Shape Sexual Violence in Japan

Abstract

Despite legal reforms and growing social media discourse, sexual violence in Japan remains underreported due to cultural taboos and the influence of insular sub-societal structures. This study examines the structural factors that sustain sexual violence, focusing on sub-societies—distinct groups with unique norms that shape attitudes and responses to such violence. Drawing on Durkheim's concept of collective consciousness, Weber's analysis of power structures, and Giddens' theory of structuration, the study explores how sub-societal norms perpetuate and conceal sexual violence. Through an interdisciplinary review of English and Japanese literature, the findings highlight power imbalances, gender inequality, and the closed nature of sub-societies as key contributors. Examples include sports clubs, fraternities, workplaces, and the entertainment industry, where internal norms often override legal standards, fostering environments that condone abuse. To counter these hidden influences, this chapter proposes the following: (i) reforming sub-societal norms to promote zero tolerance for sexual violence, (ii) strengthening whistleblower protections, and (iii) implementing audits and external monitoring, including establishing an independent national human rights institution. This study underscores the structural role of sub-societies in sustaining sexual violence, providing a foundation for further research and policy interventions.

Keywords: Sexual Violence, Sub-Society, Structure, Sociology, Norms

1 Introduction

Japan has been characterized by some observers as exhibiting a degree of social and legal leniency toward individuals convicted of sexual offenses. For instance, Johnson (2024) reports that while Japanese police claim to solve 97% of reported rape cases, systemic underreporting and selective recording obscure the reality. For every 1,000 rapes in Japan, only 10 to 20 result in criminal convictions, and fewer than half of those convicted face incarceration. While this perspective may be considered untenable, certain elements warrant consideration in the context of recent media reports of sexual violence in Japan.

One interpretation of this phenomenon suggests that it stems from a perception of a male-dominated society, exemplified by the patriarchal tenets of the older civil code before December 1947 (Johnson 2024). This hypothesis remains difficult to substantiate due to the lack of empirical evidence, posing challenges for its validation. In the context of Japanese society, discourse concerning sexual violence has historically been subject to social taboo and marginalization. A key barrier to public awareness of sexual violence is the limited availability of opportunities to educate the public on its nature and underlying causes.

An alternative interpretation is rooted in the legal perspective on sexual offenses, which presents a more concrete basis for analysis (Kemp 2020). In September 2014, Minister of Justice Midori Matsushima highlighted the peculiar fact that rape was regarded as a less grave offense than robbery, prompting a review of the Penal Code's Sexual Offenses. This review culminated in the revision of the Penal Code in June 2017, which was subsequently amended and re-enacted in July 2023, aiming to improve the handling of cases of sexual violence within the criminal justice system (Ministry of Justice of Japan 2023). However, these legislative reforms have yielded limited changes in public perceptions of sexual violence, although they have demonstrably improved the legislative framework. The long-term impact on public awareness remains to be determined.

Recent technological developments, particularly the proliferation of social media, have begun to transform public discourse regarding sexual violence. This shift has increased transparency in discussions on the subject but has also led to some confusion. These platforms enable individuals to express their opinions and share factual information.

Consequently, concerns regarding sexual violence that were previously concealed are now being brought to the fore, thereby encouraging a more extensive discourse. However, the number of women who discuss sexual violence remains limited, and the vast majority of victims of sexual violence remain silent in Japan (Japan P.E.N. Club 2024; Osawa 2025).

The term sexual violence is broad in scope, encompassing a wide range of behaviors. These include sexual assault, rape, domestic violence, dating sexual violence, and stalking (University of California, n.d.). Sexual violence is defined as any sexual act, attempt to obtain a sexual act, or other act directed against a person's sexuality using coercion, by any person regardless of their relationship with the victim, in any setting (WHO, n.d.). According to the legal definition outlined in the Penal Code of Japan, which was revised in July 2023, sexual offenses are defined as any sexual behavior that occurs without the consent of the other individual, thereby violating bodily integrity and the right to sexual self-determination (Ministry of Justice of Japan 2023). This legal definition underscores the parties' free and voluntary consent, thereby distinguishing sexual offenses from sexual violence.

In this chapter, the term sexual violence is specified herein as physical and psychological sexual abuse against adults, to narrow the scope of the discussion. Consequently, the scope of this chapter does not extend to sexual violence against minors, as it necessitates a separate and distinct systematic consideration.

Sexual violence is a serious human rights violation and must not be tolerated. A taxonomy of sexual violence perpetration processes has been identified from the narrative, categorized as follows: the surprise type, the type involving alcohol and drug use, the sexual abuse type, and the entrapment type (Saito and Okamoto 2022). Sexual violence is frequently perpetrated through the exercise of power or superiority. When addressing the issue of sexual violence, it is insufficient to solely focus on the actions of the perpetrator; the social environment and cultural background of both the perpetrator and the victim must be considered to elucidate the structural factors that give rise to sexual violence. While a multitude of social factors contribute to sexual violence (Stermac et al. 1990), this study will focus on one aspect of the mechanism of its occurrence, namely, the concept of sub-society as used in sociology.

In jurisprudence, the doctrine of partial societies holds that judicial review does not apply within such groups but covers events affecting the external legal order. For example, sanctions for violating school or company rules, like expulsion or dismissal, are internal matters, and compensation claims are not subject to judicial review (Westlaw Japan 2018). The concept of a sub-society in sociology differs from its legal counterpart. A sub-society is defined as a social group that constitutes a part of the larger society; possesses a distinct function or purpose; or is characterized by a particular regional or cultural background; and shares common values, norms, and modes of behavior. The spectrum of sub-societies is extensive, encompassing workplaces, educational institutions, associations, and local communities, among others.

Sub-societies frequently possess their own unwritten norms and standards of behavior, which exert influence on the behavior of their members. The reality of such sub-societies is often challenging for external observers to ascertain. At times, the unique norms of a sub-society are elevated above general social norms by its members and accorded precedence in terms of observance. In the event of deviations from established norms, the prevailing sentiment often suggests that the "atmosphere" of the local or community exerts considerable influence (Tanaka 1989). It is asserted that the prevailing atmosphere of a particular milieu exerts a dominant influence on its constituents, subsuming individual autonomy and the right to self-determination. Consequently, individuals find themselves constrained to adhere to the prevailing norms and regulations of that particular social group, a phenomenon that might be attributed to peer pressure.

An examination of the relationship between the prioritization of these distinctive norms and sexual violence may yield insights into the underlying causes of sexual violence and inform the development of effective prevention strategies. Sociologists such as Émile Durkheim (1858–1917), Max Weber (1864–1920), and Anthony Giddens (1938–) have explored the influence of norms within social organizations from their own perspectives. Despite the differences in their respective historical backgrounds and geographical locations, the application of these theories to contemporary Japan offers insights into the unique norms that shape sub-societies and the mechanisms through which these norms exert social influence.

This chapter, therefore, examines the silent, structural factors influencing sexual violence in Japan, with a focus on how distinct sub-societal norms contribute to attitudes that perpetuate such violence.

2 Methodology

The study's methodology constitutes a comprehensive literature survey in English and Japanese, encompassing interdisciplinary research, including sociology, social psychology, and jurisprudence. A literature survey in English and Japanese has been conducted with key words, such as "sexual violence," "sub-society," "sexual violence sub-society norms," and "sociological factors in sexual violence." The volume of Japanese literature on sexual violence is limited in scope, particularly with regard to academic analysis. To address this gap, the study incorporates public lectures related to sexual violence held in Tokyo to augment the literature survey. This study references recent Japanese translations of sociological works.

The deaths of prominent postwar figures in Japan have precipitated a shift in power dynamics, bringing to light issues that had previously been disregarded. A prominent example is Johnny Kitagawa, who held noteworthy influence over Japan's entertainment industry, encompassing television, radio, print media, live performances, music, sport events, and advertising (Kinoshita 2024). Following his demise in July 2019, allegations of sexual impropriety involving over 1,000 male minors became known, with his company now providing compensation to the victims. Another case involves a male celebrity who had a close association with Kitagawa. This individual abruptly retired from the entertainment industry following a widely publicized assault on a female television announcer. This incident resulted in criticism of Fuji Television Network and Fuji Media Holdings for their alleged failure to uphold corporate governance standards, specifically regarding the protection of employee human rights as mandated by the governance code (Ishikawa and Zheng 2025).

Due to the lack of available details, these cases are not well suited for academic analysis at this stage. Consequently, this study adopts a more expansive perspective, encompassing a comprehensive examination of the underlying mechanisms of sexual violence within the broader context of sub-society. The objective of this study is twofold: first, to identify a mechanism that explains the occurrence of sexual violence from the perspective of a sub-society and, second, to explore the discourse surrounding sexual violence as an issue of citizenship to investigate the preventive measures.

The subsequent research questions have been formulated to guide the investigation:

1. In what ways do sub-societal structures contribute to the occurrence of sexual violence, as analyzed through the lens of sociological theories of Durkheim, Weber, and Giddens?
2. What preventive measures can be implemented to address sexual violence, informed by the findings of this analysis and the identified characteristics of sexual violence?

This chapter opens with a comprehensive review of the extant literature on sub-societies and sexual violence, focusing on their distinguishing characteristics. It then moves on to analyze how the unique norms in sub-societies influence the occurrence of sexual violence. The analysis reveals that sexual violence is not merely an individual problem for perpetrators and victims; it is also associated with social and cultural factors. The chapter then considers which approaches are effective in preventing sexual violence based on the sexual violence mechanism and proposes preventive measures.

3 Sub-Societies and Sexual Violence

3.1 Specific Examples of Sub-Societies

Sub-societies are defined as small groups or subgroups within a larger societal context. These groups are distinguished by their unique values and norms and can range from everyday organizations such as families, workplaces, associations, and local communities to more exclusive groups like university clubs or business units of companies. It is important to note that the norms within these sub-societies may not always align with the legal and moral norms of general society and that in some cases, they may even contradict them. These distinctive norms can exert a detrimental influence on society and shape behavior and values within the designated sub-society (Tanaka 1989). Consequently, it is imperative to address the question of how these unique norms influence society and assess their positive and negative impacts. In order to comprehend the characteristics of sub-societies, it is imperative to provide concrete examples.

A notable example of a sub-society is represented by sports clubs. These organizations prioritize a robust sense of solidarity and teamwork, where attaining victory and accomplishing objectives are of the utmost importance. Consequently, internal norms often supersede those of the broader society. For instance, it has been documented that bullying and violence among players is rationalized in certain sports clubs as a means of strengthening team cohesion (Endo 2020). Moreover, a pervasive reluctance to report sexual violence externally, in favor of addressing such issues internally, has been observed.

A notable example of this phenomenon is the practice known as *kawaigari* ("adoration") in the sumo-wrestling world, which has been interpreted as a form of aggressive training for younger wrestlers. This practice has, in certain instances, resulted in injuries and even fatalities. A notable incident that exemplifies this dynamic occurred in June 2007, prior to the Nagoya sumo tournament, where a young wrestler was assaulted and killed by the stablemaster and others in Inuyama City (McCurry 2008).

Second, university student friendship clubs (fraternities) have been identified as a notable form of sub-society. These fraternities, particularly those found in Western universities, tend to be closed and emphasize traditional rituals and customs, fostering an environment conducive to sexual violence and harassment (Boyle 2024). Even when victims report incidents, they may be silenced to preserve the group's reputation and traditions. Thus, the unique norms in sub-societies increase the likelihood of encouraging sexual violence.

In Japan, the emergence of cult religious groups has been observed to have a significant impact on societal behavior, often exhibiting characteristics that are in opposition to established societal norms. This phenomenon draws parallels to the antisocial activities perpetrated by Aum Shinrikyo, a notable example being the sarin gas attack on the Tokyo subway that occurred on March 20, 1995 (Public Security Intelligence Agency of Japan 2020).

In the context of corporate workplaces, these environments can also be considered sub-societies due to their unique social structures and power dynamics. In workplaces with rigid hierarchies and pronounced power imbalances, the risk of sexual violence and harassment is notably elevated. The extended working hours and substantial hierarchical pressures can contribute to the cultivation of an environment where unprofessional behavior is often overlooked, thereby hindering the effective deterrence of sexual violence (Human Rights Watch 2018). If unaddressed, misconduct can lead to the normalization of violent behavior within such workplaces.

Journalist Jibu proposes a series of recommendations aimed at addressing sexual violence at both the individual and the organizational levels (Jibu 2018). At the individual level, it is essential for individuals to accept the statements of sexual violence victims as factual and refer them to support organizations, such as one-stop centers. At the organizational level, companies must administer consequences to perpetrators, reframe sexual harassment as a "diversity" issue rather than merely a "risk," and continue employing individuals who have confessed to sexual violence. This approach fosters accountability and rehabilitation within the workplace.

The entertainment industry, regarded as a distinct sub-society with its own set of norms, offers a pertinent example (Park 2023). When a major corporation engages with the entertainment industry, it holds a position of influence, enabling it to regulate its governance through contractual agreements. However, there is a possibility that the corporation might acquiesce to the unique norms of the entertainment industry, thereby impeding its own governance function. This phenomenon, if unaddressed, can potentially compromise the company's social credibility due to the failure of its internal audit or trade union to adequately cleanse.

The analysis thus underscores the reinforcement of norms within a sub-society and the subsequent divergence from the legal and ethical standards of general society, particularly in cases where a company's interaction with the entertainment industry is substantial. Furthermore, when the unique norms of one sub-society invade the domain of another sub-society, the negative effect is that their influence will be transferred to the sub-society and eventually spread, further widening the gap between the unique norms of the sub-society and the legal and ethical norms of general society. In the absence of awareness regarding these deleterious consequences, the phenomenon is likely to persist, thereby amplifying the risk of sexual violence outbreaks within sub-society.

3.2 Sociologists' Theories in the Sub-Society Context

In the event that a possibility of violence or abuse exists within a given sub-society, the question must be raised as to why sexual violence manifests itself among the various forms of violence or abuse. In order to provide a satisfactory answer to this question, it is necessary to explore the structural factors that underpin sexual violence, with reference to the sociologists' theories.

Durkheim's perspective on society as a system of norms regulating individual behavior is particularly relevant in this context (Durkheim 2018). He emphasizes that norms within a sub-society exert considerable influence on individual actions, shaping behavior through shared values and expectations. His concept of collective consciousness elucidates how these shared norms function as regulatory mechanisms, reinforcing group cohesion and guiding individual conduct. Human behavior and thought are shaped by social conventions and local customs that extend beyond individual agency, manifesting as societal expectations. Furthermore, Durkheim's theory anticipates the increasing specialization and the corresponding emergence of distinct normative frameworks within sub-societies, a phenomenon intrinsically linked to the advancement of the social division of labor.

Weber's seminal work explores the intricate relationship between societal structures and norms, providing extensive analyses of how interactions within sub-societies influence broader social dynamics (Weber 2023, 2024). His examination of bureaucracies illustrates how internally established rules and conventions not only regulate the behavior of members but also serve as mechanisms for transmitting sub-societal norms into the larger societal framework (Weber 2012). This process underscores the structured yet dynamic nature of normative diffusion. Moreover, Weber's discussion of charismatic domination highlights its potential as a transformative force, capable of disrupting established norms within sub-societies and, in some cases, reshaping societal structures at large. By juxtaposing bureaucratic rationalization with charismatic influence, Weber provides a nuanced perspective on how sub-societal norms emerge, persist, and evolve within the broader social order.

Giddens employs structuration theory to examine the dynamic interplay between sub-societies and the broader societal structure (Giddens 2015, 2021). He highlights the significance of temporal and spatial dimensions in shaping and sustaining social norms, emphasizing that while sub-societies provide individuals with a sense of security, their norms may sometimes conflict with external societal norms, leading to tensions. Within this framework, agency and structure interact dynamically—structures shape human actions, but actors simultaneously reproduce and transform these structures. Institutionalized practices persist through habitual actions, and social interactions unfold within specific temporal and spatial contexts. Furthermore, practical consciousness plays a crucial role in guiding behavior, often unconsciously reinforcing existing norms. Thus, human actions in sub-societies are not mere reflections of structure but actively contribute to its maintenance and evolution.

3.3 Sociologists' Theories Applied to Sexual Violence

A key factor contributing to sexual violence is power imbalance. According to Max Weber, power is defined as the ability to realize one's own will, even to the exclusion of the resistance of others. In this context, sexual violence can be conceptualized as a means through which those in positions of authority reinforce their dominant social position over those subject to their authority and impose their will on the subjugated. In contexts characterized by closed environments and rigid hierarchical structures, the likelihood of sexual violence as a means of control is amplified (Saito 2024). For instance, in professional settings such as workplaces and sports clubs, supervisors, managers, and senior staff may exploit their authority to perpetrate sexual violence against their subordinates and players. In such contexts, sexual violence transcends the realm of personal desires, serving as a means to wield power and control over others. The pervasiveness of such structures of control fosters an environment conducive to the recurrence of sexual violence within specific settings.

Durkheim's concept of collective consciousness offers a framework for understanding the prevalence of sexual violence in relation to cultural and social norms. Within a given sub-society, its norms are shaped by the collective consciousness shared by its members, and these norms may be interpreted and justified within the sub-society even if they contradict the legal and ethical norms of external society. For instance, within university student fellowship and sports clubs, where specific rituals and customs are regarded as traditions, sexual violence may be tolerated as an integral component of the organization's culture. When sexual violence is enacted as a rite of passage for newcomers or as a bonding act, both victims and perpetrators often rationalize it, perceiving it not as a problem. This internalization of norms, in which sexual violence becomes an accepted practice within specific social groups, contributes to its normalization (Saito 2024).

Sexual violence is intrinsically linked to gender inequality (Osawa 2023a, 2023b). Historically, social structures that have placed men in a dominant position over women have created a fertile environment for sexual violence. From a feminist standpoint, sexual violence is regarded as a manifestation of systemic gender inequality. It functions as a means to perpetuate gender inequality, with men leveraging it as a tool to dominate women. In certain male-dominated sports clubs and workplaces, for instance, women are subjected to inappropriate treatment, and sexual violence is glorified as a manifestation of masculinity. These social structures, in their role in perpetuating gender inequality, not only tolerate sexual violence but also accelerate its incidence.

The insular nature of sub-societies is a significant factor contributing to sexual violence. According to an analysis based on Giddens' theory of structuration, the temporal and spatial characteristics within the sub-society make it difficult for external intervention and contribute to the fixation of internal norms. Closed environments conceal sexual violence when it occurs and make it difficult for victims to speak out. For instance, within professional environments and sports clubs, sexual violence may be uncovered but concealed to protect the reputation of the organization as a whole. This concealment can impede opportunities for prevention, contributing to further victimization.

The analysis underscores the necessity to view sexual violence not merely as an individual problem but as a phenomenon rooted in social and structural factors. The analysis posits that the power structure in certain societies, the formation of specific norms through collective consciousness, gender inequality, closure and concealment, and other factors interact to promote the occurrence of sexual violence.

3.4 Structural Factors Contributing to Sexual Violence in Sub-Society

The preceding analysis emphasizes the importance of understanding sexual violence not solely as an individual issue but as a phenomenon embedded within social and structural contexts. Specifically, the power structures within sub-societies, as theorized by Weber, the formation of specific norms through collective consciousness, gender inequality, and the closed and concealed nature of these groups interact to perpetuate sexual violence. As previously discussed, these interactions can be distilled into three key factors that contribute to the persistence of sexual violence within sub-societal structures. The promotion of sexual violence in sub-society can be influenced by three main factors, as was discussed.

First, the preeminence of distinct norms within a sub-society can be problematic, as illustrated by Durkheim's concept of collective consciousness.

In instances where sub-societies are characterized by the predominance of their own distinct overriding norms, these norms have the capacity to supersede the legal and moral norms that are extant in general society. Consequently, these norms can serve to legitimize sexual violence. For instance, groups such as sports clubs and university student friendship clubs frequently prioritize cohesion, loyalty, and in-group cohesion. Within these groups, there is a tendency to prioritize internal norms over external norms and ethics, which can result in the concealment of reported cases of sexual violence. The emphasis on togetherness within the group may lead to an internal cover-up of the act or protection of the perpetrator when sexual violence occurs. This distinctive social environment is a probable facilitator of sexual violence.

Second, the act of whistleblowing is fraught with difficulty. In sub-societies individuals who expose malpractice or wrongdoing are frequently stigmatized as traitors, thereby discouraging external interference (Foxley 2019). This dynamic engenders a pervasive culture of silence, where victims and witnesses of sexual violence face significant challenges in articulating their experiences. Whistleblowing is often met with skepticism and resistance within the group, as it is perceived as a threat to the integrity and cohesion of the collective. The whistleblower is often subjected to social disapproval and may face disadvantages in terms of social standing, relationships, and opportunities within the group. This dynamic engenders an environment where instances of sexual violence are frequently underreported, perpetuating a cycle of harm that remains unaddressed and potentially leads to the recurrence of such violations (Stewart et al. 2024). The barriers that hinder whistleblowing contribute to the concealment of sexual violence and the avoidance of appropriate punishment for perpetrators. Furthermore, victims of sexual assault may become targets of vilification through social media. This phenomenon also hinders victims from filing charges.

Third, the complexity of external intervention represents a significant contributing factor as informed by Giddens' theory of structuration. In instances where social circles are characterized by a high degree of closure, external intervention becomes an exceedingly challenging endeavor. Even when external bodies such as law enforcement or judicial institutions initiate investigations, internal cover-ups and the destruction of evidence can impede the process. Within these sub-societies, external norms and legal authority are often not applicable, leading to underreporting of sexual violence and a lack of appropriate legal action. This environment fosters an environment conducive to the proliferation of sexual violence and increases the probability that perpetrators will evade accountability. A prime example of this phenomenon is sexual violence within the family.

The interplay of three interconnected factors—the dominance of internal norms, challenges in whistleblowing, and difficulties in external intervention—creates an environment that facilitates the persistence of sexual violence within sub-societies. The distinctive values and norms within this sub-society, coupled with its insular culture, can create a situation that conceals sexual violence and protects perpetrators, thereby encouraging its occurrence. Consequently, it is imperative to understand the existence and impact of these phenomena.

4 Sexual Violence and Its Prevention

4.1 Data and Policy for Sexual Violence in Japan

The prevalence of sexual violence in Japan is a matter of concern, particularly among younger age groups. According to data from the Cabinet Office of Japan (2024), over one in four individuals aged 16 to 24 (both males and females) have experienced some form of sexual violence, with 12.4% reporting physical contact and 4.1% experiencing non-consensual sexual intercourse. A salient feature of this phenomenon is the fact that a considerable proportion of perpetrators are known to the victims, with incidents perpetrated by strangers accounting for approximately 10% of the total. Furthermore, there has been a notable increase in the number of reported cases of forcible sexual intercourse, reaching 2,711 in 2023 (+52% from 2018). It is also worth noting that over 80% of victims are under the age of 30.

In response to these statistics, the Japanese government has strengthened its measures against sexual crimes and violence. Legal reforms, such as raising the age of consent from 13 to 16, aim to enhance legal responses. Victim support systems have been improved through the establishment of one-stop support centers, which provide comprehensive assistance and coordinate with medical institutions and law enforcement. Annually, one-stop support centers document an escalation in consultations (+97.5% between 2018 and 2023), accompanied by a substantial surge in male clients (+205% between 2018 and 2023). Efforts to prevent secondary victimization include refining evidence collection and storage procedures. Furthermore, educational initiatives like "life safety education" and campaigns such as "Youth Sexual Violence Prevention Month" seek to increase public awareness and promote societal change (Cabinet Office of Japan 2025).

However, significant challenges persist. Many victims still struggle to seek help, with over half of female victims and nearly 60% of male victims refusing to disclose their experiences (Cabinet Office of Japan 2025). Support systems for male victims and younger individuals remain underdeveloped. Addressing unreported cases remains a critical issue, necessitating enhanced early detection mechanisms and support structures within communities and schools. While Japan has made progress in addressing sexual violence through policy reforms and support initiatives, there are substantial gaps in societal awareness and robust support systems that underscore the need for continued and intensified efforts to eradicate this pervasive problem (Uchida 2020).

4.2 How Sexual Violence Has Been Addressed in Japan

In order to understand the characteristics of sexual violence, it is necessary to consider how this issue has been addressed in Japanese society. The subject of sexual violence has long been regarded as a taboo, and it has been extremely difficult for victims to make their experiences public. This is because victims often experience a state of emotional distress, finding it difficult to disclose their experiences of sexual violence due to the prevailing societal attitudes. Even when victims confide in family members, perpetrators often downplay the harm and pressure them to remain silent. Moreover, even in cases where victims do come forward, there is often a lack of acceptance of their reports by law enforcement agencies (Saito 2024; Osawa 2023a).

A salient feature of sexual violence cases is that even when victims do come forward, they are often met with defamation rather than empathy. This pervasive issue, compounded by the ambiguity surrounding its definition and the societal reluctance to address it, has led to a state of long-standing underreporting and under-acknowledgment of sexual violence. Consequently, the prevalence of sexual violence remains obscured by government statistics, effectively consigning it to the shadows (Japan P.E.N. Club 2024; Osawa 2025). In many cases, victims continue to suffer in silence. A lack of an initiative-taking stance on addressing sexual violence has contributed to a perpetuation of its harmful effects.

Recent advancements in this field commenced with the disclosure of individual experiences concerning sexual violence by victims on social media platforms as part of the feminist movement in the United States. In Japan, female victims of sexual violence also disclosed their real names, garnering societal attention. For instance, the BBC has reported on the attempted rape case of journalist Shiori Ito, which took place in April 2015. This case was featured in the 2018 BBC television documentary *Japan's Secret Shame* and later in the documentary film *Black Box Diaries*, produced by Ito. While Ito won the civil lawsuit, the suspect was not indicted in the criminal case. This outcome highlights significant challenges within Japan's legal system regarding sexual violence (Kyodo News 2022).

Research on sexual violence in Japan is gradually advancing. These analyses explore how social norms and cultural contexts influence victims' behavior (NHK 2022; Saito 2024; Osawa 2023a, 2023b). Of particular interest are studies of cases involving sexual violence within a specific sub-society where norms deviating from legal and moral standards of the general population may prevail, potentially leading to the condoning or concealment of sexual violence (Ito 2001; Maenosono 2022).

Notable examples of this phenomenon include the long-standing case of Johnny Kitagawa's sexual assault of young boys and the case of Jimmy Savile on the British public service broadcaster BBC (Saisho 2024). In these cases, the peculiar norms of the sub-society suppressed the voices of the victims, and the perpetration continued for a protracted period. In the Kitagawa case, the industry's awareness of the perpetrator's actions was widely acknowledged, even by the courts for civil law cases. However, stakeholders, including the police, did not take any preventive action.

A parallel tendency was identified in the BBC's management of the Savile case, which was denounced as an implicit endorsement of the accused's behavioral comparable tendency manifested in the Weinstein case in the United States, where Weinstein utilized his predominant status in the entertainment industry to impose a confidentiality agreement that muzzled the victim's testimony (Hagiwara 2023). This case study underscores the potential for sexual violence to be concealed within specific industries and groups.

An analysis of these cases reveals that sexual violence is not only an individual act but also a phenomenon fostered by social context and structure. In particular, in sub-societies the social environment that fosters sexual violence is established. Understanding this structure is essential for addressing the issue. To elucidate the characteristics of sexual violence, a critical analysis of the social background and structure is necessary, as well as an examination of the relationship with general society. The development of social systems and environments that empower victims to come forward and the enhancement of the transparency and reformulation of the norms of these sub-societies are crucial steps in this direction. Through these efforts, the establishment of concrete measures to eradicate sexual violence becomes attainable.

4.3 How Sexual Violence Can Be Prevented

In order to establish effective preventative measures for sexual violence, it is crucial to consider the unique characteristics of sub-societies. The rationale behind this necessity stems from the potential for closed cultural norms and unique social structures within sub-societies to foster an environment conducive to sexual violence. Consequently, it is imperative to implement preventative measures that address these distinctive characteristics. The following three approaches have been identified as effective preventative measures to address sexual violence. These approaches include a review of existing norms, the strengthening of whistleblower protection systems, and the implementation of internal audits and external monitoring. These measures are designed to address the three structural factors contributing to sexual violence in sub-society, as previously discussed.

The initial step in this process is a re-evaluation of the original norms of the sub-society. In the event that the norms within the sub-society give rise to a culture that condones sexual violence, the first step is to re-evaluate those norms and cultivate a culture that does not condone sexual violence (Perrin et al. 2019). The onus falls particularly heavily on leaders who occupy positions of influence within the sub-society. For instance, the director of a sports club or the secretary of a university student friendship club must explicitly state a policy of zero tolerance for sexual violence and ensure its enforcement within the organization. By unequivocally declaring their commitment to zero tolerance, leaders can reshape the values and codes of conduct of the entire organization, thereby generating social pressure to prevent sexual violence. This necessity extends to corporate human rights governance, where effective implementation mechanisms are essential.

Second, it is imperative to fortify the whistleblowing protection system. In a sub-society, whistleblowers are frequently stigmatized as traitors, and this can readily engender a scenario where whistleblowing is discouraged. To mitigate the risk of whistleblowers being subjected to reprisals, it is crucial to implement systems to safeguard them. Examples of such measures include the implementation of social media reporting systems, mechanisms that facilitate anonymous whistleblowing, and legal and organizational frameworks designed to prevent retaliation and defamation following whistleblowing. These measures foster a secure environment for victims and witnesses to come forward, thereby facilitating the identification and reporting of sexual violence. The enhancement of whistleblower protection is also anticipated to bolster social resistance to sexual violence and prevent cover-ups within organizational settings. It is imperative to avoid the application of the conventional "fight-or-flight" response and to adopt solutions that obfuscate the issue.

Finally, the implementation of internal audits and external monitoring can be efficacious. In the context of closed sub-societies, internal problems are less likely to be recognized by external observers, thereby increasing the likelihood of misconduct, including sexual violence, being concealed (Banyard 2020). For this reason, the introduction of mechanisms for internal auditing and external monitoring can be effective. One such mechanism could be the establishment of a national human rights institution, operating with independence from government, to oversee any transgressions within these sub-societies. This institution would be obligated to respond promptly to emerging issues and to play a role in evaluating and enhancing the situation from a neutral vantage point. The Japanese government has not accepted the establishment of a national human rights institution that would be independent from the government and based on the 1993 Paris Principles. This approach would contribute to the dissolution of the insular character of these sub-societies, thereby deterring sexual violence (Japan P.E.N. Club 2024).

The implementation of the aforementioned preventive measures will establish a solid foundation to prevent sexual violence. It is imperative to acknowledge that preventing sexual violence entails not only enhancements in individual conduct but also a transformation in societal perceptions to cultivate human capital to avoid sexual violence (Ilabaca Baeza et al. 2022). Consequently, it is paramount to undertake periodic reviews of cultural values and social norms, nurturing a culture of communication and mutual respect within a thriving society. Educational initiatives and awareness-raising activities within sub-societies have also been shown to be efficacious in deterring sexual violence. It is of the utmost importance to prioritize responses to victims of sexual violence within the community. In addition to immediate responses, the implementation of restorative justice (Keenan and Zinsstag 2022) could be a valuable approach, although this is a matter for future consideration.

5 Conclusion

This study examines the structural factors that contribute to sexual violence in Japan, focusing on how sub-societal norms shape attitudes and responses to such violence. Despite recent legal reforms and growing public awareness, sexual violence remains underreported and inadequately addressed due to entrenched social norms and institutional barriers. Through a comprehensive literature review, this study applies sociological theories from Durkheim, Weber, and Giddens to analyze the role of sub-societies—such as sports clubs, university fraternities, corporate workplaces, and the entertainment industry—in perpetuating sexual violence. These groups often develop insular norms that override legal and ethical standards, fostering environments where misconduct is tolerated or concealed.

The findings highlight key structural factors, including power imbalances, collective consciousness, and gender inequality, which sustain sexual violence within these sub-societies. Addressing these issues requires targeted interventions, including: (i) reforming internal norms to promote a zero-tolerance culture, (ii) strengthening whistleblower protections to encourage reporting without fear of retaliation, and (iii) implementing external oversight mechanisms, such as an independent national human rights institution. These measures are essential for dismantling systemic barriers and fostering a culture of accountability.

This study is limited by its theoretical approach, as it relies primarily on literature review rather than empirical data. This reflects the broader challenge of conducting empirical research on sexual violence in Japan. However, the theoretical analysis remains valuable given the scarcity of scholarship on this issue. Future research should incorporate case studies and empirical investigations to deepen understanding and inform more effective policy responses.

Acknowledgment

The author acknowledges the in-person public lecture by Machiko Osawa, sponsored by Tokyo College, the University of Tokyo, on January 21, 2025, which inspired this chapter.

AI Acknowledgment

The author acknowledges the use of the AI systems, including ChatGPT, DeepL, GEMINI, and Perplexity, for translation from Japanese to English and English editing work as well as in the preparation of this manuscript, but no use of generative AI or AI-assisted technologies in completion of the essential authoring tasks in this manuscript. The prompts used include "Please translate this sentence into English," "Please correct this sentence to align with academic writing standards," and "Please present available statistics concerning sexual violence in Japan." The output from these prompts was used for English writing, English editing, and data analysis.

Informed Consent

The authors declare that informed consent was not required as there were no human participants involved.

Conflict of Interest

The authors declare that there is no conflict of interest.

Bibliography

Banyard, Victoria L., Katie M. Edwards, Andrew J. Rizzo, Emily F. Rothman, Patricia Greenberg, and Megan C. Kearns. 2020. "Improving Social Norms and Actions to Prevent Sexual and Intimate Partner Violence: A Pilot Study of the Impact of Green Dot Community on Youth." *Journal of Prevention and Health Promotion* 1 (2): 183–211. https://doi.org/10.1177/2632077020966571.

Boyle, Kaitlin M. 2024. "Social Psychological Processes That Facilitate Sexual Assault Within the Fraternity Party Subculture." *Sociology Compass* 9 (5): 1–16. https://doi.org/10.1111/soc4.12261.

Cabinet Office of Japan. 2024. "Progress of Measures against Sexual Crimes and Sexual Violence." Material No. 2 in the National Forum on Life Safety Education Held on April 1. Accessed April 2, 2025. [in Japanese]. https://www.gender.go.jp/kaigi/senmon/boryoku/siryo/pdf/bo124-3.pdf.

Cabinet Office of Japan. 2025. "Section 2 Sexual Crimes and Sexual Violence, White Paper on Gender Equality 2024." Accessed April 2, 2025. [in Japanese]. https://www.gender.go.jp/about_danjo/whitepaper/r06/zentai/html/honpen/b1_s05_02.html.

Durkheim, Émile. 2018. *Rules of Sociological Method.* Translated by Kikutani Kazuhiro [in Japanese]. Kodansha.

Endo, Ai. 2020. "Considering Sports Harassment from a Coaching Perspective." *Tokyo Keizai University Journal of Humanities and Natural Sciences* 146: 153–60. Accessed April 2, 2025. [in Japanese]. http://hdl.handle.net/11150/11450.

Foxley, Ian. 2019. "Overcoming Stigma: Whistleblowers as 'Supranormal' Members of Society?" *Ephemera: Theory & Politics in Organization* 19 (4): 847–64. Accessed April 2, 2025. https://www.proquest.com/docview/2330592794.

Giddens, Anthony. 2015. *The Constitution of Society.* Translated by Kenichi Kadota [in Japanese]. Keiso Shobo.

Giddens, Anthony. 2021. *Modernity and Self-Identity.* Translated by Akiyoshi Mitsuru, Taro Ando, and Junya Tsutsui [in Japanese]. Chikuma Shobo.

Hagiwara, Hiroko. 2023. "A Glance at Cinema: *She Didn't Say*: What Is the Legal Principle That Forces Silence? *She Said*: Reveal the Name (directed by M. Schrader)." *Working Women's Information Magazine: Iko ✻ru* 68: 13. http://hdl.handle.net/10466/0002000437.

Human Rights Watch. 2018. "Japan: End Workplace Harassment, Violence—Labor Ministry's Draft Proposals Fail to Prohibit Abuse." Accessed April 2, 2025. https://www.hrw.org/news/2018/12/02/japan-end-workplace-harassment-violence.

Ilabaca Baeza, P., J. M. Gaete Fiscella, and F. Hatibovic Díaz. 2022. "Social, Economic and Human Capital: Risk or Protective Factors in Sexual Violence?" *International Journal of Environmental Research and Public Health* 19 (2): 777. https://doi.org/10.3390/ijerph19020777.

Ishikawa, Chihiro, and Nancy Zheng. 2025. "How Japan's Fuji TV Failed in Corporate Governance: 5 Things to Know." *Nikkei Asia*, January 28. https://asia.nikkei.com/Business/Media-Entertainment/How-Japan-s-Fuji-TV-failed-in-corporate-governance-5-things-to-know.

Ito, Yoshiko. 2001. "Analysis of Narratives Mediated by 'Others' Concerning 'Being a Victim of Sexual Violence': Identities of 'Victims of Sexual Violence'." *Women's Studies Lecture Meeting* 24: 1–29. [in Japanese]. http://hdl.handle.net/10466/00017684.

Japan P. E. N. Club, Women's Writers Committee. 2024. "Thinking About Sexual Violence and Harassment in Japan." 6th Session, September 8. Accessed April 2, 2025. [in Japanese]. https://www.youtube.com/watch?v=UnAl1pZoQLE.

Jibu, Renge. 2018. "The Unbearable 'Lightness' of the Atmosphere That Belittles Sexual Violence: What Individuals and Companies Can Do for Victims." *Toyo Keizai Online*, March 6. [in Japanese]. https://toyokeizai.net/articles/-/210354.

Johnson, David T. 2024. "Is Rape a Crime in Japan?" *International Journal of Asian Studies* Published online: 1–16. https://doi.org/10.1017/S1479591423000554.

Keenan, Marie, and Estelle Zinsstag. 2022. *Sexual Violence and Restorative Justice: Addressing the Justice Gap.* Oxford University Press.

Kemp, Poppy. 2020. "Japanese Rape Law: There's Still Work to Be Done." Cambridge University Law Society. https://www.culs.org.uk/per-incuriam/japanese-rape-law-theres-still-work-to-be-done.

Kinoshita, Koichi. 2024. "Pitfalls in Japanese Journalism: The Johnny's Entertainment Sexual Abuse." *Teikyo Journal of Sociology* 37: 157–73. [in Japanese]. http://hdl.handle.net/10682/5869.

Kyodo News. 2022. "Top Court Upholds Damages Ruling in Japan's #MeToo Symbol's Rape Case." July 10. Accessed February 5, 2025. https://english.kyodonews.net/news/2022/07/0aff9de9c110-top-court-upholds-damages-ruling-in-japans-metoo-symbols-rape-case.html.

Maenosono, Kazuki. 2022. *What Does the Story of Sexual Violence Bring?* [in Japanese]. Keiso Shobo.

McCurry, Justin. 2008. "Japanese Sumo Trainer Arrested Over Death of Pupil." *The Guardian*, February 7. https://www.theguardian.com/world/2008/feb/07/japan.justinmccurry.

Ministry of Justice of Japan. 2023. "Q&A on Legal Reforms Related to Sexual Crimes." July. Accessed April 2, 2025. [in Japanese]. https://www.moj.go.jp/keiji1/keiji12_00200.html.

NHK (Japan Broadcasting Corporation). 2022. "Thinking About Sexual Violence: Sexual Violence Survey, 38,383 Responses Received." May 27. Accessed April 2, 2025. [in Japanese]. https://www.nhk.or.jp/minplus/0026/topic059.html. (Note that the site is no longer available due to the NYK system change. This research was conducted and provided by NHK).

Osawa, Machiko. 2023a. *Building a Society Where Women Can Ask for Help: Sexual Violence and Gender Inequality in Japan*. [in Japanese]. Nishinihon Publishing.

Osawa, Machiko. 2023b. "Sexual Violence and Gender Inequality in Japan." *Asia-Pacific Journal: Japan Focus* 21 (11), no. 5, Article ID 5808. https://apjjf.org/2023/11/osawa.

Osawa, Machiko. 2025. "Why Does Sexual Violence Continue to Occur: Questioning the Social Norms Behind It." Public Lecture Sponsored by Tokyo College, University of Tokyo. January 21. [in Japanese] https://www.tc.u-tokyo.ac.jp/en/ai1ec_event/13833/.

Park, Keun-Sun. 2023. "Johnny's Issue: A System Should Be Put in Place to Protect the Rights of Talents without Treating the Entertainment Industry as a 'Special Industry'." *The Asahi Shimbun Globe*, September 27. Accessed April 2, 2025. [in Japanese]. https://globe.asahi.com/article/15009467.

Perrin, Nancy, Mendy Marsh, Amber Clough, et al. 2019. "Social Norms and Beliefs About Gender-Based Violence Scale: A Measure for Use with Gender-Based Violence Prevention Programs in Low-Resource and Humanitarian Settings." *Conflict and Health* 13 (6). https://doi.org/10.1186/s13031-019-0189-x.

Public Security Intelligence Agency of Japan. 2020. "25 Years After the Tokyo Subway Sarin Gas Attacks." Accessed April 2, 2025. https://www.moj.go.jp/psia/25years_after_the_tokyo_subway_sarin_gas_attacks.

Saisho, Reiko. 2024. "The Media and Child Sexual Abuse: A Case Study of BBC's Response." *Broadcast Research and Surveys* 74 (7–8): 50–65. [in Japanese]. https://www.nhk.or.jp/bunken/research/oversea/20240701_6.html.

Saito, Azusa. 2024. *To Think About Sexual Violence* [in Japanese]. Ichigeisha.

Saito, Azusa, and Kaori Okamoto. 2022. *Psychological Support for Victims of Sexual Violence* [in Japanese]. Kongo Shuppan.

Stermac, Lana E., Zindel V. Segal, and Roy Gillis. 1990. "Social and Cultural Factors in Sexual Assault." In *Handbook of Sexual Assault*, edited by W. L. Marshall, D. R. Laws, and H. E. Barbaree. Applied Clinical Psychology. Springer.

Stewart, Sophie, Dominic Willmott, Anthony Murphy, and Catherine Phillips. 2024. "'I Thought I'm Better Off Just Trying to Put This behind Me': A Contemporary Approach to Understanding Why Women Decide Not to Report Sexual Violence." *Journal of Forensic Psychiatry & Psychology* 35 (1): 85–101. https://doi.org/10.1080/14789949.2023.2292103.

Tanaka, Kunio, 1989. "Does 'Atmosphere' Determine Behavior?: Research and Development of Attitudes and Other Variables as Predictors of Behavior." *Annual convention of the Japanese Association of Educational Psychology*. [in Japanese]. https://doi.org/10.20587/pamjaep.31.0_L9

Uchida, Ayaka. 2020. "Issues in Sexual Crime Measures Based on the Actual Conditions of Victims (2)." *Legislation and Research* 425. House of Councillors, Standing Committee Research Office. Accessed April 2, 2025. [in Japanese]. https://www.sangiin.go.jp/japanese/annai/chousa/rippou_chousa/backnumber/2020pdf/20200708051.pdf.

University of California. n.d. "FAQ: Understanding Sexual Violence and Sexual Assault." Accessed April 2, 2025. https://sexualviolence.universityofcalifornia.edu/faq/.

Weber, Max. 2012. *Power and Domination*. Translated by Akira Hamashima [in Japanese]. Kodansha.

Weber, Max. 2023. *Power I: Bureaucracy, Patrimonialism, Feudalism*. Translated by Masahiro Noguchi [in Japanese]. Iwanami Shoten.

Weber, Max. 2024. *Power II: Charisma and Clericism*. Translated by Masahiro Noguchi [in Japanese]. Iwanami Shoten.

Westlaw Japan. 2018. "No. 133: Internal Discipline of Local Assembly and the Doctrine of Partial Society: Supreme Court Decision of April 26, 2018." Accessed April 2, 2025. [in Japanese]. https://www.westlawjapan.com/column-law/2018/180524/.

WHO (World Health Organization). n.d. "Sexual Violence." Accessed April 2, 2025. https://apps.who.int/violence-info/sexual-violence/.

CHAPTER 10

Possible Challenges to the Welfare State in a Post–COVID-19 Society: An Illustration from a Citizen's Perspective

Abstract

The chapter aims to clarify possible challenges to the welfare state in a post–COVID-19 society and to illustrate conceptual ideas on how to tackle those challenges from a citizen's perspective. This is based on interdisciplinary studies, particularly the literature survey in English and Japanese. The direct and indirect impacts of the COVID-19 pandemic in the global community have been examined from a broader perspective. The chapter clarifies that the impacts of the COVID-19 pandemic are expected to be far larger and more complicated than those originally expected. The issues regarding possible challenges to the welfare state in a post–COVID-19 society are discussed in the three contexts of (1) the vulnerability approach, (2) governmental policy priority, and (3) social distancing in a civil society. Then, some ideas are illustrated from a citizen's perspective. Through the discussion, it can be assumed that the government of each welfare state will make its best endeavors to respond to the requests of citizens but will face challenges that cannot be resolved easily with respect to the national budget, skilled human resources, technology, information, and so on. International cooperation among states would be of paramount importance to cope with a global issue like the COVID-19 pandemic. Another important consideration is that the future will be created by people in civil society embracing universal values and social ethics while maintaining a good relationship with the government. When facing inexperienced challenges, good citizenship in civil society would be a starting point because governments, parliaments, and courts cannot respond to sudden challenges. Individuals may take actions to express their ideas where the information technology of social networking services has developed.

Keywords: Welfare State, COVID-19, Vulnerability, Policy Priority, Social Distancing

1 Introduction

We live in a COVID-19 pandemic risk. This risk may differ by country and area, but it is obvious that the pandemic has had serious impacts on people's lifestyle, society, and state and will continue to have more impact. How people and government should live together with the COVID-19 pandemic is a basic question. This chapter focuses on the welfare state,[1] because the relationships among families, markets, and state as the main elements of the welfare state (Esping-Andersen 1990) have been influenced by the COVID-19 pandemic. The chapter aims to clarify possible challenges to the welfare state in a post–COVID-19 society and to illustrate conceptual ideas on how to tackle those challenges from a citizen's perspective. This is based on interdisciplinary studies, particularly the literature survey in English and Japanese.

As the research topics in question concern various ongoing phenomena directly and indirectly caused by the COVID-19 pandemic, a wide range of literature surveys have been done (United Nations [UN] 2020a, 2020b; World Health Organization [WHO] 2020a, 2020b; World Economic Forum 2020a, 2020b, 2020c; European Commission [EC] 2020; PwC Australia 2020; Prime Minister of Japan and His Cabinet 2020; Brennan et al. 2020; Institute for Advanced Sustainability Studies [IASS] 2020; Rohwerder 2020; Tashiro and Shaw 2020; Béland et al. 2020; Lu et al. 2020; Rahman et al. 2020). In fact, studies on the possible challenges to the welfare state in a post–COVID-19 society are limited (Kübra 2020; Breznau 2020; World Economic Forum 2020b; Sennet 2020). In this respect, this chapter covers a wider range of issues that surround the research questions, not only today but also throughout history, that indirectly correspond to the COVID-19 pandemic.

---

[1] The term *welfare state* refers to a form of government in which the state, or a well-developed network of social institutions, plays a central role in protecting and promoting the economic and social well-being of its citizens. It is founded on the principles of equality of opportunity, equitable distribution of wealth, and public responsibility for those unable to secure the minimal provisions for a decent life. See *Encyclopaedia Britannica*, s.v. "Welfare State."

The academic study on this topic needs further time to ensure necessary data collection and discussion, but the additional time needed does not negate the importance of this research at this stage to explore further discussion. The area of discussion is basically in Japan, but most of the discussion would presumably be relevant to global application. The following research questions will be taken up in this chapter.

1. What are the direct effects of the COVID-19 pandemic on the global community from a broader perspective?
2. What are the indirect effects of the COVID-19 pandemic on the global community from a broader perspective?
3. How will the impact of COVID-19 affect the welfare state in a post–COVID-19 society, and what will be the possible ideas to challenge the impacts?

Following the "Introduction," the part "COVID-19 Impacts on the Global Community" will review the impacts of COVID-19 on the global community, the message we can attain through the ongoing phenomenon, and what the situation is like. Those reviews may indirectly correspond to the later discussion. The part "Possible Challenges to the Welfare State in a Post–COVID-19 Society" will examine possible challenges to the welfare state in a post–COVID-19 society within three contexts: (1) the vulnerability approach, (2) policy priority of the government, and (3) social distancing in a civil society. It will discuss possible ideas to challenge the impact. And the part "In Closing" presents the conclusion.

2 COVID-19 Impacts on the Global Community

2.1 COVID-19 Impacts

The COVID-19 pandemic outbreak has had significant impacts on the global community and will continue to have further impacts from a broader perspective. The impacts of the pandemic extended not only to the national health policy but also to general policies, including politics, the economy, employment, education, people's lifestyle, and so on. The COVID-19 crisis was expected to wipe out 6.7% of working hours globally in the second quarter of 2020—equivalent to 195 million full-time workers (International Labour Organization [ILO] 2020). The latest analysis warned that COVID-19 pushed an additional 88 million people into extreme poverty in 2020 (Blake and Wadhwa 2020). The pandemic has had a great influence on international politics, immigration, and diplomacy, resulting particularly in greater diplomatic tension between the USA and China. The pandemic may leave a huge scar on the international community. There is a risk that the world's fragmentation will further accelerate due to the strength of the exclusive climate (Mitsubishi Research Institute 2020a).

The international mobility of people is largely restricted even though commodity trading, including energy resources and financial transactions, continues to occur properly. It is as if we lived in the days before the modernization of Japan began, in 1868. That was the Tokugawa Shogunate era,[2] which lasted for approximately two hundred and fifty years without trading and diplomacy with overseas countries, except for the Dutch merchants at Dejima in Nagasaki.[3] Indeed, people today live in a national isolation that is unique to their experience. People are forced to live in narrow areas, and the right to free choice has been partly restricted for human security purposes.

The world is gradually changing in every respect since the COVID-19 pandemic, and these changes might in part be the result of a degree of over-protection initiated by governments. According to some IMF analysts, the pandemic will have cost the global economy $12.5 trillion in lost output by the end of 2021 (Lynch 2020). The magnitude of those impacts on the economy can be assumed to be deeper and broader than that of the bankruptcy of Lehman Brothers, or what is commonly referred to in Japan as the "Lehman Shock." The Lehman Shock occurred in October 2008, mainly as a result of bad debt securities. And it immediately affected banking credit worldwide. In particular, the Lehman Shock disrupted the inter-banking credit line system. Consequently, numerous banks went bankrupt. Some major banks survived, but they, including Japanese major banking companies, were temporarily under government control through a bailout. At the time, the disruption was called "one

---

[2] It was the last part of the feudal era when Japan was centrally governed by the Tokugawa Shoguns from 1603 to 1868 before the modernization of Japan. The Japanese population remained unchanged at as many as 30 million during the era, which is one-fourth of the present population of Japan.

[3] The Tokugawa government issued special permission for the Nagasaki local government to trade only with the Dutch merchants in Hirado in 1601, and then the authorized place was transferred to Dejima in Nagasaki in 1641. Consequently, Portuguese and other merchants other than the Dutch were barred. Japan reopened for trading and diplomacy in 1854, first, with the US; second; Britain; and third, Imperial Russia through a bilateral treaty.

of the worst financial shocks in one hundred years."[4] After the Lehman Shock, it took the world economy six years to recover to the same level prior to the event.

The economic impacts of the COVID-19 pandemic, on the contrary, are progressing slowly but steadily, unlike the Lehman Shock in the financial sector. The social impacts of COVID-19 may well compare with the 1929 Great Depression, the impact of which lasted for more than ten years. However, the pandemic, which has squeezed the world economy due to the sudden suspension of social activities resulting from lockdowns and the like, has had a social impact that is deeper and broader than that of the Great Depression (Bremmer 2020). Countries, corporations, and people have become far more dependent on one another in various respects, such as human relations, commodities, money, capital, technology, and information. The influence of traditional and social media has expanded the psychological impact of the pandemic, particularly the sentiments of fear and desperation, by quickly spreading information to people around the world. In some cases, news contained untruthful content.

The Great Depression was ultimately resolved by World War II, which raises the simple questions of how and when the current problem will be resolved. At this moment, the magnitude of direct and indirect impacts of the COVID-19 pandemic remains unclear because all the impacts have not been fully grasped through publicly accessible national statistics.[5] Some countries may not disclose accurate national statistics or may publish false statistics with some intentions. Transparency and credibility of the national statistics may differ by country, and thus we cannot always grasp precise information on impacts based on such statistics. Moreover, the global community missed the opportunity of investigating exactly where, how, and why the COVID-19 pandemic originally started. Again,

---

[4] In Japan, the phrase "one of the worst financial shocks in one hundred years" was frequently used in media coverage and financial reports (Mitsubishi UFJ Financial Group [MUFG] 2009). MUFG's report analyzed corruption cases in the US following the Lehman Shock and discussed possible reforms to capitalism aimed at creating a more genuinely "free market" (Reich 2015).

[5] According to GDP data for April to June 2020, annualized growth rates declined by 32.9% in the US, 47.6% in the European Union, and 27.8% in Japan (*Japan Times* 2020). For the full year 2020, GDP contracted by 4.7% in the US, 6.6% in the European Union, and 4.8% in Japan, following the implementation of fiscal stimulus measures (IMF 2021). The US unemployment rate rose to 14.7% in April 2020 and fell to 6.1% by April 2021 as economic activity gradually resumed (U.S. Bureau of Labor Statistics 2021). The Biden administration released the *National Strategy for the COVID-19 Response and Pandemic Preparedness* on January 21, 2021, outlining measures to combat the pandemic and support economic recovery (The White House 2021a).

in academic research cooperation among countries to investigate these important questions seems to have been kept suspended or confidential.[6]

2.2 A Lesson from History

As a result of indirect impacts of the COVID-19 pandemic, society may undergo a structural change ; however, people cannot fully recognize what change occurs and will occur and how it happens and will happen. The international impacts of the pandemic could be clarified and summarized at the G7[7] Summit meeting or the like. At the summit, some economic sanctions and human rights issues may be considered in regard to a certain country. Solutions to the pandemic and the recovery of the world economy could also be discussed there. COVID-19 may have impacted national security. Hence, a joint movement is expected to bring about severe economic sanctions on the country suspected to have originated from the virus (Enos 2020). The former US Secretary of State Michael R. Pompeo, in his historical speech on July 23, 2020, called on the people of China, along with the rest of the world, to confront the Communist Party, which is the government of China.[8] President Biden retained this diplomacy and noted in his press conference on March 25, 2021, that this is a battle between the utility of democracies in the twenty-first century and autocracies (The White House 2021b).

This reminds us of the history of the Pacific region between 1940 and 1941, when Imperial Japan suffered from severe economic sanctions caused by the ABCD encirclement.[9] The ABCD encirclement included an

---

[6] The WHO announced that an independent evaluation of the global COVID-19 response would be presented in an interim report in November 2020 (WHO 2020c). The research experienced delays, and the WHO international team of experts ultimately visited Wuhan, China, from January 14 to February 10, 2021, to investigate the origins of the COVID-19 pandemic. The WHO's international report was released on March 30, 2021; however, it provided limited clarification, and further investigation has been deemed necessary (WHO 2021).

[7] The G7 online summit meetings were convened under the chairmanship of the US president on March 17 and April 16, 2020.

[8] A parallel can be observed between Secretary Pompeo's rhetoric ptoward China and the US attitude toward Japan after World War II. In Japan's case, the military organization and its supporters were publicly purged, yet the imperial institution, the National Diet, and the bureaucratic structure of government remained largely intact (U.S. State Department 2020).

[9] The term "ABCD encirclement" refers to the allied economic sanctions imposed on Imperial Japan, including embargoes on crude oil, oil products, iron ore, and steel goods. The name derives from the initials of the participating countries: A for America, B for Britain, C for China (the Nationalist government), and D for the Dutch. At the time, Japan's oil reserves covered only about six months of national consumption, meaning that continuation

embargo against Japan on oil and steel products due to territorial conflicts among countries around China and Southeast Asia.[10] Before the ABCD encirclement, the *Immigration Act* of 1924, or the *Johnson–Reed Act*, was enacted as a US federal law that prevented immigration mainly from Asia, set immigration quotas on the number of immigrants to the US, and provided funding and an enforcement mechanism. It was a shocking event for Asian people and governments, particularly the Japanese. The relationship between Japan and the US was generally uncomfortable, and the US position was basically the Monroe Doctrine of isolation (Levi and Tetlock 1980).[11] Thus, some similarities are seen between the then Japan–US and the current US–China diplomatic relationship, such as severe pressure from the US, restrictions on immigration to the US, and isolation policy and economic sanctions of the US.

Japan unconditionally surrendered in 1945.[12] After a terrible war with a heavy national sacrifice of some three million lives,[13] Japan changed its regime from a military state to a peaceful and democratic state aiming at economic success as a consequence of Japan's democratization programs. Those programs were initiated by the Allied Supreme Commander (SCAP) General Douglas MacArthur and his General Headquarters (GHQ) teams with the cooperation of the Japanese government from 1945 to 1951 (Sundelson 1950).[14] This change was supported by the Japanese people even though some pro-communist and socialist political movements existed. Japan then returned to being a member of

---

of the embargo would have effectively paralyzed the country's industrial and military activities. Consequently, the ABCD encirclement has often been interpreted as a quasi-declaration of war by the allied states against Japan.

[10] There is a view that such severe economic sanctions may have compelled the Japanese government to choose war with the US and its allies. The U.S. Note to Japan of November 26, 1941—commonly known as the Hull Note—was deemed unacceptable by the Japanese government, and after the suspension of diplomatic dialogue between Japan and the US was formally confirmed, war appeared to be the only remaining option.

[11] Statements made in Liaison Conferences (where policies were formulated) tended to be significantly less complex than those presented at Imperial Conferences (where policies were submitted to the emperor for formal approval).

[12] By accepting the Potsdam Declaration on August 14, 1945, Japan renounced all overseas territories, including southern Sakhalin, Korea, Taiwan, and various Pacific islands. The Japanese government formally signed the Instrument of Surrender on September 2, 1945.

[13] The death toll in the Japanese war was 3.1 million, of which 2.3 million were soldiers and the remaining 0.8 million were civilians.

[14] The American new dealers came to Japan to persuade the Japanese government to adopt socialistic public policy. For example, Carl Sumner Shoup (1902–2000) was an economist at Columbia University who led the Shoup Mission of seven economists at the invitation of General MacArthur to revise the tax system in post-World War II Japan. His Mission published the report to the GHQ, and, in fact, to the Japanese government to adopt strict progressive taxation on high-income earners for equalization of the income of Japanese people.

the international community through the *San Francisco Peace Treaty* and the *Japan–US Security Treaty* signed in 1951. Since then, Japan has lived in peace for seventy years. Therefore, it can be assumed that the COVID-19 impacts might be extended to issues of diplomacy and political regime that the war made.

2.3 Uncertainty Prevails

As COVID-19 continues to spread around the world, it seems to get worse in developing countries in South America, South Asia, and Africa. Some experts expect that the pandemic will continue to be influential until an effective global vaccine becomes available. In fact, we still live with a pandemic risk. Therefore, it can be understood that we live in a time of uncertainty with limited insight into the future. This sentiment of anxiety and frustration is largely shared among people (Ferreira et al. 2021).[15]

From a socio-psychological perspective, there is tremendous peer pressure[16] in society. The peer pressure is so harsh in Japan as a national character (Kokami and Sato 2020). This contributes positively to maintaining discipline even in natural disasters. But everyone, including children, the elderly, and person with disabilities, are forced to comply with the regulations or guidelines shared among people in daily life, such as washing hands, mask-mandates, social distancing, opening windows for ventilation, and not having conversations in closed public spaces. Those who break the regulations or guidelines, intentionally or unintentionally, tend to be heavily criticized among people, not by an authority, even when the

---

[15] The initial impacts of the COVID-19 pandemic on people's life in the US and the UK are described as follows.

Americans see the spread of disease as a top international threat, along with terrorism, nuclear weapons, and cyber-attacks. The 86 per cent say that it is particularly important to cooperate with other countries, and the 97 per cent say it is at least somewhat important to cooperate. And as the economic fallout from the COVID-19 crisis becomes clearer, Americans increasingly see the condition of the global economy as a threat (Pew Research Center 2020).

Older Americans continue to follow COVID-19 news more closely than younger adults (Pew Research Center 2020).

Of the 59.7 percent of key workers who said their work was being impacted by COVID-19, the most common concern was their health and safety at work (UK, Office for National Statistics 2020a).

Almost half (45.1 per cent) of disabled adults, compared with around a third (30.2 per cent) of non-disabled adults, reported being very worried about the effect the coronavirus (COVID-19) pandemic is having on their life. Nearly 9 in 10 disabled adults (86.3 per cent) reported that they are very worried or somewhat worried. Nearly two-thirds (64.8 per cent) of disabled adults said COVID-19-related concerns were affecting their wellbeing (UK, Office for National Statistics 2020b).

[16] *Peer pressure* refers to the strong influence exerted by a group—particularly among children or adolescents—on its members to conform to shared behaviors or norms (Cambridge Dictionary, n.d.).

regulations are not deemed illegal.[17] Anonymous posts in social networking systems are further amplifying that impact. It is an age of intolerance as if people were living in a time of war.

According to a study, the Japanese unintentionally have herd immunity against various types of COVID-19 viruses,[18] thus explaining the low ratio of COVID-19 deaths among them. If this is so proven by the academic society, it is wondered why Japan and East Asian countries have adopted similar policy restrictions , including lockdowns or voluntary restrictions on lifestyle, in response to COVID-19, as was done in Europe and the US. The restrictions would be meaningless if the Japanese had herd immunity. One expert on herd immunity recommends Japanese people to become infected with the coronavirus, as it is constantly mutating, to establish herd immunity against COVID-19 by remaining in contact with various types of viruses modifying themselves. However, this opinion is not proven by the academic society, which has a different opinion and is thus not accepted by the government. Although this opinion of herd immunity sounds interesting, it is regarded as a minority viewpoint in the research community. This has brought about a feeling of uncertainty, knowing that academic society lacks flexibility. Hence, uncertainty prevails in society.

3 Possible Challenges to the Welfare State in a Post–Covid-19 Society

Based on a discussion of the global impacts of the COVID-19 pandemic, possible challenges to the welfare state in a post–COVID-19 society will be reviewed from a citizen's perspective below.[19]

---

[17] Japan's Constitution contains no explicit state of emergency clause (Ida 2020). In response to the COVID-19 pandemic, however, the government was able to declare a state of emergency through statutory provisions. Unlike lockdowns in some other countries, Japan's measures relied primarily on voluntary compliance, requesting citizens and businesses to follow guidelines or restrictions issued under the authority of local governors, pursuant to amendments to the relevant laws in February 2021.

[18] Two Japanese public health researchers, Kamikubo and Takahashi (2020), concluded that the Japanese population may have developed herd immunity unintentionally, based on their analysis of publicly available health data.

[19] The views of one scholar (Kübra 2020) can be summarized as follows:
  (a) The economic and social consequences of the crisis will bring about deep and lasting changes in people's lives.
  (b) The weakening of social protection networks will compel states to adopt more interventionist measures, and ideologies that restrict state involvement in social and economic affairs are likely to decline following the COVID-19 pandemic.
  (c) Three main factors will determine the extent of this fundamental transformation.

3.1 Vulnerability Approach

In the post–COVID-19 society, the risk of COVID-19 or another virus will be identified, and it will become part of our consciousness. In this sense, everybody will be regarded as vulnerable. Vulnerability has been analyzed and explored by Martha Albertson Fineman, a feminist scholar.[20] Fineman's main points in her articles can be summarized as follows: Vulnerability theory challenges the concept of vulnerability as a dominant, static, and individualized legal subject and argues for the recognition of the reality of the human condition, which is finite and fragile, as well as socially and materially dynamic (Fineman 2017). The term "vulnerable" describes a universal, inevitable, enduring aspect of the human condition that should be at the heart of the concept of social and state responsibility (Fineman 2008, 8). Human beings are vulnerable to inescapable interrelationship and interdependence (Fineman 2012, 71). Human vulnerability and dependency across the life-course rely on other individuals, the family, and the state and its institutions (Fineman 2012, 111). The vulnerability approach to social justice recognizes that the relationship between the individual and society is synergetic and thus ongoing (Fineman 2020, 61–62).

Through the lessons of the COVID-19 pandemic, the elderly, people with underlying disease, and people with disabilities will be regarded as the most vulnerable, and that has proven to be the case in practice since the discovery of the virus (Chen and McNamara 2020). The state will respond by protecting those who are most vulnerable by allocating more of the national budgets and human resources to them, and this will, in turn, increase the tax burden on future residents. Due to reduced consumption of commodities, for the time being, a significant surplus of supply capacity in any industry will be a severe problem for the economy. Thus, the private sector will be forced to rationalize its surplus supply capacity, thus leading to an increase in unemployment. Consequently, the economy and society will become somewhat unstable. People will pressure the government for more large-scale public spending to rescue people in need (Curtice 2020). This naturally translates into a bigger and more active government to improve the economy and society in a way different from normal (World Economic Forum 2020a). Market mechanisms may slightly abate, and governments may increase public spending in areas

---

[20] This paragraph is based on the author's previous publication (Sakurai 2021, 22–23).

such as public health, infant and elderly care, and welfare for the poor and the unemployed.

Typical functions of the welfare state government are required to promote social business and welfare programs to take care of vulnerable people who have problems. In such cases, capable political leaders and skillful public agencies to administer those functions would be essential to manage social policy effectively. The social ethics and moral standards of political leaders and public agencies will be crucial for leadership, but this aspect may be questionable in the political parties that are deeply involved in vested interests (Scartozzi 2017). People will then need to have a new type of political leadership with a good sense of social ethics to cultivate the future. However, who will take up such leadership is unknown. Therefore, to find appropriate human resources would be challenging, and confusion would be anticipated until the situation returns to normal.

One positive aspect is expected to encourage powerful motivations for scientists, engineers, and corporate management to promote technological improvements and innovations. There is a possibility that a digital communication shift will progress all over the world where new businesses will be created (Mitsubishi Research Institute 2020a). In the 2030s, it is expected that the developed countries will shift to a new era of technology, particularly through artificial intelligence (AI). This trend would give us positive and negative effects on daily life. In fact, a product of the COVID-19 pandemic might be a surveillance society in which some security systems in society are guaranteed, but these are often based on an exchange or sacrifice of freedom and privacy. Perhaps Edward Joseph Snowden[21] alerted us to such a governmental attempt as surveillance activities, but it was not understood then and has become clear now. Thus, possible security safeguards must be simultaneously incorporated into the law systems to prevent infringement of people's privacy in a surveillance society (Mitsubishi Research Institute 2020b).

3.2 Policy Priority of Government

The COVID-19 pandemic has begun to affect national security policy and does not just remains a public health issue to be addressed by the

---

[21] Edward Joseph Snowden (born June 21, 1983, in Elizabeth City, North Carolina, US) is an American intelligence contractor who, in 2013, disclosed the existence of secret, wide-ranging information-gathering programs conducted by the National Security Agency (NSA) (*Encyclopaedia Britannica*).

Ministry of Health and medical practitioners. National security concerns will continue to grow among those in government and society (Ida 2020; The White House 2020). National security will cover a broad area, likely including military defense, public health, cybertechnology, intelligence, outer space, immigration control, and so on. Consequently, trade and capital transactions by the private sector, which have largely relied on the market, might be in part controlled by the government in accordance with its national interests. With such a defensive governmental policy, priority will often be given to national security. Therefore, social business and welfare programs will be implemented by the welfare state within the national budget after precedence is given to national security. After the Summit meeting or the like, diplomacy among the major states will revitalize international cooperation in the area of national security. If a burden-sharing policy program materializes, it would promote certain cooperation among the states. Such external commitment would have a positive effect on government, which tends to be devoted mainly to interior administration, and open the government's eyes to international relations.

With stronger governmental control of national security, the value of freedom might be partly lost, and the value of equality might prevail. But a fair implementation of social business and welfare programs will not always be guaranteed to be a fair distribution to people, and in such a case, the poor will have to demonstrate severe tolerance under the pressure of unfair distribution. Civil society may respond to improve the situation and restructure the welfare system to be more cost-effective or to shift to the universal basic income (UBI) system.[22] The spending priorities for the welfare state are focused, balancing the traditional welfare priorities and the emerging demands by new social risks (Quilter-Pinner et al. 2020).

But civil society might sometimes react in favor of totalitarianism by not properly reacting in a democratic way and instead referring to history in an extreme case. Characteristics of totalitarianism were critically advocated by Hannah Arendt in her book, *The Origins of Totalitarianism* (Arendt [1951]1973). In the book, referring to the severe lessons of World War II, Arendt analyzed that there pwas a strong and overwhelming support among the masses for political leaders and their governments

---

[22] Spain introduced the *Minimum Living Income* system, which is not a universal basic income (UBI) but rather the country's first nationwide minimum income scheme aimed at supporting low-income individuals (Rincon 2020).

demonstrating totalitarianism. Meanwhile, the people under such systems felt severely isolated and frustrated with economy and society. The political leaders influenced people's minds through democratic procedures, and some minorities of specific races, having physical/intellectual/mental disabilities, in the LGBT community, and communists became the subjects of social criticism and elimination from society. This is a risky phenomenon, but it has happened in the past and could happen again.

Democracy is an imperfect political system. It tends to be destabilized by populism arising through people's and politicians' transactions (Canovan 1999). In the worst case, the situation might be chaotic. Media and civil society should watch government and politicians to ensure that they do not conduct illegal matters. But sometimes, even media and civil society may react emotionally to the requests of government and politicians and, consequently, conduct radical actions arising from collective frustration. In a modern society, media and social networking services (SNS) will be more effective for political advertisements to influence people. Then, not only the government and its associated groups but also civil society might force people to take a specific course of action without valuing diverse input from the people (Kreitman 2020). Nazism, Italy during Mussolini days, and the Imperial Japan in 1931 to 1945 were examples.

Against such a potential risk, it must be reconfirmed that freedom of speech and freedom of expression are universal values in a democratic society. Thus, people will be encouraged to protect universal values, but those people might be thrilled by the stronger government and conservative movements of civil society. People, as members of civil society, should respond to protect human rights and social ethics from the potential risk of harm in society (Brechenmacher et al. 2020).

3.3 Social Distancing in a Civil Society

In a civil society, one thing that we must always pay attention to is social distancing. This situation may severely restrict face-to-face contact. Instead, contact among people is largely replaced by online communication. This dramatic change in contact might initially weaken the power of communication and even the freedom of speech and expression in a civil society. Aged care activities at nursing homes and the like require careful attention to social distancing as a part of public health procedures, and welfare practitioners need additional skillful training to provide such services (Kohn 2020). In fact, the data indicates the fact that certain mortality in nursing homes was associated with COVID-19 outbreaks (Comas-Herrera et al. 2020). Every care institution or public agency makes efforts to observe its own guidelines, or the guidelines shown by the government. The Office of the Public Advocate in the state of Victoria, Australia, for example, has implemented and continues to refine processes for continuing critical safeguarding work.[23]

Social distancing generally affects group activities of people, including education, sports, music, arts, and travel. It affects the physical and mental growth of children. It also affects the isolation and loneliness of the elderly and people with disabilities. Special attention is vital, particularly to vulnerable people in mental capacity treatments (39 Essex Chambers 2020).[24] In the long run, individualism and a virtual reality mindset may dominate society, and civil society may fall short of the reality to be mutually realized by human contacts. Yuval Noah Harari, an Israeli historian, noted the distrusting attitudes and behaviors of people that COVID-19 and social distancing may generate. He observed that humans have developed society and technology based on the capability of human cooperation through mutual trust and imagination (Harari 2020a). Thus, if mutual trust and imagination may fade, then the development of society and technology might slow down. Yuval also expressed his concerns about "totalitarian surveillance" and "nationalist isolation" in the post–COVID-19 world (Harari 2020b).

Concerning business, the industrial map will be largely revised in proportion to the changes in economy and society. For example, financial institutions, particularly small and medium-sized banks in Japan, will come to exist in surplus, and an unemployment risk will arise from rationalization. In such a case, it would be an idea to establish a public agency specializing in financial management for the elderly or people with disabilities, like Victorian State Trustees Limited, which is wholly owned by the state of Victoria in Australia. That public corporation may employ human resources having financial business experience, but the salary level

---

[23] These measures include: (i) contacting represented persons and service providers by phone or video link where possible; (ii) attending Victorian Civil and Administrative Tribunal (VCAT) hearings via phone or video link; (iii) participating remotely in police interviews; and (iv) conducting phone or video visits to Supported Residential Service facilities and disability group homes (Office of the Public Advocate, State of Victoria, Australia). For European countries, see Daly et al. (2021).

[24] This guidance-note, made by the Barristers' Chambers in the UK, provides an overview of the framework within which decisions need to be taken in England.

would be dramatically less. This could be a part of a Japan "New Deal Project"[25] to address large unemployment through a state initiative. A measure such as this would allow the elderly and people with disabilities to enjoy financial management services at reasonable fees.

At the time of a drastically changing social environment, a new attempt is worth considering for the future. For example, there is a case for the Ireland reform project, which focuses on the necessity of active labor policy reform in response to the pandemic unemployment crisis (McGann et al. 2020). From the government's perspective, every country/area in the world has the challenge of how to maintain a good balance between the public health policy and the activation of the economy. In the long run, welfare policy reform in each country/area would be a serious issue. The development of welfare policy reform would affect people's conceptualizations as to what the welfare state will be and what the roles of the government will be. It can therefore be assumed that this challenge would need international cooperation to share wisdom and empirical data to seek the best possible scenario for each country/area.[26] Individuals may take actions to express their ideas where the information technology of SNS has developed. Useful ideas to contribute to the public welfare by citizens' initiatives would be worth considering (Yunus 2020).[27]

4 Conclusion

In this chapter, the direct and indirect impacts of the COVID-19 pandemic in the global community have been examined from a broader perspective. The chapter clarifies that the impacts of the COVID-19 pandemic are expected to be far larger and more complicated than those originally expected. The issues regarding possible challenges to the welfare state in a post–COVID-19 society are discussed in three contexts: (1) the vulnerability approach, (2) governmental policy priority, and (3) social distancing in a civil society. Then, some ideas are illustrated from a citizen's perspective.

---

[25] The New Deal refers to the domestic program of US President Franklin D. Roosevelt's administration between 1933 and 1939, which implemented measures to provide immediate economic relief and introduced reforms in industry, agriculture, finance, waterpower, labor, and housing, thereby vastly expanding the scope of the federal government's activities (Encyclopaedia Britannica).

[26] "It is necessary to develop global solutions for global problems" (Aysan 2020, 695).

[27] Muhammad Yunus, in his message, advocates for the promotion of small and micro social businesses through the initiative and active participation of citizens. This represents one form of citizen-initiated action.

Through the discussion, it can be assumed that the government of each welfare state will make its best endeavors to respond to the requests of citizens but will face challenges that cannot be resolved easily with respect to the national budget, skilled human resources, technology, information, and so on. International cooperation among states would be of paramount importance to cope with a global issue like the COVID-19 pandemic (Evens 2020; Aoi 2020[28]).[29] Another important consideration is that the future will be created by people in civil society embracing universal values and social ethics while maintaining a good relationship with the government. When facing inexperienced challenges, good citizenship in civil society would be a starting point because governments, parliament, and courts cannot respond to sudden challenges (Pisano et al. 2020). Individuals may take actions to express their ideas where the information technology of SNS has developed.

Acknowledgments

The author thanks Piers Gooding, a research fellow at the Melbourne Social Equity Institute and Melbourne Law School, for his comments and suggestions to publish this chapter.

Bibliography

39 Essex Chambers. 2020. "Rapid Response Guidance Note: Covid-19, Social Distancing and Mental Capacity." Accessed January 18, 2021. https://www.39essex.com/rapid-response-guidance-note-covid-19-social-distancing-and-mental-capacity/.

Aoi, Yoshie. 2020. "International Order and Japan in the 'Post-Corona' Era." Issue Brief 1120: 1–10. [in Japanese]. https://dl.ndl.go.jp/view/download/digidepo_11561442_po_1120.pdf?contentNo=1.

Arendt, Hannah. [1951] 1973. The origins of totalitarianism. Vol. 244. Houghton Mifflin Harcourt.

---

[28] At the Japanese government's Advisory Panel, it was proposed that Japan take the lead in promoting multilateral cooperation—not only by strengthening relations with the United States and China but also by enhancing collaboration with countries in Asia, Europe, and Oceania.

[29] Japanese Prime Minister Suga emphasized the importance of international cooperation among states, recognizing that COVID-19 constitutes a human security crisis. The next G7 summit meeting was scheduled for June 2021, to be chaired by the UK prime minister.

Aysan, Mehmet Fatih. 2020. "Rethinking the Welfare State Social Policies During the Covid-19." In *Reflections on the Pandemic in the Future of the World*, edited by Muzaffer Seker, Ali Özer, and Cem Korkut. Turkish Academy of Sciences Publications.

Béland, Daniel, Shannon Dinan, Philip Rocco, and Alex Waddan. 2020. "Social Policy Responses to COVID‑19 in Canada and the United States: Explaining Policy Variations Between Two Liberal Welfare State Regimes." *Social Policy & Administration* 55 (2): 280–94. https://doi.org/10.1111/spol.12656.

Blake, Paul, and Divyanshi Wadhwa. 2020. "2020 Year in Review: The Impact of COVID-19 in 12 Charts." *World Bank Blogs*, December 14. Accessed January 18, 2021. https://blogs.worldbank.org/voices/2020-year-review-impact-covid-19-12-charts.

Brechenmacher, Saskia, Thomas Carothers, and Richard Youngs. 2020. "Civil Society and the Coronavirus: Dynamism Despite Disruption." *Carnegie Endowment for International Peace*. Accessed January 18, 2021. https://carnegieendowment.org/2020/04/21/civil-society-and-coronavirus-dynamism-despite-disruption-pub-81592.

Bremmer, Ian. 2020. "The Next Global Depression Is Coming and Optimism Won't Slow It Down." *Time*, August 6. Accessed January 18, 2021. https://time.com/5876606/economic-depression-coronavirus/.

Brennan, John, P. Reilly, K. Cuskelly, and S. Donnelly. 2020. "Social Work, Mental Health, Older People and COVID-19." *International Psychogeriatrics* 32 (10): 1205–9. https://doi.org/10.1017/S1041610220000873.

Breznau, Nate. 2020. "The Welfare State and Risk Perceptions: The Novel Coronavirus Pandemic and Public Concern in 70 Countries." *SocArXiv*. Accessed January 18, 2021. https://doi.org/10.31235/osf.io/96fd2.

Cambridge Dictionary. n.d. "Peer Pressure." Accessed January 18, 2021. https://dictionary.cambridge.org/ja/dictionary/english/peer-pressure.

Canovan, Margaret. 1999. "Trust the People! Populism and the Two Faces of Democracy." *Political Studies* 47: 2–16. https://doi.org/10.1111/1467-9248.00184.

Chen, Bo, and Donna Marie McNamara. 2020. "Disability Discrimination, Medical Rationing and COVID-19." *Asian Bioethics Review* 12: 511–18. https://doi.org/10.1007/s41649-020-00147-x.

Clarfield, A. M., T. Dwolatzky, S. Brill, et al. 2020. "Israel Ad Hoc COVID-19 Committee: Guidelines for Care of Older Persons During a

Pandemic." *Journal of the American Geriatrics Society* 68 (7): 1370–75. https://doi.org/10.1111/jgs.16554.

Comas-Herrera, Adelina, Joseba Zalakaín, Charles Litwin, Amy T. Hsu, Natasha Lane, and Jose-Luis Fernández. 2020. "Mortality Associated with COVID-19 Outbreaks in Care Homes: Early International Evidence." International Long-Term Care Policy Network. Accessed January 18, 2021. https://ltccovid.org/wp-content/uploads/2020/06/Mortality-associated-with-COVID-among-people-who-use-LTC-26-June-2020-1.pdf.

Curtice, John. 2020. "Will Covid-19 Change Attitudes Towards the Welfare State?" *IPPR Progressive Review* 27 (1): 93–104. https://doi.org/10.1111/newe.12185.

Daly, M., Margarita Leon, Birgit Pfau-Effinger, Costanzo Ranci, and Tine Rostgaard. 2021. "COVID-19 and Policies for Care Homes in European Welfare States: Too Little, Too Late?" *Journal of European Social Policy* 32 (1): 48–59. Accessed April 7, 2021. https://forskning.ruc.dk/en/publications/covid-19-and-policies-for-care-homes-in-european-welfare-states-t.

EC (European Commission). 2020. "2020: EU's action against coronavirus." Accessed January 8, 2026. https://commission.europa.eu/strategy-and-policy/coronavirus-response/2020-eus-action-against-coronavirus_en.

Encyclopedia Britannica. n.d.-a. "Edward Snowden." Accessed January 18, 2021. https://www.britannica.com/biography/Edward-Snowden.

Encyclopedia Britannica. n.d.-b. "New Deal." Accessed January 18, 2021. https://www.britannica.com/event/New-Deal.

Enos, Olivia. 2020. *Holding the Chinese Communist Party Accountable for Its Response to the COVID-19 Outbreak*. Heritage Foundation. Accessed January 18, 2021. https://www.heritage.org/asia/report/holding-the-chinese-communist-party-accountable-its-response-the-covid-19-outbreak.

Esping-Andersen, Gøsta. 1990. *The Three Worlds of Welfare Capitalism*. Princeton University Press.

Evens, Olaniyi. 2020. "Socio-Economic Impacts of Novel Coronavirus: The Policy Solutions." *BizCons Quarterly* 7: 3–12. Accessed January 18, 2021. https://ideas.repec.org/a/ris/buecqu/0013.html.

Farkasi, Kathleen J., and J. Richard Romaniuk. 2020. "Social Work, Ethics and Vulnerable Groups in the Time of Coronavirus and Covid-19." *Society Register* 4 (2): 67–82. https://doi.org/10.14746/sr.2020.4.2.05.

Ferreira, L. N., L. N. Pereira, M. da Fé Brás, and Kateryna Ilchuk. 2021. "Quality of Life Under the COVID-19 Quarantine." *Quality of Life Research* 30: 1389–405. https://doi.org/10.1007/s11136-020-02724-x.

Fineman, Martha Albertson, The Vulnerable Subject: Anchoring Equality in the Human Condition. Yale Journal of Law & Feminism, Vol. 20, No. 1, 2008, Emory Public Law Research Paper No. 8-40, Available at SSRN: https://ssrn.com/abstract=1131407

Fineman, Martha Albertson, 'Elderly' as Vulnerable: Rethinking the Nature of Individual and Societal Responsibility (June 20, 2012). Emory Legal Studies Research Paper No. 12-224, Available at SSRN: https://ssrn.com/abstract=2088159

Fineman, Martha Albertson. 2017. "Introducing Vulnerability." In *Vulnerability and the Legal Organization of Work*, edited by Martha Albertson Fineman and Jonathan W. Fineman. Routledge.

Fineman, Martha Albertson. 2020. "Beyond Equality and Discrimination." *SMU Law Review Forum* 73: 51–62. https://doi.org/10.25172/slrf.73.1.7.

Goul Andersen, Jørgen. 2007. "Welfare States and Welfare State Theory." Working Paper, Centre for Comparative Welfare Studies. Accessed January 8, 2026. https://vbn.aau.dk/en/publications/welfare-states-and-welfare-state-theory/.

Harari, Yuval Noah. 2020a. "This Is the Worst Epidemic in at Least 100 Years." *CNN*, March 15. Accessed January 8, 2026. https://edition.cnn.com/videos/tv/2020/03/15/yuval-noah-harari-amanpour-cnn-coronavirus.cnn

Harari, Yuval Noah. 2020b. "The World After Coronavirus." *Financial Times*, March 20. Accessed January 18, 2021. https://www.ft.com/content/19d90308-6858-11ea-a3c9-1fe6fedcca75.

IASS (Institute for Advanced Sustainability Studies e.V.). 2020. "How Is COVID-19 Affecting the Global Economic Order? Scenarios for the Global Monetary System." *ScienceDaily*, May 11. Accessed January 18, 2021. https://www.sciencedaily.com/releases/2020/05/200511112538.htm.

Ida, Atsuhiko. 2020. "COVID-19 and Emergency Declaration and Action Control Measures: Focusing on the Legislation of Each Country." *Survey and Information* 1100. National Diet Library. [in Japanese]. https://doi.org/10.11501/11499114.

ILO (International Labour Organization). 2020. "ILO: COVID-19 Causes Devastating Losses in Working Hours and Employment." Accessed January 8, 2026. https://www.ilo.org/resource/news/ilo-covid-19-causes-devastating-losses-working-hours-and-employment-0.

IMF (International Monetary Fund). 2021. IMF Annual Report 2021. https://www.imf.org/external/pubs/ft/ar/2021/eng/downloads/.

Japan Times. 2020. "GDP." Accessed January 18, 2021. https://www.japantimes.co.jp/tag/gdp/.

Kamikubo, Yasuhiko, and Atsushi Takahashi. 2020. "Epidemiological Tools That Predict Partial Herd Immunity to SARS Coronavirus 2." *medRxiv* 2020.03.25.20043679. https://doi.org/10.1101/2020.03.25.20043679.

Kohn, Nina A. 2020. "The Pandemic Exposed a Painful Truth: America Doesn't Care About Old People." *Washington Post*, May 8. Accessed January 18, 2021. https://www.washingtonpost.com/outlook/nursing-home-coronavirus-discrimination-elderly-deaths/2020/05/07/751fc464-8fb7-11ea-9e23-6914ee410a5f_story.html.

Kokami, Shoji, and Naoki Sato. 2020. *Peer Pressure: Why Japanese Society Is Stuffy* [in Japanese]. Kodansha Publishers.

Kreitman, Paul. 2020. "In the Fight Against COVID-19, Neighborhood Associations Could Be Japan's Ace in the Hole." *Japan Times*, April 26. Accessed January 18, 2021. https://www.japantimes.co.jp/news/2020/04/26/national/japan-neighborhood-associations-coronavirus/.

Kübra, Yavuz. 2020. "Effects of Covid-19 Pandemic on the Future of Social Policy." *Journal of Social Sciences* 45: 181–93. http://doi.org/10.29228/SOBIDER.42843.

Levi, Ariel, and Philip E. Tetlock. 1980. "A Cognitive Analysis of Japan's 1941 Decision for War." *Journal of Conflict Resolution* 24 (2): 195–211. Accessed January 18, 2021. https://www.jstor.org/stable/173850.

Lu, Quan, Zehao Cai, Bin Chen, and Tao Liu. 2020. "Social Policy Responses to the Covid-19 Crisis in China in 2020." *International Journal of Environmental Research and Public Health* 17 (16): 5896. https://doi.org/10.3390/ijerph17165896.

Lynch, David. 2020. "IMF Says Global Economic Collapse Caused by Coronavirus Will Be Even Worse than Feared." *Washington Post*, June 25. Accessed January 18, 2021. https://www.washingtonpost.com/business/2020/06/24/imf-global-economy-coronavirus/.

McGann, Michael, Mary P. Murphy, and Niall Whelan. 2020. "Workfare Redux? Pandemic Unemployment, Labour Activation and the Lessons of Post-Crisis Welfare Reform in Ireland." *International Journal of Sociology and Social Policy* 40 (9–10): 963–78. Accessed January 18, 2021. https://doi.org/10.1108/IJSSP-07-2020-0343.

Mitsubishi Research Institute. 2020a. "Impact of Covid-19 Infectious Diseases on World and Japanese Economy and Proposals for Economic Measures." Accessed January 18, 2021. [in Japanese]. https://www.mri.co.jp/knowledge/insight/ecooutlook/2020/20200406.html.

Mitsubishi Research Institute. 2020b. "The Future of the Surveillance Society—What the COVID-19 Response Suggests." Accessed January 18, 2021. [in Japanese]. https://www.mri.co.jp/en/knowledge/mreview/202006-6.html.

Mitsubishi UFJ Financial Group. 2009. "Why the 'Once a Hundred Year Crisis' Was Not Foreseen." Accessed January 18, 2021. [in Japanese]. https://www.murc.jp/report/rc/column/search_now/sn090406_2/.

OECD. 2020. "Social Economy and the COVID-19 Crisis: Current and Future Roles." Accessed January 8, 2026. https://www.oecd.org/en/publications/social-economy-and-the-covid-19-crisis-current-and-future-roles_f904b89f-en.html.

Office of the Public Advocate (Victoria, Australia). n.d. "Official Guidance and COVID-19 Response Measures." Accessed January 8, 2026. https://www.publicadvocate.vic.gov.au/index.php?option=com_content&view=article&id=224&catid=19.

Pew Research Center. 2020. "Coronavirus (COVID-19)." Accessed January 18, 2021. https://www.pewresearch.org/topics/coronavirus-disease-2019-covid-19/.

Pisano, Gary P., Raffaella Sadun, and Michele Zanini. 2020. "Lessons from Italy's Response to Coronavirus." *Harvard Business Review*, March 28. Accessed January 18, 2021. https://hbr.org/2020/03/lessons-from-italys-response-to-coronavirus.

Prime Minister of Japan and His Cabinet. 2020. "Ongoing Topics: [COVID-19] Government Responses on the Coronavirus Disease 2019." Accessed January 18, 2021. https://japan.kantei.go.jp/ongoingtopics/_00013.html.

PwC Australia. 2020. "The Possible Economic Consequences of a Novel Coronavirus (COVID-19) Pandemic." Accessed January 8, 2026. https://www.pwc.com.au/media/2020/pwc-australia-covid-response.html.

Quilter-Pinner, Harry, Clare McNeil, and Dean Hochlaf. 2020. "The Decades of Disruption: New Social Risks and the Future of the Welfare State." Institute for Public Policy Research. Accessed January 18, 2021. http://www.ippr.org/research/publications/decades-of-disruption.

Rahman, M. M., Jean-Claude Thill, and K. C. Paul. 2020. "COVID-19 Pandemic Severity, Lockdown Regimes, and People's Mobility: Early Evidence from 88 Countries." *Sustainability* 12 (21): 9101. https://doi.org/10.3390/su12219101.

Reich, Robert B. 2015. *Saving Capitalism: For the Many, Not the Few.* Vintage.

Rincon, Leire. 2020. "Living Minimum Income in Spain: Very Far from a UBI." Basic Income Earth Network. Accessed January 18, 2021. https://basicincome.org/news/2020/06/living-minimum-income-in-spain-very-far-from-a-ubi/.

Rohwerder, Brigitte. 2020. *Social Impacts and Responses Related to COVID-19 in Low- and Middle-Income Countries*. Institute of Development Studies. Accessed January 18, 2021. https://opendocs.ids.ac.uk/opendocs/bitstream/handle/20.500.12413/15625/EI35_Covid-19%20and%20Social%20Development.pdf?sequence=1.

Sakurai, Yukio. 2021. "Vulnerability Approach and Adult Support and Protection: Safeguarding Laws for Adults at Risk." *Journal of Aging and Social Change* 11 (1): 19–34. https://doi.org/10.18848/2576-5310/CGP/v11i01/19-34.

Scartozzi, Cesare M. 2017. "Hereditary Politics in Japan: A Family Business—Second-Generation Politicians Are Increasingly Entrenched in Japan's Diet and Government." *Diplomat*, February 9. Accessed January 18, 2021. https://thediplomat.com/2017/02/hereditary-politics-in-japan-a-family-business/.

Sennett, Richard. 2020. "Can COVID-19 Change the Welfare State?" *Foreign Affairs*, November/December. Accessed January 18, 2021. https://www.foreignaffairs.com/articles/india/2020-10-30/can-covid-19-change-welfare-state.

Sinclair, Craig, Linda Nolte, Ben White, and Karen Detering. 2020. "Advance Care Planning in Australia During the COVID-19 Outbreak: Now More Important Than Ever." *Internal Medicine Journal* 50 (8): 918–23. https://doi.org/10.1111/imj.14937.

Sundelson, J. Wilner. 1950. "Report on Japanese Taxation by the Shoup Mission." *National Tax Journal* 3 (2): 104–20. Accessed January 18, 2021. https://www.jstor.org/stable/pdf/41789858.pdf?seq=1.

Tabner, Isaac T. 2020. "Five Ways Coronavirus Lockdowns Increase Inequality." *Conversation*, April 8. Accessed January 18, 2021. https://theconversation.com/five-ways-coronavirus-lockdowns-increase-inequality-135767.

Tashiro, Ai, and Rajib Shaw. 2020. "COVID-19 Pandemic Response in Japan: What Is Behind the Initial Flattening of the Curve?" *Sustainability* 12 (13): 5250. https://doi.org/10.3390/su12135250.

The White House. 2020. "Proclamation on Declaring a National Emergency Concerning the Novel Coronavirus Disease (COVID-19) Outbreak." March 13. https://trumpwhitehouse.archives.gov/presidential-actions/proclamation-declaring-national-emergency-concerning-novel-coronavirus-disease-covid-19-outbreak/.

The White House. 2021a. "National Strategy for the COVID-19 Response and Pandemic Preparedness." Accessed April 7, 2021. https://www.whitehouse.gov/wp-content/uploads/2021/01/National-Strategy-for-the-COVID-19-Response-and-Pandemic-Preparedness.pdf.

The White House. 2021b. "Remarks by President Biden in Press Conference March 25, 2021." Accessed April 7, 2021. https://www.whitehouse.gov/briefing-room/speeches-remarks/2021/03/25/remarks-by-president-biden-in-press-conference/.

UK, Office for National Statistics. 2020a. "Coronavirus and the Social Impacts on Great Britain: 30 April 2020." Accessed January 18, 2021. https://www.ons.gov.uk/peoplepopulationandcommunity/healthandsocialcare/healthandwellbeing/bulletins/coronavirusandthesocialimpactsongreatbritain/30april2020.

UK, Office for National Statistics. 2020b. "Coronavirus and the Social Impacts on Disabled People in Great Britain." April 24, 2020 Accessed January 18, 2021. https://www.ons.gov.uk/peoplepopulationandcommunity/healthandsocialcare/disability/articles/coronavirusandthesocialimpactsondisabledpeopleingreatbritain/2020-04-24.

United Nations, Department of Economic and Social Affairs, Social Inclusion. 2020a. "Everyone Included: The Social Impact of COVID-19." Accessed January 8, 2026. https://social.desa.un.org/everyone-included-social-impact-of-covid-19.

United Nations, Department of Economic and Social Affairs, Social Inclusion. 2020b. "Policy Brief: The Impact of COVID-19 on Older Persons." Accessed January 18, 2021. https://unsdg.un.org/sites/default/files/2020-05/Policy-Brief-The-Impact-of-COVID-19-on-Older-Persons.pdf.

U.S. Bureau of Labor Statistics. 2021. "The Employment Situation—April 2021." Accessed January 8, 2026. https://efaidnbmnnnibpcajpcglclefindmkaj/https://www.bls.gov/news.release/archives/empsit_05072021.pdf.

U.S. State Department. 2020. "Secretary Pompeo Speech—Communist China and the Free World's Future." Accessed January 8, 2026. https://2017-2021.state.gov/communist-china-and-the-free-worlds-future-2/.

Watt, Laura Tamblyn. 2020. "Canada's Coronavirus Chaos." *Bifocal* 41 (6). Accessed January 18, 2021. https://www.americanbar.org/groups/law_aging/publications/bifocal/vol-41/vol-41--issue-no-6--july-august-2020-/canada-s-coronavirus-chaos/.

WHO (World Health Organization). 2020a. "Coronavirus Disease (COVID-19) Pandemic." Accessed January 18, 2021. https://www.who.int/emergencies/diseases/novel-coronavirus-2019.

WHO (World Health Organization). 2020b. "Seventy-Third World Health Assembly Resolution: COVID-19 Response." Accessed January 18, 2021. https://apps.who.int/gb/ebwha/pdf_files/WHA73/A73_CONF1Rev1-en.pdf.

WHO (World Health Organization). 2020c. "Independent Evaluation of Global COVID-19 Response Announced." Accessed January 18, 2021. https://www.who.int/news-room/detail/09-07-2020-independent-evaluation-of-global-covid-19-response-announced.

WHO (World Health Organization). 2021. "WHO-Convened Global Study of Origins of SARS-CoV-2: China Part." Accessed April 7, 2021. https://www.who.int/publications/i/item/who-convened-global-study-of-origins-of-sars-cov-2-china-part.

World Economic Forum. 2020a. "Challenges and Opportunities in the Post-COVID-19 World." Accessed January 8, 2026. https://www.weforum.org/publications/post-covid-19-challenges-and-opportunities/#:~:text=build%20back%20better.-,This%20collection%20of%20essays%20draws%20on%20the%20diverse%20insights%20of,the%20state%20of%20the%20world..

World Economic Forum. 2020b. "COVID-19 Could Change the Welfare State Forever." Accessed January 8, 2026. https://www.weforum.org/publications/post-covid-19-challenges-and-opportunities/#:~:text=build%20back%20better.-,This%20collection%20of%20essays%20draws%20on%20the%20diverse%20insights%20of,the%20state%20of%20the%20world.

World Economic Forum. 2020c. "To Build Back Better, We Must Reinvent Capitalism. Here's How." Accessed January 8, 2026. https://www.weforum.org/stories/2020/07/to-build-back-better-we-must-reinvent-capitalism-heres-how/.

Yunus, Muhammad. 2020. "Post-Corona Rebuilding Programme: No Going Back." *China–US Focus*. Accessed January 8, 2026. https://www.chinausfocus.com/finance-economy/post-corona-reconstruction-no-going-back#:~:text=Under%20the%20rebuilding%20programme%2C%20governments,Who%20Are%20Social%20Business%20Investors?

CHAPTER 11

Turkish Politics and Human Rights Law: Focusing on Transformation

Abstract

Turkey is regarded by some as a state not demonstrating a commensurate respect for human rights. But why? Our hypothesis assumes that if Turkey undergoes a transformation under the influence of Europeanization, a greater respect of human rights will flower. And without that transformation, advancement in the field of human rights would not be expected. Through literature research and interviews with experts, this chapter analyzes the relationship between Turkish politics and human rights law based on a transformation model of Turkey. Under its EU accession policy, the Turkish government has undergone a transformation to reform domestic law so that it would be in compliance with the European human rights legal system. The Turkish legal system has adopted nearly all human rights legislation of EU countries. However, in the opinion of some, human rights are not respected in Turkey. According to their argument, the Turkish government dominates the mass media and restricts freedom of expression, and the current situation in Turkey suggests that simply ratifying European human rights legislation has not necessarily led to a respect for human rights in practice. Five elements are inherent in Turkish politics, and those elements work structurally and are examined in this chapter. Some also argue that the Turkish democracy works in appearance but not in substance under the bias of the government, particularly in the electoral, media, legislative, and judicial arenas. Human rights law would fall in the legislative category.

Keywords: Turkey, EU Accession, Transformation, Human Rights Law

1 Introduction

The Armenian massacre in the Ottoman Empire, which is claimed to have occurred around 1915 (Suny, n.d.), is said to have been one of the first international human rights problems in Europe (Irie 2017). A century later, this claim continues to elicit animosity, with the Dutch House of Representatives passing a resolution on February 22, 2018 to recognize the Armenian genocide (Winter 2018). Yet the Turkish government does not officially acknowledge the massacre of the Armenians (Ministry of Foreign Affairs of the Republic of Turkey, n.d.-e), and Turkey's human rights issues continue to be a cause for concern for some to this day. In fact, after an abortive coup attempt in July 2016, a two-year state of emergency was implemented (*Hurriyet Daily News* 2018c).[1] Affiliates of Fethullah Gülen (hereinafter referred to as "Gülen") (Sanderson 2018), the supposed master of the coup, currently reside in the United States, and the Turkish government has considered Gülen to be the leader of the Fethullah Terrorist Organization (*Fetullahçı Terör Örgütü* [FETÖ]) since May 2016 (*Reuters* 2016). In June 2017, the Turkish Supreme Court of Appeals ruled that FETÖ is to be considered an armed terrorist organization (Turkish Constitutional Court 2017), and many people—including military officers, civil servants, professors, legal professionals, and journalists—have been consequently expelled, detained, and imprisoned after being suspected of being involved in the Gülen movement.[2] The detainees include EU citizens, US Embassy local staff, and international human rights NGO staff (DeYoung and Fahim 2017). International criticism of the Turkish government's actions has included accusations of international human rights infringement and has thus become a serious diplomatic issue for Turkey (Toksabay 2017).

---

[1] A state of emergency was declared in Turkey on July 20, 2016, immediately following the failed coup attempt and remained in effect until July 19, 2018, shortly after the general and presidential elections of June 2018. During this period, certain derogations from the European Convention on Human Rights (ECHR) and the International Covenant on Civil and Political Rights (ICCPR) were authorized but were formally revoked upon the termination of the state of emergency. Nevertheless, subsequent legislation was enacted that restricted public demonstrations under the justification of protecting national security, effectively curtailing a significant dimension of civil liberties. *Hurriyet Daily News*, "New Measures before Emergency Rule Ends in Turkey," July 17, http://www.hurriyetdailynews.com/new-measures-before-emergency-rule-ends-in-turkey-134645.

[2] "Some 160,000 people were detained for questioning, of which over 77,000 were formally arrested for alleged links to terror organizations, including Gulen's network and outlawed Kurdish rebels. Those arrested include military personnel, police, journalists, lawmakers, judges and prosecutors. According to Justice Ministry figures, close to 35,000 people put on trial for links to Gulen's network have been convicted so far. Around 14,000 others were acquitted" Associated Press (*AP News*) (2018).

This chapter presents a research question that asks, "Why is Turkey regarded by some to be a state that does not respect human rights?" A hypothesis assumes that if Turkey is transformed under the influence of Europeanization, a respect for human rights will flower and that without that transformation, advancement in the field of human rights would not be expected. The primary limitation of this study is its potentially limited time frame of applicability. Turkey's human rights legislation and its practice are subject to governmental policy and to change. As a result, the conditions addressed in this chapter will likely change in the future. However, this limitation does not negate the importance of academic analysis of the foregoing research question for the contemporary setting.

In the section "Methodology," the methodology applicable to this chapter is provided. The section "Modern Turkey Classified by Period," which follows, briefly reviews the history of modern Turkey and shows how it can be categorized by period. The section "Framework of Human Rights Policy in Turkey" reviews the framework of human rights policy based on the official view of the Turkish government. The types of human rights issues occurring in Turkey are then examined in "Issues Under Human Rights Law in Turkey." The section "Why Do Human Rights Issues Occur in Turkey?" analyzes why those issues have arisen. A "Conclusion" follows.

2 Methodology

Literature surveys and interviews with experts have been used for this research. This literature research encompasses approximately fifty academic books, articles, and website resources, mainly in English and Japanese, collected and reviewed between 2016 and 2018. These sources were retrieved through research in the field of Turkish Studies and International Human Rights Law, using "Turkey," "human rights law," and "Turkey's EU accession negotiations" as key expressions, following academic criteria acceptable to the Japan Association of International Relations and the International Human Rights Law Association in Japan. Previous studies include those applicable to international human rights in the specific area of Turkey (Hirai 2010; Nishii 2014), those applicable to international human rights law in connection with Turkey's accession to the EU (Hachiya et al. 2007; Bürgin 2012), and those applicable to international human rights law in general (Hopgood et al. 2018; Zalaquett 1992). However, those applicable to specific Turkish international human rights can be found only in official reports made by the UN, EU, UK, and US (United Nations Human Rights Council [UNHRC] 2018; European Commission 2018; United Kingdom 2017; U.S. Department of State 2019). Interviews were conducted with fifteen experts in Istanbul (April 2018) and Tokyo (2017–2018). These experts are attached to businesses, research institutes, universities, and public agencies. The selection criteria for the experts included extensive experience with local businesses, or academic societies. The interview process was as follows. After making an appointment to meet individually with experts, interviews were conducted in experts' offices in line with questions prepared prior to the interviews. Summary records were then written as minutes in Japanese.

The information is viewed and analyzed through a transformation model as a frame of reference, as emphasized by Keyman and Gumucu: "Transformation opens up a space for a critical analysis of this navigation in which one could take into account both potentials and risks involved in the process of making Turkish democracy consolidated and Turkish modernity plural and multicultural" (Keyman and Gumucu 2014, 17) This transformation model demonstrates advancements of the state under the influence of Turkey's EU accession policy (Ministry of Foreign Affairs of the Republic of Turkey, n.d.-g). Turkey became a candidate for EU accession in 1999, and since 2000, the country has been transformed under the influence of Europeanization. Europeanization refers to the process to accept the EU framework and its values, including establishing a legislation and institutional system that meets the Copenhagen criteria.[3] Turkey's EU accession negotiations began in 2005, but the progress of transformation was delayed, and the country's course was eventually reversed after the negotiations were nearly suspended in 2007 (European Commission, n.d.-a). Under the administration of the Justice and Development Party (*Adalet ve Kalkınma Partisi; AK Parti* [AKP]) (AKP, n.d.), the ruling party since 2002, the government's media control gradually tightened, and restrictions on freedom of expression and assembly were strengthened (Hoffman and Werz 2013). Around 2011, the public began to embrace an Islamic orientation.[4] After an abortive coup attempt in July

---

[3] Adopted by the European Council held in Copenhagen in 1993, the Copenhagen criteria stipulate the accession conditions that a country must satisfy to join the EU, including geographical, political, economic, and legislative requirements.

[4] Some examples of political and cultural changes in Turkey include primary educational reforms to offer pupils more Islamic instruction and the planned demolition of the AKM Atatürk Cultural Center to be replaced by an opera house and a mosque (Taşpınar 2012).

2016, a state of emergency was implemented and continually extended every three months until July 2018 (*Hurriyet Daily News* 2018a). During this period, the rule of law was partly lost, and a crackdown on irregular suspects was carried out for the purpose of national security (*Hurriyet Daily News* 2018b). Turkey was thus transformed during three stages of change: (1) Europeanization under the EU accession policy, (2) Discontinuation of Europeanization, and (3) Crackdowns during state-of-emergency declaration (Figure 1).

Figure 1: Transformation Model

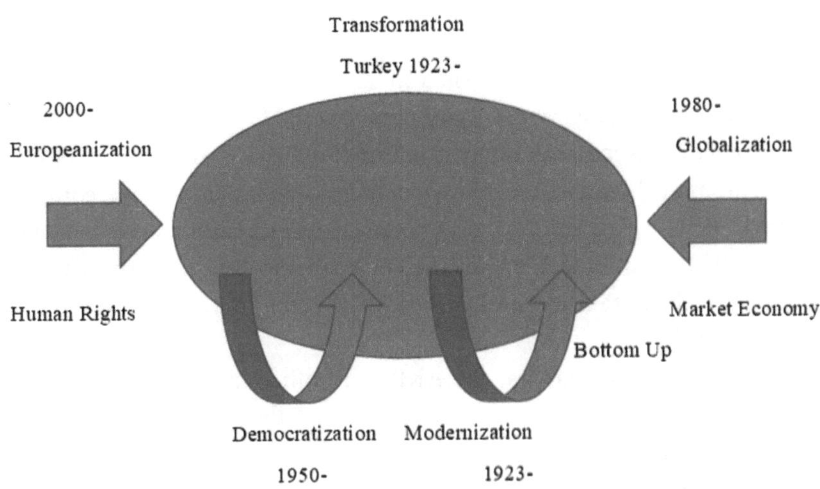

Source: Adapted by Author based on Keyman and Gumucu 2014

3 Modern Turkey Classified by Period

3.1 A Brief History of Modern Turkey

A brief review of the history of modern Turkey is provided here. The Republic of Turkey was founded in 1923 after a war of independence against foreign occupation and rule by sultans. The modernization and civilization promoted by the first president, Mustafa Kemal Atatürk ([Kemal]), are the basis of the country's subsequent national policy, a policy that is depicted by the six arrows on the CHP flag—i.e., arrows representing republicanism, nationalism, Kemalist populism, statism, secularism, and revolutionism (Arai 2001). Under this national policy, Turkey adopted a rule of law and parliamentary democracy and aimed to construct a modern nation-state, establish a society fully devoted to secularism, and create a centralized administrative system governed by political elites (Arai 2001). With this governance mechanism, a so-called tutelary democracy arose featuring a national army and a judiciary that strongly supported the national policy in accordance with the constitution (Baser and Ozturk 2017).

In Turkey, when maintaining the national policy became difficult on three occasions—namely, two military coups in 1960 and 1980, and a written military threat in 1971—the military took temporary control of the administration and then transferred power to civilians.[5] The current constitution, which was established in 1982 by the military administration, has been partially revised since then, but the fundamental parts have not changed, thus maintaining it as national policy.[6] In response to political parties that threatened secularism, strict countermeasures were implemented, including dissolution orders issued by the Constitutional Court (Algan 2011). From the 1990s to the beginning of the 2000s, the Turkish economy lacked stability, and the national economy collapsed and fell into serious disarray.[7]

Under such circumstances, the AKP took office in 2002. The AKP is a pro-Islamic political party[8] that was originally formed by Abdullah Gül and Recep Tayyip Erdoğan (Erdoğan). During that period, globalization based on the market economy progressed, and the economic

---

[5] Transfers of powers to civilian governments occurred in 1961 and 1983, respectively, following military coups in 1960 and 1980.

[6] Article 2 of the Constitution of the Republic of Turkey states: "The Republic of Turkey is a democratic, secular and social state governed by rule of law, within the notions of public peace, national solidarity and justice, respecting human rights, loyal to the nationalism of Atatürk, and based on the fundamental tenets set forth in the preamble." Article 4 provides: "The provision of Article 1 regarding the form of the State being a Republic, the characteristics of the Republic in Article 2, and the provisions of Article 3 shall not be amended, nor shall their amendment be proposed" (The Grand National Assembly of Turkey (website), 2019).

[7] "During the lost years of the 1990s, financial deepening was mainly shaped by credit expansion through public banks and creative credit expansion tactics of banks using instruments such as back-to-back credits" (Gormez and Yigit 2009, 17).

[8] Article 2 of the Turkish Constitution formally restricts party leaders from asserting that the AKP is a pro-Islamic party. Nevertheless, the party's founders, cabinet members, and even their spouses are pro-Islamic, suggesting that the AKP is potentially a pro-Islamic party. At the same time, the party has demonstrated early signs of a pro-Western orientation. As one analysis notes, "The AK Party won massive support not because voters thought it aspired to an Islamic state. The electorate gave this party its votes because they hoped and believed that the party would put an end to *yoksolluk* (poverty) and *yolsuzluk* (corruption)" (Karlsson 2008, 99–108; Celik 2017, 99–119).

growth of emerging economies was highlighted. Trade between the EU and Turkey became more active in accordance with the EU-Turkish Customs Union adopted in 1995, and Turkey began to supply industrial parts and semi-finished products to the EU, especially Germany, and became a product-assembly base in the European region (European Commission, n.d.-b). The AKP revitalized the domestic economy, promoted large-scale infrastructure projects, and achieved management stability of the financial industry, which was a key element of the national economy, and improved the credibility of the Turkish economy (Acemoglu and Ucer 2015).

In diplomacy, the AKP set out the EU accession policy and encouraged a friendly attitude toward the EU and US. The AKP appointed economic technocrats such as Ali Babacan, a Turkish minister and later deputy prime minister, and implemented innovative programs in diplomacy and economics. As a result, the domestic economy grew remarkably, attracted direct investment from EU states, assembling industries supported by the country's competitive labor, and tourists who desired tourism in an area having a moderate climate (Acemoglu and Ucer 2015). As a result, the GDP per capita in 2011 exceeded US$10,000 (Right 2012), Turkey's domestic consumption became active, and the middle class largely grew. In fact, Turkish society changed significantly due to the economic prosperity initiated by the AKP administration (Acemoglu and Ucer 2015).

Meanwhile, EU accession negotiations started in 2005, but in 2007, negotiations were eventually suspended. One of the reasons for this was a disagreement among the major states on the EU side; in particular, the leaders of both Germany and France opposed Turkey's accession (Inal and Yegenoglu 2005). Afterward, Turkey was incorporated into the EU economic partnership by the EU-Turkey Customs Union but not included in political and migration partnerships as an EU member or its substitute. Nonetheless, Turkey adhered to the EU accession policy, and European transformation of the Turkish legal and institutional system, including human rights legislation, advanced gradually (Hale 2011). Meanwhile, during the EU accession negotiations, the political issues around the legal status of North Cyprus were addressed and remained a large hurdle for Turkey to join the EU.[9] As a result, although considerable progress had

---

[9] North Cyprus is a so-called de facto state recognized only by Turkey. For this diplomatic reason, Turkey officially cannot recognize Cyprus as an independent country. This situation stems from a long-standing and sensitive diplomatic conflict between Turkey and Greece (Sertöz 2015).

been made through legislation reform, a high political hurdle that could not be cleared by legislative provision brought Turkey's EU accession negotiations to a standstill.

Also, with regard to the unsettled conflict between Turkish government and Kurdish armed forces, a ceasefire agreement that had continued from 2013 to 2015 was eventually abandoned (Tanchum 2015). Afterward, violence became more common. The battle areas of the Turkish armed forces extended into northern Iraq and northwest Syria. For this reason, diplomatic tensions arose between Turkey and the US, which had supported the Kurds strategically in Iraq and Syria (Arslan et al. 2018). Domestically in Turkey, after the AKP brought the national military under political control around 2011, the relationship between the AKP and Gülen worsened (Sanderson 2018). The conflict between the AKP regime and the Gülen movement intensified, especially after a corruption scandal involving AKP ministers and Erdoğan's son in December 2013 (Arango 2013), and an abortive coup attempt in July 2016 (Ministry of Foreign Affairs of the Republic of Turkey, n.d.-f).

3.2 Turkey Classified by Period

After 2002, the AKP administration initially enjoyed economic prosperity and placed the EU accession policy at the forefront, but as economic growth slowed and the EU accession policy was virtually aborted, an Islamic orientation began to grow (Bakner 2017, 21–46). Since the inauguration of Erdoğan as president in 2014, the Islamic orientation trend has accelerated (*Atlantic* 2016) and been carried out by the AKP with new construction of mosques (Sokollu 2013), an emphasis on religious education curriculum at schools, and the addition of religious public schools.[10] While terrorism eventually occurred in 2015 and 2016 after the ceasefire agreement was abandoned, and as the country's national security became unstable, the AKP embraced a presidential system with executive power and a constitutional revision enabling it. In the April 2017 referendum, the constitutional amendments were approved by 51.14% of the voters, and the shift to a presidential system with executive power was officially accepted (Esen and Gumuscu 2018; Sakurai 2018). Turkey has undergone

---

[10] "Since 2012, when *Imam Hatip* education was extended to middle schools for pupils aged 10 to 14, total pupil numbers have risen fivefold to 1.3 million students in over 4,000 schools" Butler (2019).

rapid transformation since the inauguration of the AKP administration in 2002. The foregoing historical progression is generally categorized by period, as follows:

1. 2002–2007: Period of transformation (democracy, economic growth, pro-EU policy)
2. 2008–2013: Period of partial transformation (competitive authoritarianism, economic stability, partial independent diplomacy)
3. 2014–2019: Period of transformation reversal (authoritarianism, economic instability, independent diplomacy)

4 Framework of Human Rights Policy in Turkey

The framework for human rights legislation and policy currently in effect is based on the official views of the Ministry of Foreign Affairs of Turkey (n.d.-a). It is assumed that Turkey developed a framework for human rights legislation under its EU accession policy. Since Turkey became an EU member candidate in 1999, legislation reform in the area of international human rights has occurred. For EU accession, it is necessary for Turkey to meet the EU accession criteria referred to as the Copenhagen criteria, which includes human rights provisions. Turkish implementations are composed of three pillars of legal improvements: "ratification of international conventions on human rights," "revision of the constitution and the domestic law system," and "improvement of the enforcement system of domestic legislation" (Ministry of Foreign Affairs of the Republic of Turkey, n.d.-a).

4.1 Ratification of International Conventions on Human Rights

The main international and regional human rights conventions ratified by Turkey are as follows:

Council of Europe
Convention for the Protection of Human Rights and Fundamental Freedoms as amended by Protocol No.11 (Originally effective May 1954)

United Nations

International Covenant on Civic and Political Rights (Effective March
  1976)

International Covenant on Economic, Social and Cultural Rights (Effective March 1976)

Convention Against Torture and Other Cruel, Inhuman or Degrading
  Treatment or Punishment (Effective June 1987)

International Convention on the Elimination of All Forms of Racial
  Discrimination (Effective September 2002)

Convention on the Elimination of All Forms of Discrimination Against
  Women

(Effective September 1981)

Convention on the Rights of the Child (Effective September 1990)

International Convention on the Protection of the Rights of All Migrant
  Workers and Members of Their Families (Effective July 1967)

Turkey has frameworks of cooperation with three international and
regional organizations, including the Council of Europe and the European Court of Human Rights (ECtHR), the UN Human Rights Council
(UNHRC), and the Human Dimension of the Organization for Security
and Co-Operation in Europe (OSCE) (Ministry of Foreign Affairs of the
Republic of Turkey, n.d.-b).

4.2 Council of Europe and ECtHR

The Council of Europe, which was established in Strasbourg, France,
in 1949 as a pan-European international agency, is the main maker and
administrator of international standards in the fields of human rights,
democracy, and rule of law. Together with Greece in 1949, Turkey became
a member of the Council of Europe. The ECtHR was founded under the
European Convention on Human Rights (1953, ECHR) and is a judicial
body of the Council of Europe, ECtHR,[11] which addresses violations of

---

[11] The European Court of Human Rights (ECtHR) is a "judicial organ established in 1959 that is charged with
supervising the enforcement of the Convention for the Protection of Human Rights and Fundamental Freedoms
(1950; commonly known as the European Convention on Human Rights), which was drawn up by the Council
of Europe. The convention obligates signatories to guarantee various civil and political freedoms, including the
freedom of expression and religion and the right to a fair trial. The court is headquartered in Strasbourg, France"
Encyclopedia Britannica Online (n.d.-b).

ECHR. As a member, Turkey has a legal relationship with the Council of Europe and ECtHR. The members of the Council of Europe have similar values and a close cooperative relationship with one another. Based on this relationship, Turkey has carried out extensive legal reforms, including changes to the Turkish constitution, civil code, and criminal law, to prepare for EU accession.

Specifically, these changes include abolition of the death penalty, prohibition of torture, freedom of religion, reform of inmates and detention centers, freedom of expression, and freedom of assembly, in addition to an emphasis on the role of justice; the relationship between civilians and the military; economic, social, and cultural freedom; and corruption prohibition. In fact, Turkey ratified 117 (53%) out of the 222 conventions adopted by the Council of Europe (Ministry of Foreign Affairs of the Republic of Turkey, n.d.-a). Further, Turkey played a leading role at the Council of Europe Convention on preventing and combating violence against women and domestic violence, i.e., the so-called Istanbul Convention held in Istanbul in May 2011 under Council of Europe sponsorship (Ministry of Foreign Affairs of the Republic of Turkey, n.d.-b).

4.3 UNHRC

The UNHRC is an organization responsible for international human rights issues in the UN. Turkey has ratified fifteen out of the eighteen human rights conventions adopted by the UN (United Nations Office of the High Commissioner for Human Rights [OHCHR], n.d.-a). In 2001, Turkey became a member of a special procedure subject to UN procedures and regularly accepted human rights inspections by individual third parties. The country is also the subject of the Universal Periodic Review (UPR) of the UNHRC, with the first review being conducted in 2010 and the second review in 2015 (OHCHR, n.d.-b).

In the first review, the Turkish government rejected the recommendation concerning ethnic and religious minorities and gender issues, with no regard being given to the issue of transferring Northern Cyprus residents to Turkey, and the concept of "minorities" under the constitution (Nishii 2014). However, except for these two points, "basically, it seems to read that the Turkish government is flexible, as it has properly expressed reservations about unacceptable points, and sophisticated responses are diplomatically provided. In the end, an effective dialogue occurred" (Nishii 2014, 57). In the second cycle review, the aforementioned correspondence did not change in principle, and the number of comments from the examining UN member states increased, including concerns about the refugee convention.

4.4 OSCE

The OSCE has fifty-seven member-countries in North America, Europe, and Central Asia and is the world's largest regional security organization (OSCE, n.d.). It is thought that problems in the economic, environmental, human rights, and humanitarian fields will also lead to security threats, so security encompasses many activities: "In addition to its primary function of being a regional security forum, OSCE assists the efforts of the participating States in the field of respect for democracy, the rule of law and human rights. Along with Permanent Council and Ministerial Council meetings within the OSCE, each year Human Dimension Implementation Meetings (HDIM); and Supplementary Human Dimension Meetings (SHDM) are organized" (Ministry of Foreign Affairs of the Republic of Turkey, n.d.-a; OSCE 2017).

The OSCE for Democratic Institutions and Human Rights (ODIHR) prepared a report from a third-party stance on international surveillance activities related to Turkey's election implementation, and the organization's recent statement related to the referendum in April 2017 questioned the fairness of an election held under a state of emergency (OSCE 2018).

4.5 Revision of the Constitution and Domestic Law System

In the current Turkish constitution, provisions on basic human rights are clearly and comprehensively stated in the preamble and "Part 2: Basic Rights and Obligations" as follows:

Preamble (partial quotation) (The Grand National Assembly of Turkey, 2019)
Every Turkish citizen has an innate right and power, to lead an honorable life and to improve his/her material and spiritual well-being under the aegis of national culture, civilization, and the rule of law, through the exercise of the fundamental rights and freedoms set forth

in this Constitution, in conformity with the requirements of equality and social justice;

All Turkish citizens are united in national honor and pride, in national joy and grief, in their rights and duties regarding national existence, in blessings and in burdens, and in every manifestation of national life, and that they have the right to demand a peaceful life based on absolute respect for one another's rights and freedoms, mutual love and fellowship, and the desire for and belief in "Peace at home; peace in the world";

Part 2: Basic Rights and Obligations (Partial quotation) (The Grand National Assembly of Turkey, 2019)

Chapter 1 General Provision (names of clauses only)

I. Basic rights and nature of freedom, II. Restrictions on basic rights and freedoms, III. Prohibition of basic rights and abuse of freedom, IV. Restrictions on basic rights and exercise of freedom, V. Status of foreigners

Chapter 2 Personal Rights and Obligations (names of clauses only)

I. Inviolability, material and spiritual existence of personality,

II. Prohibition of forced labor, III. Individual freedom and safety, IV. Secrets and protection of private life, V. Residence and movement freedom, VI. Religion and freedom of conscience, VII. Freedom of thought and opinion, VIII. Freedom to represent and disseminate thought, IX. Academic and artistic freedom, X. Regulations concerning press and publication, XI. Right and freedom of assembly, XII. Ownership, XIII. Provision on protection of rights, XIV. Right of certification, XV. Protection of basic rights and freedoms.

Article 90 of the Turkish constitution regarding ratification of international conventions regulates international conventions and their legal effect, and this chapter was partially revised in May 2004 to delineate that international conventions shall prevail over domestic law if the content of ratified international conventions on basic human rights conflict with any national law (Duvan 2015). This constitution reform would allow us to assume that Turkey is demonstrating a respect for international conventions on basic human rights as a part of legislation.[12]

---

[12] "The amendment to the Constitution, however, did not help create an automatic priority for international human rights law in practice" (Akbulut 2015, 77).

The constitution was further amended by the referendum of September 2010. Accordingly, the principle of positive discrimination applicable to women, children, the disabled, and the elderly was recognized as a constitutional right; the protection of personal data was safeguarded; the rights of children were guaranteed; the scope of the right to freedom of assembly and association was expanded; the right to information was defined as a constitutional right for the first time; the right to vote and to be elected was further strengthened; and disciplinary provisions for civil servants and other public officers were included in the scope of judicial review.

4.6 Improvement of the Enforcement System of Domestic Legislation

New mechanisms for safeguarding human rights have come into effect. The Turkish Human Rights Agency Law and Ombudsman Agency Law were enacted in June 2012, and two domestic human rights institutes began activities. A domestic human rights agency refers to an independent legal institution established for the purpose of extending and protecting the human rights of the citizens, according to the principles of the Statement of Paris 1992 on the status of domestic human rights institutes (Fujimoto 2001). The rule of law has been strengthened, the Constitutional Court and the High Council of Judges and Prosecutors have been restructured on the basis of best practices in other democratic countries, and the area of military jurisdiction has been restricted (UNHRC 2014, 2–3).

Turkish domestic human rights institutes then began to function as a domestic torture-prevention mechanism of the Convention of Torture from January 2015. After that, in April 2016, the agency was reorganized into the Human Rights and Equality Institution of Turkey (HREI) and became involved in discrimination prohibition activities. The role of the Ombudsman Institute is to deal with all problems related to human rights from an independent position and to accept individual complaints. Both institutes are expected to contribute to extending and protecting the human rights of Turkish citizens (UNHRC 2014, 4).

The individual right to apply to the Constitutional Court, "which was introduced for further protecting the individual rights and freedoms and making the implementation of the ECHR provisions more effective, came into force on September 23, 2012" (Ministry of Foreign Affairs of the

Republic of Turkey, n.d.-a).[13] The Democratization Package of September 2013 enabled political campaigning and propaganda, as well as education in private schools, in languages and dialects other than Turkish. The ban on women wearing headscarves in the public service was lifted. Hate crimes were included in the Turkish Penal Code, and the penalty for discrimination and hatred was increased (UNHRC 2015).

4.7 Summary

To sum up, "Turkey has put into effect a comprehensive reform process since the early 2000s with a view to further strengthening democracy, consolidating the rule of law, and ensuring full respect for fundamental freedoms."[14] It could be said that Turkey has implemented a basic international human rights law framework that nears those of other European states.[15] Further, the establishment of this system is considered to have been realized through transformation accompanying an EU accession policy put into action by the AKP administration.

5 Issues Under Human Rights Law in Turkey

Evaluations of Turkish human rights issues from third parties outside Turkey are provided. The third parties include the US, UN, EU, and international NGOs because those states and institutions regularly monitor human rights situations by country and publish annual reports or human rights rating analyses for the public. It is therefore understood that those evaluations are worth reviewing to gain a perspective of the worldwide human rights standard.

---

[13] The number of applications from Turkish territory to the ECtHR was 2,212 (2015), 8,303 (2016), 25,978 (2017), and 6,717 (2018). Turkey was the fourth-largest applicant territory to the ECtHR in 2018, following Russia, Romania, and Ukraine. ECtHR (2019); United Nations Human Rights Council (2015, 3–4).

[14] "Turkey has put into effect a comprehensive reform process since early 2000s with a view to further strengthening democracy, consolidating the rule of law and ensuring full respect for fundamental freedoms" (Ministry of Foreign Affairs, Republic of Turkey, n.d.-a).

[15] "The harmonization laws introduced as an extension of this process and of the judgments of the European Court of Human Rights (ECtHR) brought in developments at least on the normative level" Çınar and Şirin (2017, 1).

5.1 Historical Issues

The historical challenges include recognition of the Armenian massacre (said to have occurred during the Ottoman Empire around 1915), conflict with EU member states Greece and Cyprus over Northern Cyprus (since 1974), domestic violence in rural society, honor killings, and human rights issues concerning the status of women, which were reviewed in the UPRs by the UNHRC in 2010 and 2015.[16]

5.2 Contemporary Issues

A number of contemporary issues have been pointed out in these evaluations. For example, in the "Country Reports on Human Rights Practices for 2017" by the US Department of State (2017), the following were addressed: government activities that lack legally relevant processes under a state-of-emergency declaration are being conducted (there are no legal procedures suitable for dismissal or interrogation of a large number of civil servants, etc.); government intervention is impeding freedom of the press (140 journalists had been detained as of 2016); residents are not being properly protected (relocation and violent acts toward residents by the Kurdish Workers' Party (*Partiya Karkerên Kurdistanê*, [PKK]) in southeastern Turkey); unjust treatment in crowded jails; the hindrance of judicial officials and judicial functions; inadequate support of refugees (children cannot attend school, etc.); illegal handling of children and women; discrimination against religious minorities and LGBTI; child labor issues (especially refugees' children); and discriminatory advertising against minorities.

The 2018 EU Turkey Report pointed out that Turkey's human rights were "backsliding" significantly, specifically after a state of emergency under which Turkey partly suspended the application of the Convention for the Protection of Human Rights and Fundamental Freedoms. The report also pointed out that domestic human rights institutions in Turkey were not fully compliant with the Paris Principles and thus needed to improve (European Commission 2018).

---

[16] In UPR, Turkey is peer-reviewed, and there is interactive dialogue with UN member states (United Nations Human Rights Council 2015).

According to the latest report by Amnesty International, over 100 journalists have been arrested, and the freedom of expression by human rights defense organizations and activists has been suppressed; anti-government demonstrations have been prohibited, thus suppressing the freedom of assembly; torture and other inappropriate interrogations have been carried out; armed groups have engaged in abuse (terrorist activities); more than 100,000 workers have lost their jobs through emergency declarations; 500,000 inhabitants of the southeastern part of Turkey have lost their livelihoods due to military activities; and Syrian refugees exceeding three million people in Turkey are not being properly handled (European Commission 2015), thus creating a human rights issue (Amnesty International, n.d.).

5.3 Third-Party Evaluations

International NGOs monitoring Turkey have produced various indicators, and Turkey's ratings have been relatively poor. *Freedom House* downgraded Turkey's freedom status from "partly free" since 1999 to "not free" in 2017; the country's press freedom status was "not free" in 2016 (*Freedom House*, n.d.). In the World Press Freedom Index's annual ranking, Turkey fell from 149 (2015) to 151 (2016) and further to 155 (2017) and 157 (2018) out of 180 countries (Reporters Without Borders [RSF], n.d.). In the Rule of Law Index, Turkey dropped from 91 (2015) to 99 (2016) and then to 101 (2017) out of 113 countries (World Justice Project, n.d.). The Rule of Law Index is made by the World Justice Project, an international NGO that quantifies eight factors concerning the rule of law for each country and announces the findings annually. Turkey received low scores for its "constraints on government powers" and "fundamental rights," and the country's scores for "order and security" and "criminal justice" fell, all of which negatively affected Turkey's results. The Committee to Protect Journalists announced in its 2017 survey that seventy-three journalists in Turkey had been imprisoned. In fact, Turkey was the greatest transgressor in this area, followed by China (forty-one) and Egypt (twenty) (Committee to Protect Journalists, n.d.).

The sharp response to Turkey's human rights issues has not been limited to international NGOs. The international media, governments such as the US, UK, Germany, Austria, and the Netherlands, and regional organizations such as the EU, the Council of Europe, and the OSCE have also been critical of Turkey's international human rights violations. In fact, at the EU Turkey Leaders' Meeting held in Varna on March 23, 2018, the EU president told the Turkish president that the EU could understand the importance of national security in response to the abortive coup in July 2016, but the EU was concerned about democracy and the rule of law in Turkey, suggesting that Turkey make use of the Council of Europe to resolve problems (European Council, n.d.). A US State Department spokesperson mentioned on May 4, 2018, that due to a Turkish national army campaign in Afrin, northwest Syria, many local Syrian residents had lost their homes, thus becoming refugees and creating a human rights problem (US Department of State, n.d.; Ministry of Foreign Affairs of the Republic of Turkey 2018). The UNHRC has also investigated the actual condition of human rights suppression against residents in southeastern Turkey since July 2015 and published a report in March 2017 (OHCHR 2017) and another report in March 2018 (OHCHR 2018) discouraging the state-of-emergency renewal, the restraint and imprisonment of suspects related to Gülen's movement or the PKK, and the torture of suspects.

5.4 Summary

In summary, third-party evaluations affirm concerns about restrictions on freedom of expression in Turkey, the detention and imprisonment of numerous suspects under a state-of-emergency declaration, and human rights issues, including torture, involving Kurdish and Syrian citizens. Serious concerns have been repeatedly brought up at the UN (OHCHR 2019). The Turkish case has thus apparently demonstrated that the acceptance of a human rights law system does not necessarily materialize into a respect for human rights.[17]

6 Why Do Human Rights Issues Occur in Turkey?

A question arises, namely, why do human rights issues occur in Turkey? When Turkey accepted a European transformation and crafted an EU accession policy, the driving force to accept an international human rights

---

[17] "These normative changes were not sufficiently reciprocated in practice and were not sufficiently internalized by public mechanisms, in particular the security forces" Çınar and Şirin (2017, 1).

law framework appeared to function well. As a result, a constitution, national legal system, international and regional conventions, national human rights agencies, and an international human rights cooperation system were formally developed, and Turkey could thus respond to diplomatic activities including the UPRs of the UNHRC in 2010 and 2015, in addition to high-level meetings with the Council of Europe.

Since then, however, the EU accession negotiations have come to a standstill, and as the domestic political base of the ruling AKP gradually becomes stronger, the freedoms of expression and assembly have been restricted through the detention of many journalists, the closure or sale of media outlets to pro-governmental enterprises (Jones 2018), and the rise of competitive authoritarianism (Baser and Ozturk 2017; Uno 2015). In 2014, all AKP politicians except Erdoğan, who has led the AKP since his inauguration in 2001, resigned from office due to an internal regulation limiting assembly members to three terms. While the absolute leadership of Erdoğan in the AKP has been established, authoritarianism has gradually increased (Baser and Ozturk 2017; Esen and Gumuscu 2018). It may thus be inferred that the violations of human rights in Turkey are structurally tied to elements inherent in Turkish politics.[18] If that is so, what are those elements?

6.1 Five Elements

First, a competitive authoritarianism is rising in Turkey, which means "although elections are regularly held and are generally free of massive fraud, incumbents routinely abuse state resources, deny the opposition adequate media coverage, harass opposition candidates and their supporters, and in some cases, manipulate electoral results" (Baser and Ozturk 2017, 260). In other words, democracy works in appearance but not in substance under the bias of the government, particularly in the electoral, media, legislative, and judicial arenas (Levitsky and Way 2002, 2010; Sakurai 2018). Competitive authoritarianism has become prevalent in Turkish politics. Competitive authoritarianism often ignores the will of citizens who are not supporters if the support of a majority of the

---

[18] Doğru and Şirin argue Turkish human rights violation from judicial system viewpoints; however, this article argues it from political viewpoints Doğru and Şirin (2017).

people in the parliamentary democracy is achieved through votes. And even if competitive authoritarianism cracks because of some opposition, political stability can be easily maintained. Turkish politics appears to be in a transformation from a democracy to a competitive authoritarianism and then becoming authoritarianism, as the human rights of the people are becoming less protected (Baser and Ozturk 2017). Turkish citizens are generally afraid of government crackdowns, which were severe after the Gezi Park protests in 2013 (*Hurriyet Daily News* 2013) and the abortive coup attempt in 2016,[19] and thus citizens now hesitate to express their own political opinions in public, some having even left Turkey for European countries or the US.[20]

Second, European transformation has faded. In the current Turkish constitution, Article 2 prescribes Turkish nationalism and a respect for human rights in the republic (defined in Article 1), peace of mind, solidarity of the people, and solidarity of justice in the desire for justice based on the basic principles mentioned in the Preamble. The constitution stipulates democratic, secular rule of law (Article 2), constituting the whole consisting of indivisible land and citizens (defined in Article 3). However, interpretations of those provisions are allowing an Islamic orientation promoted by the AKP to become a reality. Along with this, political leaders need not absolutely seek Europeanization; it seems to be thought that the values of Islam are acceptable to some extent by the people.[21] For this reason, rather than absolutely respecting the European values that are often considered to be the foundation of international human rights, the majority seems to be of the mindset that European values have become relative and should be balanced with the values of Islam (Karlsson 2008, 99–108; Interviews with the author, Istanbul 2018). This point of view is assumed to be largely influenced by President Erdoğan's unique politi-

---

[19] "The situation in Turkey has become even more difficult since the July 2016 coup attempt and after the declaration of the state of emergency. There are gross violations of human rights" (Yinanç 2018). However, the Turkish government states that "during the State of Emergency (SoE), Turkey has acted in full awareness of its obligations arising from international conventions and respected the principles of democracy, human rights and the rule of law" (Ministry of Foreign Affairs, Republic of Turkey, n.d.-a).

[20] "Some 113,000 Turks emigrated in 2018, a sharp increase over the previous year, when more than 69,000 left the country, according to the Turkish Institute of Statistics" (Gall 2019).

[21] "Religious people are more likely to consider heteronomy values like obedience and respect as important child qualities in their children. Moreover, the relationships between religious predictors and child-rearing traits are robust across education levels and household income" (Aydogdu and Yildiz 2016, 38–50). For adults, there has been a dramatic rise in the popularity of Ottoman Empire soap dramas on Turkish TV and impact the daily lives of Turkish people (Toksabay 2012).

cal views.[22] A new word, Erdoğanism, has come into usage. The integral pieces of Erdoğanism are composed of political Islam, authoritarianism, and Turkish nationalism (Cagaptay and Aktas 2017). This could only partly, not fully, explain Erdoğan's unique political style and philosophy and his strong character and powerful political leadership. It is assumed that Erdoğanism means that Turkish citizens rely on one man, President Erdoğan, as an autocrat or dictator (Sakurai 2018).

Third, Turkey's domestic politics are having a detrimental impact. Turkey has had a de facto AKP single party system since 2002. The opposition parties are, in fact, powerless and thus cannot compete politically with the AKP (Baser and Ozturk 2017). Although the strong political leadership of the president is fully supported by half the population, the other half opposes this direction. Turkey has considerable division among the citizens in terms of political and social orientation. The current division among the citizens in politics is between those who are pro-Erdoğan and others who are anti-Erdoğan. Erdoğan has a charismatic speaking ability, and he can understand ordinary citizens' minds by speaking the same words as they do (Cagaptay 2017). This is why Erdoğan is highly appreciated by pro-Erdoğan supporters. However, he has little mind to communicate with those who do not give him their support. Therefore, his political attitude leaves the division of the people in a serious, unsolved state (Sakurai 2018). In such a political situation, enormous energy is being invested in national security issues, such as fights with PKK; a military campaign in northwest Syria; and fights against the Democratic Union Party (PYD) and its armed wing, the People's Protection Units (YPG) in Syria as well as other terrorists.[23] Under the banner of national security, a consensus has been established in society presuming that the partial and temporary suspension of human rights protections is inevitable. As a result, human rights are not being properly safeguarded (Interviews with the author, Istanbul, 2018).

Fourth, the state of emergency that had been in effect from July 2016 until July 2018 has had a negative influence on the rule of law. The state

---

[22] Erdoğan's (1996) well-known statement at the Muslim Arab Youth Association Conference 1996 that "democracy can never be a goal, rather, it can only be considered a useful tool with which to re-shape a society from one that is secular-democratic to one that is Islamic."

[23] "PYD/YPG's affiliation with PKK is clear. PYD/YPG was set up under the control of a PKK terrorist organization in 2003. They share the same leadership cadres, organizational structure, strategies and tactics, military structure, propaganda tools, financial resources and training camps" (Ministry of Foreign Affairs, Republic of Turkey, n.d.-c).

of emergency has resulted in temporary but serious effects leading to the rule of law being neglected,[24] including some regional human rights conventions, and has prolonged human rights transgressions. In such a situation, counter-democracy activities by the citizens may eventually occur (Rosanvallon 2006), as in the Gezi Park protests in 2013, or in even more radical ways. However, the Turkish government maintains strict authoritarian control over Turkish citizens who may protest against the government, and many suspects related to the FETÖ were detained, captured, and labeled as terrorists under a state of emergency (Ministry of Foreign Affairs of the Republic of Turkey, n.d.-d). There is also a possibility that the state of emergency was used as a tailwind for the ruling AKP administration, leading up to the general/presidential co-election on June 24, 2018 (Naito 2018). Addressing this concern would first involve fostering awareness that human rights are universal values protected by the dignity of the nation itself. Second, a European transformation of Turkey from both the inside and the outside would need to be revitalized by citizens and the international community. If these concerns are not addressed, Turkey should expect to receive severe criticism by UN members and international NGOs in the coming 2020 UNHRC UPR (third cycle) (UPR Info, n.d.). It is thus assumed necessary for Turkish political leaders to make some efforts to harmonize with the international community.[25]

Fifth, civil society in Turkey is seemingly not growing but rather shrinking and not offering much public opinion under the extreme pressure of the Turkish government (Keyman et al. 2017; Keyman and Gumucu 2014, 156–162). Turkish citizens must make the ultimate decisions about national affairs, but Turkish citizens seem to simply support the AKP and Erdoğan in large numbers. Turkey has considerable division among the citizens in terms of political and social orientation. The current division among the citizens in politics is between those who are pro-Erdoğan and others who are anti-Erdoğan. In such a situation, there is no effective political mechanism for minority opinions. In this respect, due to the shrinking civil society and the loss of a pub-

---

[24] "The political order has been ravaged by coup since antiquity. During the confusion, it is often the case that the ruling government is unable to fully guarantee the rights of its subjects. Such a situation, however, has also been taken advantage of in order to purge political opponents or establish absolute rule. Therefore, human rights law must still be respected in such circumstances, and every derogation must strictly follow the conditions that are laid in the respective convention, whether it is a threat to the life of the nation or simply public security" (Nugraha 2018, 202–03).

[25] International cooperation in human rights activities by inter-cities would be one of the possibilities not requiring a large expenditure (Sakurai 2019, 22–37).

lic opinion theater, a social environment now exists in Turkey that makes it difficult for those in Turkish society to offer a minority opinion in public (Interviews with the author, Istanbul, 2018). A fair public opinion theater in Turkey has not been properly established or ever fully dismantled by the AKP.[26] This theater could contribute to building some consensus within society and narrowing gaps of understanding in various respects. This is the basic foundation of democracy. Without this mechanism, it is hard for citizens to understand the situation properly and to exchange views freely in public. As a consequence, many citizens do not trust mass media under AKP control and largely rely on social media (Bulut and Yoruk 2017). This situation, including many possible suspected cases of human rights violations, would be a malfunction of a proper democracy tasked with respecting public opinion and the views of both the majority and the minority regardless of class, leading to certain frustrations or unjust feelings being shared by the citizens (Sakurai 2018; Interviews with the author, Istanbul, 2018).

6.2 Discussion

In Turkey, these five elements are structurally embedded in political practice and therefore constitute underlying factors contributing to the emergence of human rights problems. Put differently, if Turkish political actors were to modify these elements and pursue policies aimed at maximizing respect for human rights protections, the severity of such problems could be mitigated to some extent. Although Turkey has established a formal legal framework for the protection of human rights, its effectiveness ultimately depends on the presence of genuine and sustained political will. Accordingly, the critical question is whether political will in Turkey truly supports the meaningful protection of human rights. In principle, political will should reflect the collective conscience of Turkish citizens; however, in practice, it appears to be shaped primarily by the intentions of the AKP and President Erdoğan. Consequently, decisions regarding the protection or violation of human rights law in Turkey are largely controlled by the AKP and Erdoğan under the current regime. This concentration of power lies at the core of contemporary Turkish authoritarianism, in which democratic institutions operate formally but not substantively, as government

---

[26] As an example: *New York Times* (2018).

bias undermines key arenas such as elections, the media, the legislature, and the judiciary (Levitsky and Way 2002, 2010).

The Turkish implications may be applied, more or less, to other countries such as Russia, Venezuela, and the Philippines. It might thus be possible to generalize the relationship between politics and human rights law in modern Turkey, particularly with the five politics elements, as a political theory framework for authoritarian country comparison analysis (Nisnevich and Ryabov, n.d.). However, this must be a future task since this argument requires a wide range of analysis by country, which is beyond the scope of this chapter. Instead, we can only touch on the political concept of "modern authoritarianism" (*Freedom House* 2014) as follows: "Central to the modern authoritarian strategy is the capture of institutions that undergird political pluralism. The goal is to dominate not only the executive and legislative branches, but also the media, the judiciary, civil society, the commanding heights of the economy, and the security forces. With these institutions under the effective if not absolute control of an incumbent leader, changes in government through fair and honest elections become all but impossible" (Mochtak 2017; Puddington 2017). These passages explain what "modern authoritarianism" is like, specifically with reference to Russia, but could be perfectly applied to Turkey as well. It follows that "the toxic combination of unfair elections and 'majoritarianism' is spreading to illiberal leaders in what are still partly democratic countries. Increasingly, populist politicians—once in office—claim the right to suppress the media, civil society, and other democratic institutions by citing support from a majority of voters."[27] As a consequence, human rights law is no longer respected by the government.

7 Conclusion

The relationship between politics and human rights law in modern Turkey has been examined, and a considerable gap between the desired direction of the AKP ruling party and the direction encouraged by human rights law appears to exist. An EU accession policy brought a European transformation to Turkey and played an important role in narrowing this gap, but this

---

[27] "Given the presence of a large constituency that seems to have internalized populist values and an excessive concentration of power in the executive, we can expect populism to continue to be the dominant pattern of rule in Turkey for the foreseeable future" (Aytaç and Elçi 2019, 106; Puddington 2017).

transformation has weakened since the suspension of Turkey's EU accession negotiations. Human rights problems may thus become more prevalent in Turkey, and conflicts both inside and outside Turkey could intensify.

The Turkish case implies that simply ratifying international human rights legislation will not necessarily lead to respect for human rights in practice. In fact, authoritarianism in Turkish politics currently dominates society, and a European transformation of Turkey cannot be expected to occur as long as Turkey has a de facto AKP single party system. The state of emergency has resulted in temporary but seriously negative effects, leading to the rule of law being neglected. Turkish civil society also cannot be expected to become active in dissent at this time. With the five politics elements in Turkey discussed previously, democracy works in appearance but not in substance under the bias of the government, particularly in the electoral, media, legislative, and judicial arenas. Human rights law would fall in the legislative category.

In closing, Turkish citizens must be mindful that Turkey has implemented a human rights law system and that the system could work if positive political will is available to support human rights protection. Therefore, it is ultimately questioned whether political will in Turkey genuinely supports human rights protections. In a democratic society, any political leader must rely on support from a majority of voters, and thus Turkish citizens should determine the choice of violation or protection of human rights law through votes in a democratic process. It is assumed that Turkish citizens could change the direction, if they wish, even though it would likely take time.[28] It is always darkest before the dawn.

Acknowledgments

The author wishes to acknowledge the Early-Career Researcher's Network for Human Rights Japan—held April 22, 2018, in Osaka, Japan—and the 5th World Congress Middle Eastern Studies (WOCMES 2018)—held July 16–20, 2018, in Seville, Spain—for the stimulation to draft this chapter, and Michael Hassett for his constructive review and editing of the material.

---

[28] Some political changes occurred in 2019. Mayors in Ankara and Istanbul from non-AKP candidates were elected, pending official approval by the High Election Board (YSK) (*Hurriyet Daily News* 2019).

Bibliography

Acemoglu, Daron, and Murat Ucer. 2015. "The Ups and Downs of Turkish Growth, 2002–2015: Political Dynamics, the European Union and the Institutional Slide." NBER Working Paper No. 21608 on International Trade and Investment, National Bureau of Economic Research, Cambridge, MA, October 2015. https://doi.org/10.3386/w21608.

Akbulut, Olgun. 2015. "Turkey's Reaction to the Judgements of the European Court of Human Rights." *International Journal of Multidisciplinary Thought* 5 (2): 75–86. Accessed January 8, 2026. https://www.researchgate.net/publication/291692639_Turkey's_Reaction_to_the_Judgments_of_the_European_Court_of_Human_Rights.

AKP (*Adalet ve Kalkınma Partisi*). n.d. "AK PARTi." Accessed January 8, 2026. https://x.com/Akparti on X and https://www.instagram.com/akparti/ on Instagram.

Algan, Bülent. 2011. "Dissolution of Political Parties by the Constitutional Court in Turkey: An Everlasting Conflict Between the Court and the Parliament?" *Ankara Üniversitesi Hukuk Fakültesi Dergisi (AUHFD)* 60 (4): 809–36. Accessed January 8, 2026. https://doi.org/Hukfak_0000000001

Amnesty International. n.d. "Amnesty International Annual Report 2017/2018." Accessed January 8, 2026. https://www.amnesty.org/en/latest/news/2018/02/annual-report-201718/.

AP News. 2018. "A Look at Turkey's Post-Coup Crackdown." August 30. Accessed November 1, 2025. https://www.apnews.com/dbb5fa7d8f-8c4d0d99f297601c83a164.

Arai, Masami. 2001. *Turkish Modern History: From Islamic Empire to National State* [in Japanese]. Misuzu Shobo.

Arango, Tim. 2013. "Corruption Scandal Is Edging Near Turkish Premier." *New York Times*, December 25. https://www.nytimes.com/2013/12/26/world/europe/turkish-cabinet-members-resign.html.

Arslan, Defne, Pinar Dost, and Grady Wilson. 2018. "US-Turkey Relations: From Alliance to Crisis." *Atlantic Council*, August 7. https://www.atlanticcouncil.org/blogs/new-atlanticist/us-turkey-relations-from-alliance-to-crisis.

Atlantic. 2016. "How Erdogan Made Turkey Authoritarian Again." July 21. Accessed November 1, 2025. Accessed January 8, 2026. https://efaidnbmnnnibpcajpcglclefindmkaj/https://jisc.thebrpi.org/journals/jisc/Vol_4_No_2_December_2016/4.pdf

Aydogdu, Ramazan, and Muhammed Yildiz. 2016. "The Impact of Islam on Child-Rearing Values in Turkey." *Journal of Islamic Studies and Culture* 4 (2): 38–50. Accessed January 8, 2026. //efaidnbmnnnibpcajpcglclefindmkaj/https://jisc.thebrpi.org/journals/jisc/Vol_4_No_2_December_2016/4.pdf

Aytaç, S. Erdem, and Ezgi Elçi. 2019. "Populism in Turkey." In *Populism Around the World*, edited by D. Stockemer. Springer.

Bakner, Onur. 2017. "How Did We Get Here? Turkey's Slow Shift to Authoritarianism." In *Authoritarian Politics in Turkey: Elections, Resistance and the AKP*, edited by Bahar Baser and Ahmet Erdi Ozturk. I. B. Tauris.

Barçın, Yinanç. 2018. "Turkey Has Failed to Adapt to Europe's Legal Sphere: Former ECHR Judge Rıza Türmen." *Hurriyet Daily News*, November 20. http://www.hurriyetdailynews.com/turkey-has-failed-to-adapt-to-europes-legal-sphere-former-echr-judge-riza-turmen-122657.

Baser, Bahar, and Ahmet Erdi Ozturk. 2017. *Authoritarian Politics in Turkey: Elections, Resistance and the AKP*. I. B. Tauris.

Bulut, Ergin, and Erdem Yoruk. 2017. "Digital Populism: Trolls and Political Polarization of Twitter in Turkey." *International Journal of Communication* 11: 4093–117. http://ijoc.org/index.php/ijoc/article/view/6702/2158.

Bürgin, Alexander. 2012. "Disappointment or New Strength: Exploring the Declining EU Support Among Turkish Students, Academics and Party Members." *Turkish Studies* 13: 565–80. https://doi.org/10.1080/14683849.2012.746434.

Butler, Daren. 2019. "With More Islamic Schooling, Erdogan Aims to Reshape Turkey." *Reuters*, January 25. Accessed November 1, 2025. https://www.reuters.com/investigates/special-report/turkey-erdogan-education/.

Cagaptay, Soner. 2017. *The New Sultan—Erdogan and the Crisis of Modern Turkey*. I. B. Tauris.

Cagaptay, Soner, and Oya Rose Aktas. 2017. "How Erdoganism Is Killing Turkish Democracy: The End of Political Opposition." *Foreign Affairs*, July 7. Accessed November 1, 2025. https://www.foreignaffairs.com/articles/turkey/2017-07-07/how-erdoganism-killing-turkish-democracy.

Castaldo, Antonino. 2018. "Populism and Competitive Authoritarianism in Turkey." *Southeast European and Black Sea Studies* 18 (2): 1–21. https://doi.org/10.1080/14683857.2018.1550948.

Celik, Emrah. 2017. "Power and Islam in Turkey: The Relationship Between AKP and Sunni Islamic Groups, 2002–16." In *Authoritarian Politics in Turkey: Elections, Resistance and the AKP*, edited by Bahar Baser and Ahmet Erdi Ozturk. I. B. Tauris.

Çınar, Özgür H., and Tolga Şirin. 2017. "Turkey's Human Rights Agenda." *Research and Policy on Turkey* 2 (2): 133–43. https://doi.org/10.1080/23760818.2017.1350354.

Committee to Protect Journalists. n.d. "Record Number of Journalists Jailed as Turkey, China, Egypt Pay Scant Price for Repression." Accessed March 29, 2019. https://cpj.org/reports/2017/12/journalists-prison-jail-record-number-turkey-china-egypt.php.

DeYoung, Karen, and Kareem Fahim. 2017. "U.S.-Turkey Tensions Boil over After Arrest of Consulate Employee." *Washington Post*, October 9. Accessed November 1, 2025. https://www.washingtonpost.com/world/turkey-summons-another-us-consulate-employee-as-crisis-deepens/2017/10/09/5fbaecf6-ac7b-11e7-9b93-b97043e57a22_story.html.

Doğru, Osman, and Tolga Şirin. 2017. "Human Rights Paradox of Turkey: Punishment for Victims and Impunity for Suppressors." *Research and Policy on Turkey* 2 (2): 225–43. https://doi.org/10.1080/23760818.2017.1350357.

Duvan, Ayşe Özkan. 2015. "The Judicial Application of Human Rights Law in Turkey." *Journal of Penal Law and Criminology (Ceza Hukuku ve Kriminoloji Dergisi)* 3 (1): 59–73. Accessed January 8, 2026 https://www.researchgate.net/publication/332459413_Turkish_Politics_and_Human_Rights_Law_Focusing_on_Transformation.

ECtHR (European Court of Human Rights). 2019. *Annual Report 2018*. ECtHR. https://www.echr.coe.int/Documents/Annual_report_2018_ENG.pdf.

Encyclopedia Britannica Online. n.d.-a. "European Court of Human Rights." Accessed March 29, 2019. https://www.britannica.com/topic/European-Court-of-Human-Rights.

Encyclopedia Britannica Online. n.d.-b. "European Court of Human Rights." Accessed November 1, 2025. https://www.britannica.com/topic/European-Court-of-Human-Rights.

Erdoğan's Statement at the Muslim Arab Youth Association Conference. 1996 (in Turkish). Accessed November 1, 2025. YouTube. https://www.youtube.com/watch?v=oQ-Zqn8-wF0.

Esen, Berk, and Sebnem Gumuscu. 2018. "The Perils of 'Turkish Presidentialism.' " *Review of Middle East Studies* 52 (1): 43–53. https://doi.org/10.1017/rms.2018.10.

European Commission. 2015. *EU-Turkey Joint Action Plan*. European Commission. http://europa.eu/rapid/press-release_MEMO-15-5860_en.htm.

European Commission. 2018. *Commission Staff Working Document: Turkey 2018 Report*. European Commission. https://ec.europa.eu/neighbourhood-enlargement/sites/near/files/20180417-turkey-report.pdf.

European Commission. n.d.-a. "European Neighbourhood Policy and Enlargement Negotiations: Turkey." Accessed January 8, 2026. https://enlargement.ec.europa.eu/countries/turkiye_en.

European Commission. n.d.-b. "Turkey: Trade Picture." Accessed November 1, 2025. http://ec.europa.eu/trade/policy/countries-and-regions/countries/turkey/.

European Council. n.d. "EU-Turkey Leaders' Meeting in Varna (Bulgaria), 26 March 2018." Accessed January 12, 2019. https://www.consilium.europa.eu/en/meetings/international-summit/2018/03/26/.

Freedom House. 2014. "FREEDOM IN THE WORLD 2014." chrome-extension://efaidnbmnnnibpcajpcglclefindmkaj/https://freedomhouse.org/sites/default/files/FIW2014%20Booklet.pdf. Accessed January 8, 2026.

Freedom House. n.d. "Freedom in the World 2018: Turkey." Accessed January 8, 2026. https://www.refworld.org/reference/annualreport/freehou/2018/en/120309.

Fujimoto, Koji. 2001. *Domestic Implementation of International Human Rights Law and Domestic Human Rights Institutions* [in Japanese]. Gendai Jinbunsha.

Gall, Carlotta. 2019. "Spurning Erdogan's Vision, Turks Leave in Droves, Draining Money and Talent." *New York Times*, January 2. Accessed November 1, 2025. https://www.nytimes.com/2019/01/02/world/europe/turkey-emigration-erdogan.html.

Gormez, Yuksel, and Serkan Yigit. 2009. "The Economic and Financial Stability in Turkey: A Historical Perspective." *SEEMHN Papers* 12: 17. Accessed January 8, 2026. https://ideas.repec.org/p/nsb/mhnsee/12.html

Hale, William. 2011. "Human Rights and Turkey's EU Accession Process: Internal and External Dynamics, 2005–10." *South European Society and Politics* 16 (2): 323–33. https://doi.org/10.1080/13608746.2011.577953.

Hale, William, and Ergun Özbudun. 2010. *Islamism, Democracy and Liberalism in Turkey: The Case of the AKP*. Routledge.

Hirai, Yukiko. 2010. "Turkey's EU Accession Negotiation and Kurdish Human Rights Movement—Examples of Promotion of Domestic Reform Using External Pressure." *Middle East Study* 504: 80–110. Accessed November 1, 2025. [in Japanese]. https://ci.nii.ac.jp/naid/40016740777.

Hoffman, Max, and Michael Werz. 2013. *Freedom of the Press and Expression in Turkey*. Centre for American Progress, May 14. Accessed

November 1, 2025. https://www.americanprogress.org/issues/security/reports/2013/05/14/63159/freedom-of-the-press-and-expression-in-turkey/.

Hopgood, Stephen, Jack Snyder, and Leslie Vinjamuri. 2018. *Human Rights Futures*, reprint. Cambridge University Press.

Human Rights Watch. n.d. "Turkey: Events of 2018." *World Report 2019*. Accessed March 29, 2019. https://www.hrw.org/world-report/2019/country-chapters/turkey.

Hurriyet Daily News. 2013. "Timeline of Gezi Park Protests." June 6. Accessed November 1, 2025. http://www.hurriyetdailynews.com/timeline-of-gezi-park-protests--48321.

Hurriyet Daily News. 2018a. "State of Emergency Will End 'Within a Few Days': Justice Minister." July 16. Accessed November 1, 2025. http://www.hurriyetdailynews.com/state-of-emergency-will-end-within-a-few-days-justice-minister-134618.

Hurriyet Daily News. 2018b. "Turkey's State of Emergency Commission's Term Extended." December 26. Accessed November 1, 2025. http://www.hurriyetdailynews.com/state-of-emergency-commissions-term-extended-140028.

Hurriyet Daily News. 2018c. "New Measures Before Emergency Rule Ends in Turkey." July 17. http://www.hurriyetdailynews.com/new-measures-before-emergency-rule-ends-in-turkey-134645.

Hurriyet Daily News. 2019a. "The referendum is over; now what about the tension?" April 19. https://www.hurriyetdailynews.com/opinion/selin-nasi/the-referendum-is-over-now-what-about-the-tension-112202. Accessed January 8, 2026.

Hurriyet Daily News. 2019b. "Council of Europe to observe Istanbul rerun elections." June 20. https://www.hurriyetdailynews.com/council-of-europe-to-observe-istanbul-rerun-elections-144346. Accessed January 8, 2026.

Inal, Nuray Nazli, and Duden Yegenoglu. 2005. "German and French Leaders' Views on Turkey's EU Membership." *Washington Institute: Policywatch* 1007, June 27. Accessed November 1, 2025. https://www.washingtoninstitute.org/policy-analysis/view/german-and-french-leaders-views-on-turkeys-eu-membership.

International Crisis Group. 2017. *Managing Turkey's PKK Conflict: The Case of Nusaybin*. Europe Report No. 243. International Crisis Group, May 2. Accessed January 8, 2026. https://www.crisisgroup.org/europe-central-asia/turkiye/243-managing-turkeys-pkk-conflict-case-nusaybin.

Irie, Akira. 2017. "Nagasaki in the Global History." *Journal of Global Humanities and Social Sciences, Nagasaki University* 3: 53-61. Accessed January 8, 2026. [in Japanese]. Accessed January 8, 2026. http://hdl.handle.net/10069/37261.

Jones, Dorian. 2018. "Turkey's Ruling Party Extends Control Over Media." *VOA News*, March 23. Accessed November 1, 2025. https://www.voanews.com/a/turkeys-ruling-party-extends-control-over-media/4312760.html.

Karlsson, Ingmar. 2008. "Turkey's Historical, Cultural and Religious Heritage: An Asset to the European Union." In *European and Turkish Voices in Favour and Against Turkish Accession to the European Union*, edited by Christiane Timmerman, Dirk Rochtus, and Sara Mels. European Policy Series No. 38. P. I. E. Peter Lang.

Keyman, E. Fat, and Sebnem Gumucu. 2014. *Democracy, Identity, and Foreign Policy in Turkey: Hegemony Through Transformation*. Palgrave Macmillan.

Keyman, Fuat, Nathalie Tocci, and Michael Werz. 2017. *Trends in Turkish Civil Society*. Centre for American Progress, July 10. Accessed January 9, 2026. https://www.americanprogress.org/article/trends-turkish-civil-society/

Levitsky, Steven, and Lucan A. Way. 2002. "The Rise of Competitive Authoritarianism." *Journal of Democracy* 13 (2): 51–65. Accessed January 9, 2026. https://www.journalofdemocracy.org/articles/elections-without-democracy-the-rise-of-competitive-authoritarianism/

Levitsky, Steven, and Lucan A. Way. 2010. *Competitive Authoritarianism: Hybrid Regimes After the Cold War*. Cambridge University Press.

Ministry of Foreign Affairs of the Republic of Turkey. 2018. "QA-36, 5 May 2018, Statement of the Spokesperson of the Ministry of Foreign Affairs, Mr. Hami Aksoy, in Response to a Question Regarding the Statement of the US State Department Spokesperson Claiming That the People of Afrin Are Not Allowed to Return." May 5. Accessed November 1, 2025. http://www.mfa.gov.tr/sc_-36_-afrin-halkinin-geri-donusune-izin-verilmedigi-yonundeki-aciklama-hk-sc_en.en.mfa.

Ministry of Foreign Affairs of the Republic of Turkey (Official Website). n.d. "Human Rights." Accessed November 1, 2025. http://www.mfa.gov.tr/%C4%B0nsan-haklar%C4%B1.en.mfa.

Ministry of Foreign Affairs of the Republic of Turkey (Official Website). n.d.-b. Human Rights, 2. A) Council of Europe (CoE). Accessed November 1, 2025. http://www.mfa.gov.tr/%C4%B0nsan-haklar%C4%B1.en.mfa.

Ministry of Foreign Affairs of the Republic of Turkey (Website). n.d.-c. "PKK." Accessed November 1, 2025. http://www.mfa.gov.tr/pkk.en.mfa.

Ministry of Foreign Affairs of the Republic of Turkey (Website). n.d.-d. "No: 38, 8 February 2018, Press Release Regarding the Resolution of the European Parliament Entitled 'Current Situation of Human Rights in Turkey.' " Accessed November 1, 2025. http://www.mfa.gov.tr/no_-38_-ap-nin-turkiyede-mevcut-insan-haklari-durumu-baslikli-karari_en.en.mfa.

Ministry of Foreign Affairs of the Republic of Turkey (Official Website). n.d.-e. "Controversy Between Türkiye and Armenia About the Events of 1915." Accessed January 9, 2026. https://www.mfa.gov.tr/controversy-between-turkey-and-armenia-about-the-events-of-1915.en.mfa.

Ministry of Foreign Affairs of the Republic of Turkey (Official Website). n.d.-f. "JULY 15 COUP ATTEMPT IN TURKEY AND PEOPLE'S VICTORY." Accessed January 9, 2026. chrome-extension://efaidnbmnnnibpcajpcglclefindmkaj/https://tokyo-be.mfa.gov.tr/Content/assets/consulate/images/localCache/12/57bc673b-f313-4e37-97bd-87cb26173aa6.pdf.

Ministry of Foreign Affairs of the Republic of Turkey. n.d.-g. "Turkey-EU Political Dialogue Meeting at Ministerial Level was held in Brussels." https://www.mfa.gov.tr/turkey_eu-political-dialogue-meeting-at-ministerial-level-was-held-in-brussels.en.mfa. Accessed January 9, 2026.

Mochtak, Michael. 2017. "Modern Authoritarianism as a Security Threat to Central and Eastern Europe." *Panorama of Global Security Environment 2015–2016* (2017): 539–48. In book following the pages: Peter Bátor and Róbert Ondrejcsák (eds.), Panorama of global security environment 2015-2016. STRATPOLE.

Naito, Masanori. 2018. "Comments." Presented at the Turkey Seminar, Japan-Turkey Society, Tokyo, May 17, 2018.

New York Times. 2018. "Turkish Media Group Bought by Pro-Government Conglomerate." March 21. Accessed November 1, 2025. https://www.nytimes.com/2018/03/21/world/europe/turkey-media-erdogan-dogan.html.

Nishii, Masahiro. 2014. "Actual State of the Universal Periodic Review (UPR) of the UN Human Rights Council—Focusing on the First Turkish Review." *Journal of Osaka Jogakuin 4year College* 11: 45–63. Accessed January 9, 2026. [in Japanese]. https://cir.nii.ac.jp/crid/1520853833559614080?lang=en.

Nisnevich, Yuliy Anatolievich, and Andrey Vilenovich Ryabov. n.d. "Modern Authoritarianism and Political Ideology." Working Papers Series: Higher School of Economics Research Paper No. WP BRP 44/PS/2017. Accessed January 9, 2026. https://ssrn.com/abstract=2916078.

Nugraha, Ignatius Yordan. 2018. "Human Rights Derogation During Coup Situations." *International Journal of Human Rights* 22 (2): 202–3. https://www.tandfonline.com/doi/full/10.1080/13642987.2017.1359551.

OHCHR (Office of the United Nations High Commissioner for Human Rights). 2018. "Turkey: UN report details extensive human rights violations during protracted state of emergency." OHCHR. Accessed January 9, 2026. https://www.ohchr.org/en/press-releases/2018/03/turkey-un-report-details-extensive-human-rights-violations-during-protracted.

OHCHR (Office of the United Nations High Commissioner for Human Rights). 2019. *Turkey: UN Report Details Extensive Human Rights Violations During Protracted State of Emergency*. OHCHR. Accessed November 1, 2025. https://www.ohchr.org/SP/NewsEvents/Pages/DisplayNews.aspx?NewsID=22853&LangID=E.

OHCHR (Office of the United Nations High Commissioner for Human Rights). n.d.-a. "Status of Ratification Interactive Dashboard: Turkey." Accessed November 1, 2025. http://indicators.ohchr.org/.

OHCHR (Office of the United Nations High Commissioner for Human Rights). n.d.-b. "Universal Periodic Review—Türkiye." Accessed November 1, 2025. https://www.ohchr.org/EN/HRBodies/UPR/Pages/TRIndex.aspx.

OSCE (Organization for Security and Co-Operation in Europe). 2017. "Statement of Preliminary Findings and Conclusions, International Referendum Observation Mission Republic of Turkey-Constitutional Referendum, April 16." Accessed November 1, 2025. https://www.osce.org/odihr/elections/turkey/311721.

OSCE (Organization for Security and Co-Operation in Europe). 2018. *Turkey, Early Presidential and Parliamentary Elections, 24 June 2018: Final Report*. OSCE Office for Democratic Institutions and Human Rights. Accessed January 9, 2026. https://odihr.osce.org/odihr/elections/turkey/397046.

OSCE (Organization for Security and Co-Operation in Europe). n.d. "*About Us*." Accessed November 1, 2025. https://www.osce.org/who-we-are.

Özbudun, Ergun. 2015. "Turkey's Judiciary and the Drift Toward Competitive Authoritarianism." *International Spectator* 50 (2): 42–55. https://doi.org/10.1080/03932729.2015.1020651.

Puddington, Arch. 2017. *Breaking Down Democracy: Goals, Strategies, and Methods of Modern Authoritarians*. Freedom House Special Report, June 2017. Accessed January 9, 2026. https://freedomhouse.org/sites/default/files/June2017_FH_Report_Breaking_Down_Democracy.pdf

Reuters. 2016. "Turkey Officially Designates Gulen Religious Group as Terrorists." May 31. Accessed January 9, 2026. https://www.reuters.com/article/world/turkey-officially-designates-gulen-religious-group-as-terrorists-idUSKCN0YM17F/

Right, Robin. 2012. *The Islamists Are Coming: Who They Really Are.* US Institute of Peace Press.

Rosanvallon, Oierre. 2006. *Counter-Democracy: Politics in an Age of Distrust (The Seeley Lectures).* Translated by Masaki Shimazaki. Iwanami Shoten.

RSF (Reporters Without Borders). n.d. "RSF Index 2018: Hatred of journalism threatens democracies." Accessed January 9, 2026. https://rsf.org/en/node/79170.

Sakurai, Yukio. 2018. "Turkey's Possible Future Directions After the 2017 Referendum: Autocracy or Democracy?" *International Journal of Interdisciplinary Civic and Political Studies* 13 (1): 33–45. https://doi.org/10.18848/2327-0071/CGP/v13i01/33-45.

Sakurai, Yukio. 2019. "Cooperation Among International Cities to Advance Global Concerns About the Ageing: A Possible Cooperation Among Tokyo, Singapore and Istanbul." The International Journal of Aging & Social Change 9(3): 13–24. doi:10.18848/2576-5310/CGP/v09i03/13-24.

Sanderson, Sertan. 2018. "From Ally to Scapegoat: Fethullah Gulen, the Man Behind the Myth." *Deutsche Welle (DW)*, April 6. Accessed November 1, 2025. https://www.dw.com/en/from-ally-to-scapegoat-fethullah-gulen-the-man-behind-the-myth/a-37055485.

Schmitter, Philippe C., and Terry Lynn Karl. 1991. "What Democracy Is... and Is Not." *Journal of Democracy* 2 (3): 75–88. https://doi.org/10.1353/jod.1991.0033.

Sertöz, Gökhan. 2015. "The Challenges and Prejudgements Turkey Has Exprienced Through Accession Process to the European Union." Law & Justice Review, Year:6, Issue:10: 75-109. Accessed January 9, 2026. chrome-extension://efaidnbmnnnibpcajpcglclefindmkaj/https://lawandjustice.taa.gov.tr/yuklenenler/dosyalar/dergiler/law/law-10/law10.pdf.

Sokollu, Senada. 2013. Controversial mosque. *Deutsche Welle (DW)*, August 23. Accessed January 9, 2026. https://www.dw.com/en/mosque-construction-sparks-controversy-in-istanbul/a-17041396.

Suny, Ronald Grigor. n.d. "Armenian Genocide." *Encyclopaedia Britannica Online.* Accessed November 1, 2025. https://www.britannica.com/event/Armenian-Genocide.

Tanchum, Micha'el. 2015. "New Kurds on the Block." *Foreign Affairs*, September 23. Accessed November 1, 2025. https://www.foreignaffairs.com/articles/turkey/2015-09-23/new-kurds-block.

Taşpınar, Ömer. 2012. "Turkey: The New Model?" *Brookings*, April 25. Accessed November 1, 2025. https://www.brookings.edu/research/turkey-the-new-model/.

Tezcür, Güneş Murat. 2013. "Political Islam in Turkey." In *The Oxford Handbook of Islam and Politics*, edited by John L. Esposito and Emad El-Din Shahin. Oxford University Press.

The Grand National Assembly of Turkey. (Website). 2019 "Constitution of the Republic of Turkey." Accessed January 9, 2026. chrome-extension://efaidnbmnnnibpcajpcglclefindmkaj/https://www.anayasa.gov.tr/media/7258/anayasa_eng.pdf

Toksabay, Ece. 2012. "Turkish PM Fumes over Steamy Ottoman Soap Opera." *Reuters*, November 27. Accessed November 1, 2025. https://www.reuters.com/article/us-turkey-show-suleiman/turkish-pm-fumes-over-steamy-ottoman-soap-opera-idUSBRE8AQ11H20121127.

Toksabay, Ece. 2017. "U.S., Turkey Restart Issuing Visas but Tensions over Detentions Fester." *Reuters*, November 7. Accessed November 1, 2025. https://www.reuters.com/article/us-usa-turkey-visa/u-s-turkey-restart-issuing-visas-but-tensions-over-detentions-fester-idUSKBN1D-61VQ.

Transparency International. n.d. "Corruption Perceptions Index 2018." Accessed March 29, 2019. https://www.transparency.org/en/cpi/2018.

Turkish Constitutional Court. 2017. "PLENARY ASSEMBLY JUDGMENT." *Constitutional Court of the Republic of Turkey (Official Website)*, June 20. Accessed January 9, 2026. chrome-extension://efaidnbmnnnibpca-jpcglclefindmkaj/https://www.anayasa.gov.tr/media/2723/2016-22169.pdf

UNDP (United Nations Development Programme). 2018. *Human Development Report 2018: Turkey*. UNDP. http://hdr.undp.org/en/countries/profiles/TUR.

UNHRC (United Nations Human Rights Council). 2014. *National Report Submitted in Accordance with Paragraph 5 of the Annex to Human Rights Council Resolution 16/21: Turkey*. UNHRC. Accessed January 9, 2026. https://digitallibrary.un.org/record/788715?v=pdf

UNHRC (United Nations Human Rights Council). 2015. *Report of the Working Group on the Universal Periodic Review: Turkey*. UNHRC. Accessed November 1, 2025. https://www.ohchr.org/EN/HRBodies/UPR/Pages/TRindex.aspx.

UNHRC (United Nations Human Rights Council). 2018. " Turkey: UN report details extensive human rights violations during protracted state of emergency." https://www.ohchr.org/en/press-releases/2018/03/turkey-un-report-details-extensive-human-rights-violations-during-protracted#:~:text=%E2%80%9CThe%20numbers%20are%20just%20staggering,with%20making%20the%20country%20safer.%E2%80%9D. Accessed January 8, 2026.

United Kingdom, House of Common. 2017. Human rights and the political situation in Turkey. March 6. chrome-extension://efaidnbmnnnibpcajpcglclefindmkaj/https://researchbriefings.files.parliament.uk/documents/CDP-2017-0077/CDP-2017-0077.pdf. Accessed January 8, 2026.

United States Department of State. 2019. *2018 Country Reports on Human Rights Practices: Turkey*. U.S. Department of State. Accessed January 8, 2026 https://www.state.gov/reports/2019-country-reports-on-human-rights-practices/turkey.

Uno, Yoko. 2015. "The Position of the Istanbul-Gezi Movement in the Political History of the Republic of Turkey: Seeking New Political Alternatives." *International Relations Studies* 41: 45–58. Accessed November 1, 2025. [in Japanese]. https://ci.nii.ac.jp/naid/40020405704.

UPR Info. n.d. "Turkey Next Review: 2030." Accessed November 1, 2025. https://www.upr-info.org/en/review/Turkey.

US Department of State. 2017. *Country Reports on Human Rights Practices for 2017: Turkey*. US Department of State, 2017. Accessed November 1, 2025. https://www.state.gov/documents/organization/277471.pdf.

US Department of State. n.d. "Department Press Briefing—May 3, 2018." Accessed January 9, 2026. https://2017-2021.state.gov/briefings/department-press-briefing-may-3-2018/

Winter, Chase. 2018. "Dutch Parliament Recognizes 1915 Armenian 'Genocide.' " *Deutsche Welle (DW)*, February 22. Accessed November 1, 2025. https://www.dw.com/en/dutch-parliament-recognizes-1915-armenian-genocide/a-42702730.

World Justice Project. n.d. *Rule of Law Index: Turkey*. Accessed January 9, 2026. https://worldjusticeproject.org/rule-of-law-index/country/2024/T%C3%BCrkiye/

Yavuz, M. Hakan. 2003. *Islamic Political Identity in Turkey*. Oxford University Press.

Yavuz, M. Hakan, and Bayram Balcı, eds. 2018. *Turkey's July 15th Coup: What Happened and Why*. University of Utah Press.

Zalaquett, Jose. 1992. "Balancing Ethical Imperatives and Political Constraints: The Dilemma of New Democracies Confronting Past Human Rights Violations." *Hastings Law Journal* 41 (1): 1425–38. Accessed January 9, 2026. chrome-extension://efaidnbmnnnibpcajpcglclefindmkaj/https://repository.uclawsf.edu/cgi/viewcontent.cgi?article=3088&context=hastings_law_journal

Conclusion

This volume has explored one of the defining governance challenges of the twenty-first century: how democratic societies sustain vitality, authority, and legitimacy amid crisis, interdependence, and pervasive structural change. By integrating three thematic dimensions—democracy and resilience, sovereignty and citizen well-being, and human rights and social structures—within a broader conceptual framework of pluralism, the book offers both an analytical diagnosis of contemporary political developments and a set of normative insights for strengthening democratic practice.

The comparative analysis of Japan and Turkey demonstrates that democratic strain manifests across diverse institutional settings. Japan illustrates a pattern of incremental erosion—driven by bureaucratic predominance, juridified governance, demographic pressures, and informational centralization—yet without overt institutional breakdown. Turkey, by contrast, reveals a more rapid concentration of executive authority and restructuring of institutional checks under a populist–majoritarian logic. Taken together, these cases show that democratic backsliding is neither linear nor uniform; it can emerge through subtle legal adaptations as readily as through explicit institutional redesign.

Key Contributions

1. **Democracy and resilience:** The findings underscore that formal institutions alone cannot secure democratic resilience. Meaningful resilience depends on transparent and trustworthy information flows, accountable political leadership, and social conditions that protect the expression of plural voices—particularly amid technological and geopolitical disruptions.

2. **Sovereignty and citizen well-being:** Sovereignty is shown to be relational, contingent, and embedded within global interdependence. Reconciling national autonomy with ethical obligations to safeguard citizen welfare is essential to sustaining democratic legitimacy in an era where security, economic policy, and human rights traverse national boundaries.

3. **Human rights and social structures:** Codified rights require institutional support, cultural openness, and ethical recognition of vulnerability and interdependence in order to function in practice. The study highlights pluralism as a foundational condition for transforming rights from formal guarantees into lived realities.

Future Tasks

The analysis identifies several pressing avenues for further research and policy engagement. Scholars should continue investigating how digital technologies and artificial intelligence reconfigure public discourse, political persuasion, and the epistemic foundations of democracy. Theories of relational sovereignty require refinement to address the tension between autonomy and interdependence in contemporary governance. Comparative inquiries should extend beyond Japan and Turkey to encompass a wider set of regional and regime contexts. Democratic theory, in turn, must incorporate concepts such as vulnerability, relational autonomy, and social interdependence to better protect marginalized groups and strengthen democratic inclusion. Practically, strengthening civic education, ensuring media independence, and designing participatory institutional reforms are crucial steps toward embedding pluralism within everyday governance.

Concluding Reflections

The central lesson of this study is that democracy's most substantial threat lies not in sudden breakdown but in gradual erosion disguised by legal continuity and procedural normalcy. Yet democratic resilience remains attainable. It requires cultivating transparency, reinforcing independent institutions, fostering ethical and accountable leadership, and sustaining active citizenship capable of contesting concentrated power. Pluralism—understood not merely as an abstract ideal but as a lived democratic practice—forms the normative and institutional foundation that enables democracies to adapt, endure, and flourish under conditions of uncertainty. By engaging with the intertwined themes of resilience, relational sovereignty, and substantive rights, societies can confront emerging challenges, harness opportunities for renewal, and preserve democracy not only in form but also in practice.

This volume has examined one of the defining challenges of the twenty-first century: how democratic societies can sustain vitality and legitimacy amid crisis, interdependence, and evolving governance. By integrating three thematic dimensions—democracy and resilience, sovereignty and citizen well-being, and human rights and social structures—under the conceptual framework of pluralism, the book offers both diagnosis and guidance for understanding contemporary democratic life.

KEY TERMS INDEX

www.ingramcontent.com/pod-product-compliance
Lightning Source LLC
Chambersburg PA
CBHW030454240726
48654CB00001B/1

9 781969 318313